Running Free:
My Battle with Anorexia

Rebecca Quinlan

SRL Publishing Ltd

Running Free:
My Battle with Anorexia

Rebecca Quinlan

SRL Publishing Ltd
London
www.srlpublishing.co.uk

First published worldwide by SRL Publishing in 2022
Copyright © REBECCA QUINLAN 2022

ISBN: 978-1-915073-08-2

1 3 5 7 9 10 8 6 4 2

A CIP catalogue record for this book is available from the
British Library

SRL Publishing is a Climate Positive publisher, removing more carbon
emissions than it emits.

Dear Reader,

This is a story about my battle with anorexia. I have written this book with complete honesty and openness as I want to provide a truthful account of what living with an eating disorder is like. However, because of this, you may find some of the content triggering. There are times when I have been very, very ill and my book reflects this.

To explain how deeply entrenched my anorexia was, I have conveyed my disordered thinking and feeling at the time as it is an important part of understanding my story. I also feel this honest portrayal is essential to reflect how far I have come through the journey of recovery in order to provide hope and inspiration to others. I want to stress that, in no way whatsoever, am I promoting 'Pro-Ana' thinking and behaviour in others. I do not condone my behaviour when at the depths of anorexia, but that behaviour is an important part of my journey. I urge you, please, not to use this book for tips on being 'Pro-Ana'. The detail is there solely to describe my illness at the time and to act as a source of comparison along the journey of recovery.

I also wanted to provide this detail to show how destructive and demonic anorexia is. I hope that, in writing this, I can deter others from stumbling down that same, life-destroying path. If I can prevent just one person from entering the devastation of anorexia, or help one person fight for a life without anorexia, then writing this book will have served a purpose.

I have included weights and Body Mass Index (BMIs) which I know can be triggering for some. These have been included to show that, no matter how ill you get, no matter how low your weight gets or how chronic you are, recovery is always possible. Also, I felt it important to include these details to highlight to the general public how physically dangerous eating disorders can be.

Recovery will mean different things to different people. I am not suggesting that my pathway and my version of recovery should be followed by others; I simply want to show that life can get better when you make anorexia smaller despite how ill you have been. No matter how hard it is or how much you feel you can't do it, you CAN make positive changes. Recovery is a long, hard process which I am still undergoing and I hope my story can inspire others. There is a life worth living for all of us. We just have to find the strength to fight for it. Remember, being brave doesn't mean you don't get scared. It means you don't let fear stop you.

To those struggling with an eating disorder – you are braver than you believe. Never give up.

Love, Bex xxx

She sat there broken, a shadow of what she once was.
The lights had faded and the cold was overwhelming.
She wanted to escape herself, fly away from all that she had become.
For someone to mend her broken wings and help her to soar
High above the pain and sorrow that darkened her world.
The butterfly had once been beautiful.
She had feared no heights; no cloud could stop her from reaching her heaven.
But one day the clouds became too big, forming one grey blanket under which she could not breathe.
The butterfly had begun to ebb away, her bright colours dimmed into nothingness,
The butterfly became a moth, cocooned in her world of sadness,
A world from which she could not escape.
So there she lay, waiting in hope for the return of the warmth that had fled her heart.

I would like to thank and dedicate this book to my family and to Nikki Grahame. I wouldn't be where I am today without you. I would also like to acknowledge and thank the staff in The Priory for their incredible care.

Chapter 1
Where Did It Go Wrong?

Organ failure. Resuscitation Unit. Death. What causes someone to starve themselves to the brink of death? To starve themselves to the point where they can't walk, can hardly talk, and where their heart is barely beating to keep them alive? The answer? Anorexia.

I was twenty-two years old and had been rushed to A & E and the Resuscitation Unit. My organs were failing and I had hypothermia. I was told I faced imminent death. As each minute passed, it was doubtful if I would live to see the next. I was hooked up to every machine and every drip possible. Doctors and nurses were working their hardest to keep me alive. My parents stood helpless by my bedside, ghostly pale as they watched their daughter dying in front of their eyes.

My heart rate was averaging less than twenty beats per minute and I was drifting in and out of consciousness. The nurses wrapped my body in heated blankets.

"You have severe hypothermia," a nurse said. "Your body temperature is critically low and your whole body is shutting down. We need to raise your temperature immediately or your heart is going to stop."

That was the reality – I was being told I was in organ failure and could die any minute. But the reality in my mind? I didn't care. I didn't care about anything other than my weight. I was about to die, but I was so happy that I had reached a new all-time lowest weight.

This wasn't the first time I had been in this state. My organs had nearly failed and I had nearly died several times over the previous two years. This was now my third admission.

Three years before, I was a nineteen-year-old athlete ranked in the Top 30 in the UK for my age, aspiring to run for Great Britain as a professional. How did it all go so terribly wrong? How had my one lifetime dream of becoming a professional athlete turned into the living nightmare of anorexia?

Chapter 2
The Beginning

I had always been sporty, stubborn, and determined – characteristics that all help to fuel anorexia. But I wasn't born with an irrational fear of weight gain, an intense desire to lose weight, an obsession with calories and exercise, and rock bottom self-esteem. These developed sometime over my childhood and adolescence. There was a time when it wasn't like that. There was a time when I was happy and free.

My childhood was the best I could have wished for. I always felt loved, I always had fun, and I was happy. I had two loving parents, a fun older sister, Nicola, who I got on with (most of the time), and wonderful grandparents who I saw regularly. I also had a nanny, Jenny, who looked after me when my parents went to work and, once I had started school, when school finished until my parents got home. Jenny was great and we had lots of fun. She always gave me so much love. It was like having a second mum. I was lucky to have this loving and extended family, including Jenny, as I was growing up.

When I wasn't at school, you could find me playing outside with the other kids that lived down my road. We always had a great time, making up dance routines, riding our bikes, playing football, board games, going to the park – you name it, we did it. There was never a moment that wasn't filled with fun. From the age of five, I was playing out in the street virtually every weekend. The weekends were also special because my mum and dad would take us into town and we would go to Debenhams for cake. I always had a sticky bun and Nicola had a Belgian bun.

On a Sunday, I would spend my £1 pocket money on a pack of Spice Girls photos to glue into my Spice Girls scrap book. If we were really lucky, we were allowed to go round to the corner shop and get a bag of penny sweets. Food at that age was fun. We generally ate healthily but were allowed treats like this. We always ate together as a family and meal times were enjoyable occasions. It wasn't until later that this started to change.

When I was seven, my nanny Jenny became pregnant with her first child. When Jenny's daughter, Laura, was born, it was like having a younger sister. Every afternoon when Jenny picked me up from school, I couldn't wait to go back to their house and play games, play with dolls and just have more fun. I absolutely loved being a child and I never wanted to go grow up.

From a very young age, I was a fiery, determined and stubborn character. My dad used to call me 'fierce Bex' because my determination and stubbornness could make me hot-headed. When I was about three, and my dad was trying to teach me how to ride a bike, I got so angry with him when he let go of my saddle and I fell off. Then there was the time – I was still about three years old – when I hit my sister over the head with a brick because she hadn't let me join in her game.

My mum always says that once I set my mind to something that is it, I do it. It was clear that my strong mind and determination were there from a young age. I channelled a lot of this determination into sport.

My passion for playing sport really grew during junior school. In Year 4, I started playing netball and I absolutely loved it. I played Centre because you get to run around the most – I loved running. I seemed to have a natural ability to run fast. Every sports day in primary school, I would enter the sprint race. Then I went on to the District Sports where I raced against girls from all the other local primary schools. And I always won those races. My mum, seeing that I had potential, encouraged me to join the local athletics club, which I did with my friends in the summer holidays after Year 6. But when we started secondary school and were all in different classes, we stopped going to the athletics club together. My mum encouraged me to keep going, which I did every now and again, but I hated going on my own.

I found the transition from primary to secondary school very hard. I went from being popular with lots of friends in primary school to virtually being an outcast in secondary school. In Year 7, I lost touch with all my old friends and I struggled to find a group of girls that I could call my friends. Break and lunch times were spent on the edge of a group of girls that I really wanted to be friends with. But I would stand there, on the edge of the circle, not uttering a word. Just listening to their conversations and feeling completely lonely.

"Why don't you speak?" Tina said.

She was the most popular girl in the year, and she was best friends with girl I wanted to be best friends with. I just shrugged my shoulders. I was too scared to speak. I didn't have the confidence and, deep down, I knew they didn't like me. I was a tag-along and someone they would rather be without.

But, in Years 8 and 9, I formed a new friendship group. It comprised a girl who lived down my road, Vicky, and her best friend, and another girl, Jess, who I had become good friends with through our Maths lessons. I felt like I fitted in and we always had fun. It was great because we also met up sometimes on weekends and, if we didn't make plans, Vicky and I would simply play out in the street. There was, however, an unspoken acknowledgement that Vicky and her friend from primary school were best friends, and me and Jess were best friends.

In Year 8, I started going to the athletics club regularly with Vicky. Vicky and her sister Mia had moved to my road when we were all about nine years old and they instantly joined the group of us playing outside together all the time. As we got a bit older, the numbers of us playing out in the street started to dwindle but Vicky, Mia, and I always continued. We had sleep overs, went to pop concerts, did everything and anything together. One of our favourites was the board game 'The Game of Life.' We would spend hours playing this, going backwards and forwards, trying to get the best house, the best job, and as many children as we could - for whom we meticulously planned names. For years I planned on calling my first daughter Britney, after my obsession with Britney Spears! Vicky and I were in a lot of the same lessons at school and, because we were always playing out together, it made sense for us to go to the athletics club together.

Every Tuesday and Thursday night, aged around thirteen, we went to the athletics club together where we would run and train in the young sprints group. Every sports day at secondary school, I raced in the 100 metres (m). I always won the race, then set a school record and went on to win the District Sports A race. I was the fastest girl from all the local secondary schools. This was a routine that occurred every year. In the summer, I would sometimes compete for the athletics club at weekends in the sprint races and high jump for my age group. I always did quite well. When I kept doing well and kept running quick times, it made me stop and think that actually I might be quite good at running. But it was around this time that I also became very conscious of my size and weight.

My periods started when I was thirteen and I was absolutely devastated. I cried for hours that evening. I couldn't bear the changes my body was going through. I hated having a period, I hated my body becoming like an adult, I hated that I was losing my childhood. It was with my periods starting that I became concerned with my size. In reality, my body shape and size were perfectly normal, but I felt fat and a lot bigger than other people. More importantly though, I started to think my athletic performance would improve if I lost some weight. My athletics was going well and I really enjoyed it. I dreamt about becoming a professional athlete. That was the career I wanted to pursue. Sometimes during half-term when I would go to Jenny's for the day, on my ten-minute walk to her house, I would imagine myself being interviewed on the radio – Rebecca, the Great British athlete and the story of my rise to success. It was my dream and I was determined to achieve it.

To do this, I knew I needed to train properly and I was convinced I needed to lose weight. In Year 9, aged fourteen, I rarely missed a training session. Vicky had stopped coming by this stage. On top of athletics, I was doing netball training once a week, with a match on a Saturday. I was also in the school netball, basketball, swimming, athletics, and rounders teams, which all involved regular training and fixtures. Every bit of training I did was good because it helped me feel like I was working towards my dream. I cut back a bit on what I was eating, in an attempt to lose weight to help me run faster. Not much: only the odd spoonful of Coco Pops at breakfast or chocolate after dinner in the evening.

With the large amount of exercise I was doing, coupled with my slight energy restriction, my periods stopped. I couldn't have been more pleased. Little did I know, this was probably one of the first signs that anorexia was starting to lay its foundations. At the time, I saw it only as a positive thing. Without periods, I might be able to stop my body changing into an adult and I thought that must be a good thing for my running. I knew it must mean I had lost a bit of weight, but I imagined there would be loads of professional athletes who didn't have periods.

When it was clear that my periods had definitely stopped and it wasn't simply a case of them being irregular, my mum took me to the doctor, worried that something could be wrong. The doctor dismissed her concerns and explained that many athletes do not have periods. With the amount of exercise I was doing, the doctor said not having periods was common and nothing for me to worry about. So then, in my mind, not having periods was not only a good thing because of the inhibition of adulthood, it was an absolute *must* for the achievement of becoming a professional athlete. I *had* to keep my periods away and I *had* to lose some more weight. I was convinced this was the only way to get faster.

With my determination to become a professional athlete growing stronger, in November 2003, aged fifteen, I plucked up the courage to ask the elite sprints coach if I could join his group. He welcomed me and I hoped this would be the start of the dedicated training I needed to fulfil my dream. The amount of training I was doing increased significantly. I went from doing the fun sessions twice a week to having sessions on a Tuesday and Thursday, along with weight training on a Sunday and often another running session on a Saturday.

There were some really quick sprinters in the group, and I wanted to be as fast as them. With my growing desire to get faster, so my desire to lose weight grew. The fastest girls in the group were all very slight, so the answer seemed logical to me: to become as fast as them, I needed to get as slim as them.

Monday 12ᵗʰ Jan 2004

I'm trying to lose weight because everyone at athletics is skinny and I'm fat. I want a flat stomach like the other girls in the group. I really hope I do get to be an athlete when I'm older because you only get one life and that's what I want to do in it. If I get to go to Loughborough Uni then I'll be happy. I've just done 35 sit-ups, 25 triceps dips and 100 leg raises – hopefully take some calories off me! The only meal I can cut down on is lunch because all the others my mum is there, but I feel guilty wasting food. My eyes are bigger than my belly.

Anorexia was starting to lay its roots in my mind. I didn't realise it then but, looking back, I can see my behaviours were characteristic of someone with anorexia. Though my desire to lose weight and get thinner was triggered by my desire to get faster at running, at the same time as I made the move to the elite running group, I was also becoming increasingly unhappy at school, making me more and more vulnerable to the clutches of anorexia.

At the start of Year 10, Jess found a new best friend and left our foursome to join another group. This was really hard to deal with. It confirmed my feelings that I was a completely boring and unlikeable person. I wasn't fun, outgoing, chatty or bubbly, so no one was ever going to want to be my best friend.

Sunday 25ᵗʰ January 2004,

I slept round Jess's on Friday with Chloe. They've done a friendship box and in it Jess wrote a letter to Chloe saying 'you're my best mate'. It made me sad. I wonder if I'll still be friends with Jess, Vicky, and Louise when I'm eighteen? One thing's for sure – we won't be a four anymore. I wish we could go back and be like that again. It's really weird thinking about the future because I have no idea what's going to happen. I just want Chloe and Jess to break up. I know it sounds horrible and it will probably be me and Jess that break up. I'm depressed now. Why does Jess have to be friends with Chloe? I will just have to be my own best friend.

So, at the same time my training was increasing, my friendships and my self-esteem were crumbling. I felt so lost and alone. But the one thing I was certain of – I had to lose weight. Jess had the perfect figure and the girls at running had perfect figures. They were all popular and I was a reject. Losing weight seemed to not only be the answer to getting faster at running, but also to becoming more likeable and popular. Anorexia preyed on my loneliness. I didn't have a best friend and anorexia was slowly working its poison. Little did I know that 'just having to be my own best friend' was actually anorexia starting to form the deadliest friendship with my vulnerable mind.

I began to record what I was eating. That way, I could objectively see what I might take out in order to help me lose weight.

17ᵗʰ May 2004,
Breakfast: Coco Pops and a toasted muffin
Lunch: One and a half tuna rolls, cucumber and carrot sticks, an apple and a Brunch bar
Dinner: Pasta and veg, Chocolate cheesecake, three Rolo chocolates.
What can I cut out? I don't have any discipline. I'll try and leave some Coco Pops, leave a chunk of apple and not eat chocolate after dinner.

And so the slippery slope began. Cutting out and hiding food. I started giving or throwing away part of my lunch at school, and I would hide cereal in my dressing gown at breakfast. I was competing in events such as The South Of England's, where I was ranked 13ᵗʰ, and this provided me with some hope that one day, my dream would come true. Losing weight seemed to be the answer to all my problems. In reality, my body was now actually slightly underweight though pretty athletic. But this was not the reflection I saw in the mirror. I not only hated my body – its fatness and the way it looked – but also my whole being. I hated *me*. Focusing on losing weight and trying to get thinner not only helped me work towards my dream, but it also, subconsciously, eased the pain and loneliness I was feeling.

Chapter 3
Building the Dream

As I entered Year 11 in September 2004, life continued to get harder and increasingly stressful. I was trying to deal with the workload associated with GCSEs, alongside increasing training schedules. The days of spending my time either at school or playing in the street had been replaced by either being at school or in training. I didn't mind though; I wanted to train. It helped me feel like I was working towards my dream. Plus, my training group were a really nice group of girls. At school I felt alone and isolated, at training I felt like I belonged. The track had become my second home. In fact, I was spending more time at the track than at home. But I was unhappy with my limited progress. I had to get faster. I know now that my weight loss only served to hinder my athletic performance. But at the time, I felt the only way for me to get faster was to lose weight.

I replaced my Coco Pops with 30g of Special K and stopped having the toasted muffin at breakfast and cereal bar with my ever-decreasing lunch. I did manage to lose a bit of weight - this did not go unnoticed by my mum and she did try to make me eat more.

Sun 31st October 2004,
I want to lose weight, but Ma keeps making me eat. When she wasn't at home during half-term, I'd have 30g cereal but yesterday she made me have loads more and have a hobnob after lunch. I'm not going to run fast if

I'm fat.

With the start of the new year came a bit more weight loss. Before Christmas, I had weighed 9 stone (st) 3 pounds (lb), and by February 2005 I was 9st. With my height being 1.77m, this made my BMI just over 18 which was considered underweight. While I was very happy with the weight loss, it didn't make me run any faster. It did, in fact, have the opposite effect. I still had good endurance but with the slight weight loss, I was no longer able to run as fast as I used to. So I decided that, rather than focus on the 100m, I would focus on the 300m as this didn't require quite as much speed.

I told my mum I wanted to give up puddings for Lent but, to my frustration, she wouldn't let me. To an outsider, my 'healthy' eating habits could have been dismissed as an athlete looking after what they ate. It is often more difficult to spot eating disorders in athletes because typical signs such as restrictive diets and excessive exercise can be masked by following 'an athlete diet' or completing hard training sessions. In hindsight, I can see in myself that anorexia was starting to grow at this point. Anorexia was building its strength so that, in a few years, it would well and truly strangle me of life.

The competitive athletic season and GCSE revision and exam period, both incredible sources of stress, started in April 2005. It was at this time that my weight dipped below the 9st mark. On the one hand, I was very happy to have hit 8st 13lb; on the other, my running was still not improving as much as I wanted. Both my mum and my coach were convinced my loss of speed was due to me losing weight and told me I needed to put it back on.

18th April 2005,
I really don't want to put on weight, I still think I need to lose it, I haven't got a flat stomach. I hate being slow and I wonder why I have got so much slower. Ma reckons it might be my hormones, but I don't as I didn't have them last year either. My coach and Ma think I need to put on weight but I'm 100% sure I don't.

Despite my weight loss, the summer competitive season of 2005 saw me win the Essex Schools and compete in events such as the Essex Championships, South of England Championships, and the Nationals (AAAs). The weekend of the 2005 AAAs is one of my fondest memories. My mum and I travelled to Birmingham on the Friday afternoon and we stayed at the Innkeeper's Lodge. Attached to the lodge was a Toby Carvery. I had never been to one before and I couldn't believe the glorious-looking food. Everything on the menu sounded delicious. In the few days before competitions, I never restricted my food. I ate what I was meant to because I wanted to get in as much fuel and energy as possible. Subconsciously I must have known that my limited food intake the rest of the time was not supportive of good athletic performance. But nothing could shift the thought that if I lost weight I could run faster.

So, for that meal in the Toby Carvery, I wanted something that would help me perform well. The previous year when we had stayed in a different hotel, I remembered I had eaten scampi and chips, and I had performed dreadfully the following day. This thought was in the back of my mind when I was choosing my meal. I chose beef in red wine sauce which I had with roast potatoes and vegetables from the carvery. It was delicious. When I looked round the restaurant, I remember thinking that everyone was so overweight with mountainous plates of food piled high with roast potatoes and Yorkshire puddings. I couldn't believe that people could eat so much. I vowed to myself that I must *never* be like that.

That evening we had an early night because my race the following day was one of the first events. Driving to the stadium next morning, we played my mum's cassette of Randy Crawford in the car. Whenever I listen to her music now, particularly 'Street Life' and 'One Day I'll Fly Away,' it reminds me of that trip to Birmingham. I was in Lane 3 for the first heat of the 300m hurdles. I felt sick with nerves. But, over the years of competing, I had come to learn that nerves were a good thing. They helped me perform. When I didn't have the adrenaline surging through my body, I never performed at my best. So nerves were a good sign.

Racing against the best in the country, I had no expectations. I knew I wasn't one of the best, but I had qualified to compete against them and that in itself was an achievement. I didn't mind if I came last, I just wanted to perform well for me. During the race, as I entered the final 100m, the home straight, I could see I wasn't at the back of the pack. I was up there near the front. I couldn't believe it. I stumbled over the last hurdle and nearly lost my balance. Somehow, I managed to keep on my feet and gave it one last kick towards the finish line. There was nothing left in my legs, but they kept running round. I never imagined in a million years that I would come third in my heat with a Personal Best (PB) and reach the semi-final. But that is what I had achieved. I was absolutely overjoyed. I had never expected I was capable of achieving that and my dream of becoming a professional athlete seemed more possible. I had made it to the top sixteen in the country and this was one of the best feelings I have ever felt. True happiness. It makes me wonder now how good I could have been had I been eating properly and taking in enough energy to fuel my training and competitions.

I had developed a plan in my mind that going to university would be the start of really setting about achieving my dream. I knew if I could get into a good sporting university like Loughborough, I would receive the excellent coaching I needed and, most importantly, it would be my opportunity to lose weight and attain the slender athletic figure I was convinced I needed in order to succeed. Going to university would mean my mum wouldn't be there to make me eat. I imagined everything would fall into place at university – my weight, my athletics, my dream. Until then, I told myself I just had to wait.

The summer of 2005 was also when Great Britain won the bid to host the 2012 Olympic Games, fuelling my hope and motivation.

Thursday 7th July 2005,
Yesterday we won the Olympic bid for 2012! It has made me really determined to be in them and I'm really going to train hard because I have a funny feeling inside me.

Clearly my body knew something was going to happen. Something major, something important. I thought it would be the realisation of my dream. But it was quite the opposite. That funny feeling was trying to tell me something. Yes, something important and major was going to happen. But, instead of becoming a professional athlete and achieving my dream, I became a professional anorexic and lived the nightmare.

Chapter 4
The Storm Brews

The next two years at college studying for my AS Levels and A Levels followed a similar pattern to before. My life was dominated by studying, training, worrying about having no friends, and wanting to lose weight. Jess had another new friendship group, and Vicky and her best friend had a new group now as well. Wherever I was, I was on the edge and felt left out.

Looking back, I think this is where my depression properly started. I would look around and see that everyone was thinner than me, prettier than me, more popular than me. I felt invisible, like no one would notice or care if I wasn't there. I was rarely invited to things. To have to listen to your 'friends' every break and every lunchtime talking about evenings out and weekends together, when you have not been invited, is soul-destroying. I desperately wanted a best friend and, as I struggled to make friends in reality, my relationship with what was to become my best and only friend, anorexia, was growing.

As for the athletics, I increased my training and, despite my continuing under-fuelling, I participated in and won some important competitions, and ranked in the top thirty in the UK at my event for my age. This gave me hope that I might yet become a successful athlete. In retrospect, I am sure I would have been capable of running much faster had I been fuelling myself properly. But I will never know for sure.

A new development at this time, which I now realise was

symptomatic of my growing anorexia, was when my sister visited home from university. She had lost a huge amount of weight and I found it incredibly difficult to deal with. The morning after she arrived home, I forced her onto the scales. My mum also wanted to weigh her because she was worried about her significant weight loss. The scales read 9st. That had to be a good two stones less than her previous weight. I was devastated. I could not believe she weighed the same as me. That was not how it was meant to be. To me, despite us weighing the same and being the same height, she looked far thinner than me. Throughout our whole lives, I had always been the thinner one, and I could not bear it when she became thinner than me. I was furious and jealous, and the only solution I could think of was to vow to lose more weight.

Friday 7th April 2006,
I hate Nicola being so skinny! And the fact that she can't see it. She's so hypocritical! I have been eating slightly less this week, but so has she and she's been going on the exercise bike every day! Why can't she see how thin she is? It's so annoying. I want to be thinner than her and I can't stop thinking about it. It's really getting to me.

I would look at my sister of 9 stone and see a walking skeleton. But then I would look at myself, also around 9 stone, and see a fat, cellulite lump. Isn't it ironic that I had commented on her hypocrisy, her inability to see herself as she truly was? But anorexia was clouding my vision, not blocking it at that moment, but very much clouding it. That is the thing with anorexia, it convinces you that you are bigger than everyone else and manipulates your mind so that you can't see how thin you are. To my relief, over the next few months my sister regained the lost weight and has maintained a healthy size ever since.

My new year's resolutions for 2006 were:
1. Lose weight,
2. Do not waste time or wish time to pass,
3. Treat each day like it's my last.

My breakfast and lunches became smaller or, in the case of my lunch, sometimes non-existent. From waking up in the

16

morning to dinner time in the evening, I did not consume more than 500 calories. Now I know you're probably thinking, if I was only eating 500 calories during the day and doing so much training, how was I not losing vast amounts of weight? The answer is that my dinner in the evening was always a decent size and every night I had a pudding.

I loved puddings, particularly my mum's home-made apple crumble or spotted dick, or Aunt Bessie's Jam Roly Poly. But I hated myself for eating them. I wished I had the self-discipline and willpower to turn them down, but I couldn't. My mum was so concerned I was underweight and under-fuelled, she knew dinner time was one occasion when she got to get some food into me. In my mind, I had to compensate for my dinners and puddings, where there was no possibility of restricting, by not eating much for breakfast and lunch. It is clear to me, looking back now, that these were anorexic thoughts and they were influencing my eating habits. However, they had not completely taken over and I was not fully subordinate to anorexia. That was to come later.

As I approached my eighteenth birthday in September 2006, I was filled with utter dread. I wished I could be like Peter Pan – the child that never grows up. I didn't feel ready to think about going to university; I didn't feel ready to face life. Everyone around me wanted to be eighteen. They wanted to go out partying, they wanted to go out drinking, they wanted to be an adult. Not me.

Summer 2006,

I so don't feel old enough to be 18! I still feel like a kid – I still WANT to be a kid. I want to stay a child forever. I don't want to be an adult. I hate it. Why does it have to happen? Why can't I just be 15 again? I don't feel old enough to go to uni and leave home. It's going to be so scary!

I had a bouncy castle party for my birthday which I really enjoyed, and I spent the day with my family and was treated to a professional massage, manicure, and pedicure. I had my favourite dinner in the evening: my mums home-made chicken chasseur followed by her speciality chocolate cake. This was the last birthday meal I chose, that I looked forward to, that I really enjoyed. That was my penultimate birthday before anorexia truly set in. From then on, birthdays became just another day. From then on, anorexia dominated everything. There is only room for one thing in a life with anorexia. And that isn't a birthday.

At around the same time as I turned eighteen, I had to start deciding what university I wanted to go to. To help me decide, I attended several open days at some of my choices – Loughborough, St Mary's, Bath, Birmingham, and Cardiff Metropolitan University (UWIC). Loughborough had always been my preferred choice as it is the top university in the country for sport science and has the highest calibre athletics coaches. The open day at Loughborough was my first and I went with my sister. I had gone in with such high hopes but, looking around, I absolutely hated it.

As Nicola and I inspected one of the halls-of-residence, I turned to her with tears welling in my eyes. "I'd rather sleep in a tent," I said. "This is horrible."

On the train journey home I told Nicola there was no way I would go to Loughborough. I attended the rest of the open days with my dad. I didn't like any of the universities and looking round, I felt daunted by the prospect of having to move to one of those places and establish a new life there on my own. I would look at the other prospective students looking round, and they all seemed so much older than me and excited by the prospect of moving out.

"I am not like these people," I told myself, "I can't imagine living here or coping here."

I felt like a child. I felt like I needed my parents by my side. I was terrified to face the big, wide world alone. But going to university felt like the only option for me. If I was going to achieve my dream, I needed to go to university. I was desperate to get the decent training I had been longing for, that would set me on the path to turning dream into reality. And of course, I had to go to university as soon as possible to start losing weight. Going to university felt like the only way I would lose the weight to make me run faster. And I did not want to delay the process any longer. As much as I had hated it, I knew Loughborough would be the best for my athletic development; I was determined I had to go there.

My weight towards the end of 2006 and start of 2007 remained pretty steady, around 9 stone or just under, and my training regime was as before. However, I was upset that my training wasn't going very well and it felt like my dreams were slipping away.

I would often complain to my mum, "All I want is to lose weight, train harder and run faster. But I'm getting worse. I used to be fast back in the early years of secondary school. I want to get back to that."

"The difference between then and now, Bex, is that you were bigger then. You had more power and energy to run fast. You've lost too much weight and, because you've lost weight, you've lost muscle so your speed has gone," my mum would reply, trying to give me encouragement and hope. And, most importantly, trying to encourage me back to a healthier weight.

This was a fairly frequent conversation and I would always leave the exchange questioning whether perhaps she was right, but quickly deciding no, she must be wrong.

I would think to myself, 'I do not need to put on weight. If I need to put on weight, then why I am I still so big? I wouldn't be this fat and have this huge stomach if I needed to put on weight. No, I need to *lose* weight. I need to get a flat stomach: that will help me run faster.'

My stomach is my big bugbear. It always has been, and I imagine it always will be. I would look at other athletes and see they all had six-packs and completely flat stomachs. That was what I wanted. I hated that mine stuck out so much. Jess, who I still desperately wanted to be friends with, who was popular amongst lots of the girls and all of the boys, had, in my eyes the perfect figure. Her stomach was washboard flat and she had a six-pack. She had the type of stomach you see in magazines.

"If she can get a stomach like that then so can I," I would tell myself. "Lots of sit-ups and fewer calories."

I convinced myself that if I had a flat stomach I'd be more attractive and people would like me more. All the boys fancied Jess. She would often go out to clubs and could have any man

19

she wanted. Whereas me? I was a freak. I was eighteen, never had a boyfriend, never kissed a boy. I struggled to even hold a conversation with the male species. When I would go out with Jess and her friends, as I started to do occasionally, she would receive all the attention, both from the group of girls we went out with and all the surrounding lads with their mates. I was a reject, a nobody. If I hadn't been there, no one would have noticed any difference. That was how I felt all the time. That nobody would actually care if I wasn't there. I was left feeling destroyed, convinced I was a completely unlikeable person and a freak. My self-esteem was shattered.

I have no doubt that this sense of rejection throughout my teenage years, is one of the reasons why I have clung so firmly onto anorexia. Anorexia has felt like my friend when no one else did. Anorexia convinced me I couldn't have real friends but that it didn't matter, because I could have anorexia instead. However, I was soon to discover anorexia would destroy every friendship and relationship to get its own way. Anorexia is not a friend, but an enemy.

Throughout the spring and early summer of 2007, I was spending nine to ten hours a day revising for my A Levels. The revision, coupled with my athletics training, occupied my whole time. I would walk up and down the garden path for an hour a day, reading and reciting my revision notes. That way I could revise *and* burn calories at the same time. You would think that with the importance of these exams and the need to perform well in them, I would consider the revision period an important time where I needed to be functioning at my best, with full concentration and energy. But I was very anxious about sitting down so much, so I never ate lunch and had only a handful of cereal for breakfast. This would fuel me for the whole day until dinner which, when I had training, wasn't until 9pm. I couldn't justify eating during the day when I had been sitting down. The fear of gaining weight was too strong to allow me to eat. And it seemed logical, if I was sitting down all day, I was not burning calories, so I *had* to eat less.

After my A Level exams finished, I joined another athletics club as well as my old one, so I was training every day of the week except Fridays. Joining the new club was a terrifying prospect as it meant training with much faster people and at a much higher intensity. My first few competitions of the season didn't go too well, and my times were nowhere near what I had hoped for and needed. I spent the whole winter trying to train hard. I tried 100% in everything I did. I left no training session without giving it my all. And then to find that this wasn't good enough to make any improvements from the previous year – it was gutting. I felt like a failure. This made getting into Loughborough University ever more important. It was my only chance to get the decent training I needed and to be able to lose weight and so allow me to fulfil my dreams.

I got a practice run of how I would be able to take control of my eating at university when I went on holiday with my friends in the summer of 2007. I spent most of the holiday wishing I could be closer to Jess, jealous of her always being with her best friend, Allana, and feeling like a nobody. It was a difficult time but, in my mind, I was focused on losing weight.

I was really pleased with myself that I ate minimally on the holiday. I proved to myself that I could do it, and it was a promising sign for my quest to diet at university. One day on the holiday, I only ate a tuna roll, a banana, and a rich tea biscuit. This provided the reassurance and proof I needed that if my mum wasn't cooking for me and wasn't around, then I *could* eat less. I may not have had the discipline at home but, when left to my own devices, I could be strict with myself and I was sure I would lose weight. In the one week I was on holiday, I lost nearly half a stone. I was very happy, but the downside was that my athletics performance on return was shockingly bad. I acknowledged that this may in part have been due to my lack of eating on holiday – I probably hadn't eaten enough, but I was still convinced I needed to lose weight.

It was confirmed, in August 2007, that I would go to Loughborough University. I'd achieved the A Level grades I needed and my plan to lose weight, and get faster, could now be implemented. But part of me must have known something bad might happen. My mum had continually said to me over the past few months that she thought I should take a gap year, and part of me knew she was right. When I got my results and it was confirmed I was going to Loughborough, I doubted my decision to go.

Monday 3rd September 2007,
I'm now starting to think it's not the right decision and that I should have taken a gap year. I so don't feel ready to leave home... I'm dreading going!

But I was impatient, and I didn't want to waste another year of not losing weight and not improving my running. In my head I had no choice but to go to university straight away, so I could start losing weight, training hard, and achieving my dream.

Chapter 5
Starting Out at Loughborough

D-Day occurred on Thursday 27th September 2007 – the day I moved to Loughborough. I was swamped with feelings of worry, sadness and fear. I said goodbye to my mum at home, both of us with tears welling in our eyes. It was then a three-hour car journey with my dad to arrive at my destination. The start of the journey wasn't too bad as I knew I still had a few hours until I got there. I hoped for a really long car journey, the longer the better.

But those few hours passed too quickly, and 'Loughborough' started to appear on the motorway signs. The radio was on, but I wasn't taking any of it in.

"If Loughborough is on the road signs, we must be near," I thought.

An overwhelming feeling of dread encompassed me. Then I saw the signs to my hall-of-residence and, low and behold, within several minutes we were pulling into the driveway of very old-looking buildings with hundreds of people around. I saw students with their parents unloading suitcases from their cars, knowing this was going to be me in a few minutes. These people all appeared excited, happy, chatting away. Not me: I wanted to hug my dad and get him to take me home. But we got out of the car, found our way over to the registration queue and proceeded to walk down the line, collecting leaflets, information brochures, goodie bags, and at the end of the queue, the key to my halls and my bedroom.

"19 Cedar Lodge," the boy at the desk said. "That's in the halls on the opposite side of the road, about fifty metres down."

We got back in the car and drove over to my halls. The setting was quite pretty with grand trees lining the driveway and scattered about on the grass between buildings. My block was at the end of the driveway and there was no escaping it now. We were there, and I had to go in.

I found my bedroom up the stairs near the end of a corridor in a flat of seven other bedrooms. I could see another bedroom door open, voices coming from inside, boxes stacked high on the floor. I scurried into my room with my dad; I didn't want to see anybody. The room was basic but perfectly pleasant, with a bed, a desk, a wardrobe and a window looking out onto the grass and trees. But the acceptableness of my bedroom did nothing to ease my fears and worry. My dad tried to be enthusiastic, "Cor, this is nice, isn't it? Look, you've got a nice big desk, a good view out of the window."

Despite his enthusiasm (for which I was grateful), I was fighting hard not to burst into tears. We decided to start transferring all my stuff from the car to my room. And believe me, there was a hell of a lot of stuff. When you move away to university, you literally have to transfer your whole life. Not only do you need the essentials like clothes, pillows, pots and pans, but you need the nice little extras, the nick-nacks to make your bedroom your home, as essentially this is what it becomes. You need all the photos frames, the cushions – those things that make it yours, that try and make living away from your real home less painful. For me, that meant having everything (and by everything I do mean everything) in my bedroom pink. If I was going to have to live there, I would have the pink bedroom I had always wanted. It was a mild form of compensation.

With everything piled into my bedroom, I carried my kitchen utensils into the communal kitchen. My dad helped me find a cupboard I could claim as mine, where I could store all my pink plates and cups. He went to fetch more saucepans from my bedroom as I unloaded my crockery.

A girl walked into the kitchen. She was stunning, with

shoulder-length brown hair and immaculate make-up. We exchanged a nervous 'Hello' and I rushed out as quickly as possible, feeling shy and very awkward. I later learnt that her name was Selin, and little did I know then that she would become one of my dearest friends.

With my cooking equipment all in my kitchen cupboard, and everything else packaged up in my bedroom, I told my dad he might as well go home and leave me to unpack. I hugged him, gripping him tightly as we said goodbye. My bedroom door closed behind him and I stood frozen in my bedroom. I was completely alone and I burst into tears. All I wanted was my mum and dad, to be at home with them. But I was there, alone and terrified.

I unpacked with tears rolling down my face. Eventually my room was ready, my little pink home. I braced myself and summoned up all my courage to head to the kitchen where I heard voices. There were several girls sitting round the table. We all introduced ourselves and tried to make conversation. For our first night out as freshers we had been given bright green t-shirts with our hall-of-residence name 'Harry French' on the front and a picture of Borat. We sat round the table and customised our t-shirts. Seven girls from different walks of life thrown together to start a new chapter in our lives. Surprisingly, we got on with ease. I almost instantly had a favourite, Bethan, and – me being typical me – immediately decided that I wanted her to be my best friend and, importantly, that I become her best friend. As it happened, we got on really well. She came across as chatty, kind, fun; a really lovely person. We were doing the same course (I was studying Sport and Exercise Science, she was studying Sport Science with Management) so I hoped this meant we would spend a lot of time together.

Freshers' Week is such an artificial environment. Take that first night for example. There we were – a group of seven girls who had never met before. We didn't know if we had anything in common and we were meant to go out together, partying, having fun… the sort of stuff people would have done at home but with friends they'd had for years. And we were meant to do this every night. Looking around, I could see that some students were in their element. They were like caged animals being set free into the wild. Being away from home, no parents, partying and drinking all night, lazing around all day… it was like heaven to them. One big, non-stop party.

This was not a life I was used to or a life I enjoyed. I felt like a fish out of water; an ugly Quasimodo in a world filled with stunning blonde Barbies.

There were no lessons during Freshers' Week. We were left with nothing to do all day then expected to party all night. For many, the day times were used to sleep, nurse hangovers and take that embarrassing walk of shame back to halls after a one-night stand.

Luckily, the girls in my flat weren't as 'sociable' as many others appeared to be. Yes, they liked a drink, liked to party, liked to have a good time, but they weren't 'wild'. None of them minded that I didn't drink. I was still very much included and, on a few occasions during that first week, we didn't even stay out past midnight. I don't think I could have fallen in with a better group of girls. A late addition to our group, Kate, arrived on the sixth day of Freshers' Week, having transferred from another hall. She neatly fitted into our group and was someone who, like Bethan, I instantly got on well with.

Mid-way through Freshers' Week, Bethan and I went for a walk around the area. We talked about how desperately homesick we were and how we'd believed we were the only person to feel like that. What a relief and comfort it was to know I wasn't alone in my feelings, I wasn't a freak. For someone as bubbly, chatty, and friendly as Bethan to be feeling that way, it must be ok for me to feel like that too.

While I missed home desperately, I knew I needed to stay if I was to have any hope of achieving my dream. My weight loss plan started immediately and, although being away from home was difficult, I threw myself into my new life – making friends, studying hard and, most importantly, starting intense and dedicated athletics training. Being a 400m hurdler, I joined the 400m/400m hurdles group which had a nationally renowned coach. I was ranked in the top thirty in the UK and I was eager and excited to start the training I had been wanting for so long. It was nerve-wracking to begin with. I didn't think it was appropriate for me to be a part of this group, to be training with the likes of such elite athletes. I wasn't good enough. I was scared. I simply wouldn't be able to do the training or, if I did, I would be a million miles behind everyone else and it would soon become apparent I didn't belong.

There was an 'elite' group of Olympians and Commonwealth games athletes which was part of our wider training group. We trained with them on a Monday and Saturday, and I couldn't believe I was actually accepted into this group. My group who trained together all the time, although not considered the 'elite' group, had some pretty good athletes in it. I knew who they all were from the athletics circuit and they were well up there in the rankings. For the first few sessions I was overwhelmingly nervous and anxious. I feared my lack of ability was going to be obvious and would lead to yet another rejection, and from the group I had so longed to be in. Literally, what I wanted to achieve in my life depended on how I performed as part of this group.

We went out for a few runs on the road and longer sessions on the grass for the first few weeks (interval training for those sports people out there). And I was amazed. I wasn't merely a tag-along to their training group, doing the same training as them but at the back of the pack, struggling to keep up. I was completing all the sessions and keeping up with the group. I knew I had a long way to go, but if I was already keeping up with the athletes in my group, what might I be able to achieve with three years of this professional training?

I had to get everything right. I had to be committed and train 100% all of the time. To start with, I was training five times a week. The training sessions were incredibly intense and would last several hours. They pushed me further than I'd ever gone before, making me feel pain (and lactic) like I never knew possible. As part of my course, I also had one hour of basketball and one hour of swimming per week, which I treated as good opportunities to burn calories. I also had netball training on a Tuesday evening after my athletics training. The athletics training was normally about 6-8pm and then I would walk back to my hall, before heading out on the fifteen-minute walk with Kate, to start netball training at 9pm for an hour and a half. It was an absolute killer. But I got a kick out of feeling exhausted and pushing my body to the limit. It became my expectation for myself: I must exercise and push myself as hard as I could, *all* of the time. The saying 'no pain no gain' rang very true in my mind.

All this exercise was coupled with a slowly decreasing diet. It didn't take much effort to lose weight. The pudding I had been eating every night at home was the first to go. It wasn't practically possible to have a pudding every night. My mum wasn't on hand to make them and I certainly wasn't going to go out and buy one. And despite my need to have one at home, I found it surprisingly easy to cut it out. I didn't miss my puddings. Maybe because I was missing home so much, I wasn't capable of missing anything else.

I had made all my meals smaller and this, coupled with the huge amount of exercise I was getting, allowed the weight to gradually fall off, which in my eyes, was a good thing. I needed to lose weight and at last I was in control. Everything I ate was carefully monitored, everything weighed out. My mum wasn't there to make me eat. I could do as I wanted. And I wanted to become an athlete, so this meant losing weight to get the figure of an athlete.

Everything I did had the focus of burning calories and losing weight. Going to lectures provided an opportunity to walk and burn calories. Shopping was another opportunity to exercise. Going out partying in the evening several times a week was a good opportunity to limit food and burn calories (I couldn't possibly eat a meal before going out and we had to walk to the venues and danced until the early hours of the morning). This shows how intrusive and poisonous anorexia is. Most people enjoy going out and having fun with their friends, being young and care-free. I, on the other hand, was edging closer and closer to my prison cell of anorexia, and was soon to be completely locked inside. I was not care-free. I wasn't free in any sense of the word. I was slowly falling under the dictatorship of anorexia. I couldn't do anything without thinking about how many calories I was consuming or burning. But it all felt necessary. At this stage, I was doing it purely to achieve my athletics ambition. There was no ulterior motive. It had all started as an innocent attempt to run faster. Little did I know that I was falling into anorexia's trap.

stage, I was doing it purely to achieve my athletic ambition. There was no ulterior motive. It had all started as an innocent attempt to run faster. Little did I know that I was falling into anorexia's trap.

Chapter 6
The Devil Grows

On Tuesday 27th November 2007, two months after my arrival in Loughborough, I weighed in at 53.7kg (8st 6lb). I had lost nearly half a stone in the first two months and this made me happy. I was training hard and losing weight. I wanted to lose even more weight to try and improve more.

There was another aspect to my life in Loughborough that was making me happy alongside the weight loss – my relationship with my housemates. I finally had the friends I had been so desperate for throughout my time at school and college. My housemates were fantastic and I couldn't have asked for any better. The eight of us got on really well (some more than others) and I had my two best friends, Bethan and Kate, who gave me the friendship I had longed for. The eight of us would go out clubbing and shopping, watch films and TV, and cook together... I loved this. To have spent years not invited to anything, feeling rejected and left out, to now being included in everything and having friends literally on my doorstep.

I remember one Friday evening, when most of the students of Loughborough were out partying until the early hours of the morning, we all stayed in our flat, not wanting to go to the bother of getting ready and going out. We gathered in one room and watched Titanic on DVD. We sat there together, gathered in Selin's room swaying our Pringles pot in the air as we belted out 'I will always love you' by Celine Dion. Now don't get me wrong, we did like going out and having fun, but we weren't hard-core party animals every night, and we could as much enjoy a night in as a night out.

I loved that there were always people around me. At any time, I could pop out my room, knock on one of their doors and have some company. They gave me something I had never had before. As sense of belonging. I really did enjoy my time with those girls. They accepted me for who I was and they actually seemed to like me. For once, I was never left out; I was never put to the back of the pack because they had made new friends, or because I wasn't drinking alcohol. I thought I had made my best friends for life. But this was cruelly taken away from me by anorexia. I had finally made close friendships, but this is not allowed by anorexia. There is only room for one thing in your life when you have anorexia. And that is anorexia itself.

While my friendship situation had changed drastically from college, my relationship with men had not. I was still incapable of holding a conversation with a member of the opposite sex. I would simply clam up and panic. The girls in my flat were all beautiful with personalities to match, and they easily attracted male attention. I, on the other hand, was never given a second glance. I wasn't capable of having a boy as a friend, let alone be able to have one as a boyfriend.

"Why would anyone want me?" I would ask myself, "I'm fat, ugly, boring, shy… none of which has any appeal." I had been hoping that at university I might be able to find a boyfriend, or at the very least, have some males that I got on with. But men simply weren't interested in me. And because I found it so difficult to talk to them, when I did happen to be in male company, I would sit there as if the cat had caught my tongue. I was nineteen years old, a virgin, never been kissed, never been on a date. And these issues did trouble me, confirming my view that I was a freak and a social reject.

My athletics performance was continuing to improve in the build-up to Christmas and, by the start of December 2007, my desire to lose more weight was growing ever stronger. I started to make my portions smaller and made promises to myself that I would be good by limiting my food as much as possible. Every

31

Wednesday when we had our weekly night out to 'Hey Ewe' at the student union, I would have ten-calorie soup for my dinner, after only having eaten a small bowl of cereal for breakfast and a pitta bread with tuna for lunch. I just knew I needed to lose weight.

I was looking forward to going home for Christmas and having four weeks exactly where I wanted to be – with my family and my home comforts. I would speak to my mum on the phone every day when I was in Loughborough, telling her about my training sessions, how things in general were going. I loved telling her about the good stuff, the really hard training session I'd completed and done well in, the exam I had sat and achieved a decent mark for. I missed my mum and dad immensely and talking on the phone was the closest I could get to them.

While I did tell my mum the good stuff, my running and my friends, often our conversations over the phone involved my feelings of homesickness and negativity. I was finding university stressful and I missed home. Also, although my running was improving, I would worry it wasn't improving enough. I was convinced the only way to get it to improve more was to lose more weight.

At a time where everything was stressful, losing weight gave me a real feel-good feeling. I got such a kick out of standing on the scales and seeing the numbers go down. I was achieving something. If I had a bad training session or felt overwhelmed by the workload of the course, and all I wanted to do was burst into tears and go home for a cuddle with my mum and dad, I would make myself feel better by setting my focus on losing weight. Losing weight would make me a better person in every sense. Life would be better if I could just lose more weight.

I arrived home for Christmas at 8st 5lb, with a BMI just under 17, which I was very pleased about. However, my parents expressed their concern for my weight loss. I didn't tell them what I weighed but they said they could see I had lost weight. I told them I was fine, and I ate normally while I was at home. I didn't want to show them any signs that I was restricting food and that I was hell bent on losing weight. I worried greatly about the weight I would gain but I knew, for those four weeks, I had to get on and do it. Then I could go back to Loughborough and start my mission again.

I met up with Jess, Allana, and Sarah over Christmas, all catching up about our times at university, all of them saying how much fun they were having. 'They are having a lot more fun without me', I would tell myself. I was jealous that they were all making new friends, worried I would be forgotten about even more. It was all a too familiar feeling of rejection that I had felt over the years. It did please me though that they commented on my weight loss.

Jess said. "When I was looking at your photos, I could see you were getting thinner. Look at this photo," Jess said as she got a Facebook photo up on the computer, "look how thin your arms are. You mustn't lose any more weight."

They also commented on one of the other girls in our group having lost a bit of weight and this angered me. I couldn't let her be thinner than me. For so long I had felt like the nobody, forgotten about in the background, but now I was determined I had to be the 'thin one'. Being known as the 'thin one' gave me someone to be and gave me an identity. I wanted to be the thin one both with my home friends and uni friends.

By the time I went back to university after Christmas, my weight had crept up to 8st 8lb, which I hated. This added to my stress at a time when I was trying to focus my mind on my exams. With the start of term in February 2008, my mood started to deteriorate. I could feel myself getting more and more obsessive about calories, exercise, and weight loss. My running had stopped improving and I was finding it increasingly difficult.

Tuesday 12th February 2008,

I'm back in Loughborough. Being home was nice, but training didn't go too well - I just feel so slow and with the training I've been doing I should be getting better not worse! It's really getting me down more than it's ever done before... I'm even considering giving up! I hate life at the moment. When I got home I was 8st 5, and by the end I was 8st 8. I know by being this light it's probably not doing my athletics any good but there's nothing I can do about it... I just can't eat much more. I'm trapped in a calorie counting world.

I was now training six times a week, as well as the netball training and sport lessons for my course. I was also making a concerted effort to walk a lot more, going for extra walks after training sessions and at weekends, extra runs round the streets and on the treadmill. I also started to restrict my food further. My bowl of bran flakes for breakfast became smaller, lunch was an apple except for when I knew I had a hard training session so would allow myself a pitta bread, and dinner was a plate of vegetables though sometimes I would allow myself some protein to go with it.

My world had become overpowered by restricting food, counting calories, burning calories, and weight loss. My training was getting worse and worse. The conversations with my mum over the phone had also taken a turn for the worse. Having been our main source of conversation for years, we no longer spoke about athletics. I knew I had become worse and I couldn't bear to tell my mum about this. We would only end up arguing, so it was best not to talk about it at all. I carried on trying to train as hard as I could, I couldn't give up on my dream. It was the one thing in life I had wanted, but it felt like it was getting further and further away from me. I was slipping more and more into the grips of anorexia. It became a vicious cycle – the more anorexia took over, the more my dreams faded, and the more my dreams faded the more I turned to weight loss to make myself feel better. I told myself if I couldn't have anything else in my life, at least I could be thin; and the more dominant anorexia became.

Also, although I still enjoyed going out with my friends, that feeling of rejection had crept back in. I couldn't help but think that my two best friends, Bethan and Kate, preferred each other to me and I started to feel left out. When I sat alone in my room and heard some of the girls talking, I immediately got that feeling of desertion. "Why aren't I included? They don't like me. They prefer each other to me." Was this anorexia making me paranoid? Making me feel like I needed anorexia? Not that I knew anorexia as an entity at that time, I simply knew that if I couldn't have friends, if I couldn't have my athletics, I would have to be thin instead. That would be my consolation.

Chapter 7
A Lost Dream & A New Focus

By March 2008, I was weighing myself every week in Boots on their digital scales. It was part of my routine on a Sunday. After a run, I would then go for a long walk through the town and stop off at Boots on the way. Sometimes I couldn't resist the temptation to weigh myself during the week as well. I worried that I would have gained weight from the previous week and that I had not been disciplined enough with my food. But each week I was pleasantly surprised. A few more pounds knocked off.

On Friday 14th March 2008, I weighed 7st 12lb. I was overjoyed to have broken the eight stone mark. I'd never imagined that I could get into the seven stones, but now I had reached it, there was no way I was going to go back up into the eights. No way. Seven stone was my new benchmark. Whilst reaching 8st 5lb a few weeks ago had felt incredible, the thought of going back up to that now seemed unbearable. That is the thing with anorexia, you never can get thin enough. You have a target in your head and yes, you do feel achievement when you reach it, but it doesn't stop there. Once you reach one target you instantaneously have a new one. You can always lose a bit more weight. No matter how much you think you will reach your target, be happy and stop there, it just doesn't happen. You always have to lose more weight, to see how much lower you can get. If you can get down to one number, then surely you can get lose a bit more… and a bit more… and a bit more.

The weight loss with anorexia will not stop until you die. In the eyes of anorexia, weight loss is limitless. People with anorexia feel superhuman and indestructible, like nothing can hurt them or stop them. In a sense, this is true. Left to myself, nothing would have stopped me. I was possessed, pushing my body beyond exhaustion, feeding it nothing but the absolute bare minimum. Yet I still managed to carry on. Anorexia sufferers are capable of pushing their bodies to extents that most can't even imagine. But there is a limit and there is only so far they can push until they are knocking on death's door. No one can defy death and eventually, once anorexia makes you knock on death's door, you can be sucked in and reach the end of your limits. Anorexia will not stop until you reach this.

While I was happy to see the number fall on the scales to 7st 12, I immediately started to worry that I was going to put the weight straight back on, and then some, especially as I was going home for the four-week Easter holidays. I told myself I must try to be even more disciplined, try and lose a bit more and not gain any back. I *had* to be more disciplined. I just had to. I despised myself when I felt like I lost my discipline. I felt guilty, greedy and disgusting. I would occasionally find myself picking at cereal in the morning, having a handful extra from the box, or having a spoonful of one of my friend's left-over dinners in the fridge. I would feel completely and utterly ashamed of myself.

"How could I do that?" I would ask myself, "How could I be so fat and greedy? It's disgusting. I must get my discipline back. I need to lose weight, I shouldn't be eating."

These were the thoughts that would race through my mind. However, I wasn't being greedy or undisciplined at all. I was surviving on only a few hundred calories a day and exercising intensely for hours. Quite simply, my body was eating itself. I wasn't providing it with the fuel it needed to function, so it had to get this from elsewhere. It had to eat away at my muscle, tissues, and organs. So, when I did find myself eating that handful of cereal, it wasn't greed or a sign of weakness, it was a reaction to starvation. An attempt to stay alive.

I think there is a general public belief that people with anorexia don't eat anything. This was certainly the thought I had.

I had put this idea of 'anorexia' on a throne. To be anorexic was, in my mind, the ultimate achievement. It was a status that I desperately desired. To be anorexic would make me fulfilled. Anorexics are thin, determined and disciplined. To me, they were beings above normal human beings. And I wanted to be one. But because I had this idea in my mind that anorexics didn't eat (which in fact they do, and most actually like food), I felt like I was failing and that I wasn't achieving anorexic status because I was passing food through my mouth. I thought any amount of food was too much; too much for weight loss and too much for anorexia. I would be riddled with guilt when I ate, feeling ashamed that I was giving into food when to be anorexic you have to consume nothing. I was greedy, a glutton and I lacked willpower or control, so my mind would tell me. Food passing my lips meant I was failing at being anorexic. Everything else in my life also felt like it was failing and now I was failing at my ambition to be anorexic. There was only one solution to this. I had to try harder. I had to eat less.

My portion of cereal in the morning became even smaller, lunch was scrapped completely, and dinner was a small plate of vegetables. I was still exercising excessively. On Sundays, when I didn't have training but would go for a run and a long walk, I wouldn't eat all day until dinner when I allowed myself one Quorn sausage and vegetables.

But my desire to be anorexic conflicted with my lifelong dream of becoming an athlete. I knew my low weight was severely detrimental to my running and I should probably eat more if I wanted to run faster. But anorexia now had its grip on me and, although I could understand the logic and reason to this argument, I couldn't change my behaviour, I couldn't act on it. I couldn't eat more. It was a very confusing time with my mind split in two: one half wanting to be anorexic, one wanting to be an athlete, and both requiring polar opposite behaviours. This was a constant source of conflict, a daily, hourly, non-stop mental battle. Knowing the right behaviours to achieve what had been my dream for years, but not being able to carry them out.

On 15th March 2008, I went home for the Easter holidays, full of dread. Four weeks of not being in complete control of what I ate and having to eat more because my mum would make me. I was a lot weaker by this point. I can remember struggling with my suitcase round the train stations, trying to find enough strength in my ever-depleting muscles to lift it up and down stairs. When I arrived at my home station, my mum was there waiting for me. When I saw her, I wanted to burst into tears. I was physically and mentally exhausted. My world was crumbling around me, my one dream was rapidly slipping away and I felt completely out of control. I knew I needed to eat, but I simply couldn't. I was terrified. I wanted my mum to hug me and make everything better. I wanted her to make all this bad stuff go away. I wanted to tell her everything that had been happening and how I couldn't eat.

But as much as I wanted to say all this, to surrender and have her help me, when it came down to it, anorexia took over again. Anorexia is a secretive, destructive illness. It doesn't want people to know your restriction habits and that you are losing weight. Anorexia was my secret, and no one must know. Sufferers will try their best to appear normal, to disguise any weight loss, to try to come up with believable excuses to avoid food and to sneak in more exercise. If I had told my mum exactly how I was feeling and what I had been doing, that would have been it: my weight loss mission would have been stopped dead in its tracks. While a big part of me so desperately wanted help and to stop and rest, anorexia would not allow this. It is demonic and once it has started it will not stop. It has a power over your subconscious that completely takes over and dictates your life.

So, in that moment when I was reunited with my mum, I tried my best to keep my secret. But my mum looked horrified at the shrunken frame in front of her.

"My God, Rebecca, you have lost so much weight," she gasped with worry. "What have you been doing?"

"I'm fine, there's nothing wrong. I haven't lost weight," I said matter-of-factly to try and stop her worrying.

This was a conversation that occurred regularly during the four weeks I was at home. Her expressing worry at my weight loss, me declaring I hadn't lost any weight; her trying to make me eat more, me hiding food or saying I had already eaten or was far too full.

Throughout my whole time at home during the Easter holidays, all I could think about was how much weight I was going to gain and how I needed to keep my food intake as low possible. I could no longer fake normal eating when I went home. I had fallen deeper into the grips of anorexia. I no longer wished I could have the discipline to restrict the food; there was not one part of me that wanted to eat anything. My mum's delicious dinners had gone from being considered a treat and something tasty I could just about allow myself to have in the short time I was home, to being a dirty, repulsive, terrifying thought. How could I possibly put this food into my mouth? It made me feel disgusting. I didn't want anything in my stomach.

When my mum served up her chicken chasseur, the dinner I had chosen for my eighteenth birthday because it was my favourite, I felt nothing but fear. A plate of food had me terrified. I tried my best to hide that I was struggling, but I ate nothing during the day and only very small portions for dinner, and my parents and Nicola could see I was deteriorating. Nicola had a friend stay with us for a few days and I overheard them talking about me, her friend saying how dreadfully thin I looked.

On one occasion during those holidays, I was baking some cakes for my former nanny Jenny and her girls (she now had twins as well as Laura). I was hoping the fact that I was busy would make my mum forget about lunch. But later in the afternoon she barged into the kitchen.

"You need to eat lunch. You need to have something," she demanded.

But I had planned for this eventuality and I had placed two cake cases with crumbs in the bin.

"I've already eaten," I said calmly as I carried on with my baking.

"No you haven't," she said angrily, "you haven't eaten anything."

"I have eaten. I had two of the cakes I made," I said, trying to remain calm and disguise the fact I was lying.

"I don't believe you. Don't lie to me!" My mum was now shouting.

I opened the bin and showed her my two wrappers. "See, I have eaten."

There was nothing my mum could do. She continued to argue with me but, when it came down to it, she couldn't make me eat. I always had an excuse or an answer, or a carefully placed crumb on my placemat. The more this went on, the more helpless, frustrated and desperate my mum became.

The fact I wasn't eating a normal dinner anymore only heightened her worries. Her daughter was shrinking in front her and she didn't know what to do. She shouted at me time and time again to eat more and every time I would refuse. She was at her wits' end; she was helpless and didn't know how to save her daughter. I can understand why she lost her temper with me, she didn't know what else to do and she was worried out of her mind. But nothing, absolutely nothing, could have made me eat more

After one terrible argument, my sister said to my mum, "There's no point shouting at her. She has a psychological issue and needs psychological help. It's gone a lot further than simply trying to lose weight."

It is interesting that my sister recognised this before anyone else. Everyone else thought I was dieting to the extreme and that I was simply choosing not to eat. I was being stubborn, like I had been as a child. But this was not the case. It wasn't a case of 'I don't want to eat', but more of 'I can't eat'. I was terrified of gaining weight and I was desperate to lose more weight. I had no option, I had to eat less. Despite my fears of gaining lots of weight at home, my weight stayed the same over those four weeks and I returned to Loughborough at 7st 10lb.

Within two weeks of returning to uni, I had lost a further half a stone and was down to 7st 4lb. I was ecstatic. I couldn't quite believe I had got that low. And now I was that low, there was no way I was going to let it go back up. Anorexia had fully taken hold and was working away at me with venom. My restriction had become even more extreme – only vegetables and ten-calorie soup were allowed. I was exercising at every opportunity but, by this point, I wasn't able to complete my athletics training anymore. Trying to run repetition after repetition, lift heavy weights at the gym: these were tasks I felt capable of – my mind felt capable of everything, nothing could stop me – but I wasn't physically capable of completing the sessions like I'd used to. Believe me, I tried. But to sprint round a track requires muscle, power and speed endurance. And I had lost all of mine. To live, my body had to get its energy from somewhere, and I certainly wasn't eating enough to supply this, so it had to eat its own muscle.

I kept trying to complete the sessions but the more I tried, the more destroyed I felt inside. I had to accept that my dream had gone.

Friday 2ⁿᵈ May 2008,
My weight loss is doing my running no good, but I think I have gone past the point of no return.

Because I couldn't run properly anymore and my lifetime dream was ruined, I changed my plan. I decided to forget my dream of being a professional athlete, knowing that had well and truly gone. Instead, I was to focus everything on losing weight. That was all that mattered now.

It had started out as a diet to try and improve my athletic performance. Faster running was my aim and weight loss was deemed the way to achieve it. But now the running didn't matter. The weight loss didn't improve my performance and I was well aware of that. But anorexia had grown stronger than my childhood dream. I had worked my whole life to try and achieve my running ambition, years spent training, competing, living to be an athlete and now, here I was, so entwined in the anorexic web, so caught in its malicious spell, that I could not fight for my dream. My mind told me my dream didn't matter anymore. The only thing that mattered was weight loss. Losing weight was my compensation for losing athletics and made me feel better when faced with the harsh reality of a lost ambition.

The strength of anorexia is indescribable. When most people have a dream they will do what they can to achieve it and, if they know something is preventing it from happening, they will do their best to eliminate the obstacle. But I couldn't eliminate anorexia. At the time, I didn't even know I had anorexia, so I didn't know there was anything to eliminate. Anorexia takes over your mind, body and soul. It wasn't a case of me and anorexia: I was anorexia and I couldn't stop. I had to lose weight.

But I knew I was struggling, and I knew things weren't right. I couldn't walk to lectures without having to stop for a break every few minutes. My legs simply couldn't carry me. However, I did discover I could cycle, with difficulty, on the exercise bike. So this became a substitute for my running on the track. I would tell the coach I didn't feel too well and would ask for a session on the bike. The form of exercise didn't matter; I just needed to burn calories.

The coach of the elite group asked me to meet him at the start of May 2008 because he had noticed I was 'struggling with my running'. The idea of this terrified me. This was a world-renowned coach who worked with some of the most elite British athletes and I had an appointment with him. Me, on my own, because of my running. I didn't need anybody to tell me I was struggling with my running, I was well aware of that myself. The fact that I couldn't sprint 200m anymore, or go for a jog, or even walk normally to lectures was prominent in my mind. But I hadn't thought anyone else was paying attention. I mean, why would they? Here I was with Great British Olympians who were gearing up for the Beijing Olympics in a few months' time. I was insignificant amongst these.

But it turns out I wasn't insignificant to him and he actually took the time out of his busy schedule to try to help me. He offered me support and advice and was going to arrange for me to see a nutritionist. I sat there quietly nodding throughout the meeting, agreeing to the things he was saying. It wasn't that I wasn't grateful for his offer of help, but I was too far gone. I was gripped too tightly by anorexia, so intent on my mission of weight loss that on leaving the meeting, I had absolutely no intention of acting on his advice.

It wasn't only his advice I was ignoring. I had fallen out a few weeks earlier with one of my best friends, Kate. It was after my usual circuit training on a Monday, which finished at about 7pm. I had managed to drag myself for a stop-start jog in the morning and had walked during the day. On the walk home from circuit training I happened to bump into Kate, so we walked back to our hall together. Then I went for an extra half-hour walk, which had now become part of my normal routine because I had to burn extra calories.

Again, this was something I didn't think anyone was noticing. I knew I was exercising more and more, but I didn't realise my flat mates had become aware of it. That is the thing with anorexia: your world becomes so narrow, so focused on weight loss, calories, and exercise, you become oblivious to everything else. In my mind, my behaviour wasn't extreme and I wasn't doing anything wrong. I was simply doing what I had to in order to lose weight and there was nothing wrong with that. But Kate pulled me up when I told her I was going for an extra walk. She said I had just done a training session and shouldn't be doing any more. But I told her I needed to get something from the supermarket and walked off down the street.

On returning to my room with my bag of iceberg lettuce which was going to form the main part of my dinner, along with a bit of broccoli and carrots, Kate was waiting for me. We had a big argument; the first argument I had ever had with a friend. She told me I wasn't eating enough, that I was doing too much.

"Look at your skinny legs," she said, "there's nothing of you anymore."

But I was furious. I was convinced that I was eating plenty and that I wasn't doing too much exercise; I was doing what was necessary. I felt like my secret, my little mission to lose as much weight as possible, had been exposed. I worried that, now she knew, she would stop me achieving my goal. I stormed off to my room, telling Kate she had no right to interfere, because what I did was my business and I was not doing anything wrong.

Since I had given up on my dream of becoming an athlete and had changed my focus to losing as much weight as possible, I had set it as my goal that, until my end-of-year exams were completed in June, I had to put every effort into losing weight. I wanted to lose it hard and fast. I wanted to lose as much weight as possible before the end of term to see what I could achieve. I wanted to see how low I could get. That was all that mattered to me now, and I didn't want Kate, or anyone, interfering with this.

Anorexia was causing me to destroy the friendships I'd been desperate to have after so long feeling lonely and rejected. At the time, I couldn't see it and, to be honest, in my mind at that moment it didn't matter. Friendships were no longer important to me, certainly not more important than losing weight. Isn't this a cruel way to infect someone's mind? To finally be building relationships you have only ever been able to wish for but then to be robbed of this opportunity, making you self-destruct and care for nothing and nobody.

There was not a moment of the day when I wasn't thinking about what exercise I needed to do and how many calories I had consumed; beating myself up for not exercising more and eating less. I didn't think it was possible to hate myself any more than I already did, but now my self-hatred had entered a completely new level. I detested and loathed every part of my being. And I deserved this hatred – I was fat, weak, greedy, and lazy. There was no worse a human being than me. And the best way to change this? Lose more weight. If I could only be disciplined, if I could just show that self-control, I would be a better person. Being thin and losing weight was everything to me. Anorexia was the perfect person and I wanted to achieve that. Any behaviour I exhibited that wasn't in line with this, any crumb of food I put into my mouth, any exercise I felt too tired to do, acted as fuel to the fire of my self-hatred.

Friday 16th May 2008,

I'm feeling guilty because I haven't exercised as much today so there's no way I can lose weight. I hate myself. Normally every Wednesday and Friday I go on the treadmill for 15 minutes and burn 100 calories but today I just couldn't face it and I'm so annoyed with myself. I'm really struggling to exercise at the moment. I feel totally exhausted, but I know I have to do it. I went for an extra 15-minute run on Monday so now I feel I have to go for one every Monday but I'm not sure I'm physically capable of it. But I will have to.

I didn't actually *want* to exercise; I didn't want to have to walk, or run, or cycle in every spare waking moment of the day, but I thought, if I didn't, this meant I was failing at being anorexic because I was convinced anorexics would *want* to be doing it. I had to put in more effort, I had to keep pushing my body… remember the saying 'no pain, no gain'. After I went home for the weekend at the start of May, I returned to Loughborough at a new low of 7st 2lb.

Some might ask why I was doing this. If it was making me so miserable, why didn't I just stop? But I couldn't. Anorexia had complete control of my mind and body. I thought that anorexia and losing weight would make me happy. But anorexia does not make anyone happy. It may cause moments and give glimpses of apparent happiness, but this is not real happiness. Not like happiness that comes from going out with friends or having them round for movie nights, happiness from gaining qualifications or getting a job, driving a car, spending Christmas at home with the family, going on holiday. Anorexia and happiness are juxtaposed. It lures you in, letting you think it will make you happy, that with every weight loss you will be that little bit happier, but it is an illusion, a false promise. It chips away, removing everything in life that does bring true happiness until you are left with nothing. You are left with nothing but the anorexia. And that makes you feel like you need anorexia because it is all you have and all you will ever have to make you happy. But real happiness can re-appear, it can rebuild into a life, you just have to start to let go of anorexia, as terrifying as that may be. It would be many years until I realised this.

Chapter 8
Barely Living

I started looking at Pro-Ana websites. I wanted to be anorexic, eat less, and burn more calories, so I googled 'How to be anorexic' and it led me to these sites. I didn't know them as Pro-Ana sites at the time, I didn't even know those types of sites existed. I was naïve to the world of anorexia. Although I wanted to be 'anorexic', I didn't understand what this actually entailed. To me at the time, to be anorexic meant being thin and showing discipline and willpower to restrict food. That was all I wanted. I had no idea it was a mental illness and would lead to what it did; all that pain and suffering; that it had the power to destroy lives and to kill. And I certainly hadn't recognised that I was suffering from it and that it had well and truly taken over my being.

I was innocently looking at those websites for tips on how to lose weight. Well, it felt innocent at the time: however, it was anything but. It was anorexia's manipulative way to suck me further in.

I would like to make it quite clear here that I 100% *disapprove* of these websites and would actively discourage anybody from using them. They feed into the anorexia and they make people like me, who have no idea of the 'anorexic world,' fall deeper and deeper into the destruction of anorexia. And for people who actually know what they are doing, who know they are anorexic and what this truly entails, to be encouraging easily manipulated minds to

behave in a likewise way and to be promoting anorexia, is utterly despicable. They are aware of the devastating effects of anorexia and there they are, trying to promote it, trying to sicken already ill minds. It is unacceptable and sites like these need to be banned.

My weight loss was becoming more rapid, severe and life threatening. By mid-May 2008 I weighed 6st 11lb. That was a loss of three pounds in one week which, considering my already very small frame, was a dangerous proportion of weight to be losing. I had been desperate to get into the six stones. I was convinced it would make me happy. And yes, standing on the scales and seeing the number six did give me a hit, a buzz. But by the time I stepped off the scales this feeling had been overridden with anxiety.

Monday 18ᵗʰ May 2008,
There's no way on hell's Earth I can sustain it. I'm going to end up gaining it all back, especially as I'm struggling to exercise so much.

The euphoria was short-lived. What I thought was going to make me happy had not and anorexia hit the accelerate button again to get me to lose more weight. If I had managed to get this low, how much lower could I go?

I had gone from writing my diary on a monthly basis to writing practically every day, documenting what I had eaten, what exercise I had done, how much I hated myself for eating and not doing enough exercise, how I so desperately wanted to lose more weight. It is quite apparent how much I was struggling, both physically and mentally. My mind was torturing me. There was not a spare moment when I was not engulfed by the anorexia; worrying about food, exercise, weight loss (and potential weight gain). I knew something wasn't right. I knew the fact I couldn't even walk 100 metres without stopping was a danger sign, that this wasn't how it should be. But I could not stop. I was in great distress, I was scared of myself, and I just wanted to be wrapped up by my mum and looked after. I wished she could take away this mental torture and save me from this life I had found myself in.

I did recognise that at some point I had to stop. I knew my behaviour could not continue as it was. I didn't realise though that I was suffering from anorexia and that it isn't something you can simply switch off. I had every intention of losing as much weight as possible until the end of term and then I would go home, rest and regain weight. That was what I had planned on doing. I would go home for the summer holidays at the end of June, return to normal eating, gain back all the weight I had lost, and everything would be back to how it should be. I could start my athletics training again and I could re-focus on my lost dream. I would strive again to be that professional athlete. But, in the meantime, until the end of term, everything had to be dedicated to losing weight. I truly thought this was what I was going to do. I was totally unaware that anorexia had grown so strong and I was completely trapped.

I ordered one-calorie noodles online from Japan to be delivered in the next week. 'Great,' I thought, 'this will help me lose weight. I can eat these some days and the rest of time I will eat nothing'. I couldn't wait to start my days of not eating anything. But I knew I wouldn't be able to sustain it for very long, hence why I planned to initiate this at the start of June when I only had a few weeks left of my mission. I was convinced that going days without eating would make me feel incredible. It would make me superior and prove I wasn't weak, or undisciplined, or greedy. I was desperate to feel that sense of achievement and be finally able to prove to myself that I could do it. I could push my body further than anyone else; I could be strong when everyone else couldn't. This felt like it would be the stairway to heaven. I did not realise I was heading straight to hell's gates. I continued to strive towards my ultimate weight loss.

Thursday 22nd May 2008,
I have been feeling faint and weak all day, I'm struggling to even walk but I'll get over it. I'm going to make sure I don't pick today. I must be strong!

Saturday 24th May 2008 was my hall of residence summer ball. It was a dressing-up occasion, everyone wanting to look glam in their lovely dresses with nicely styled hair and make-up. It was held in a big marquee on the grass outside the main halls on the other side of the road. There was going to be a large spread of buffet food and a hog roast. Everyone was looking forward to it; the food, the drink, getting glammed up and going out with friends… everything you should enjoy doing when you're nineteen years old experiencing your first year of uni.

But I was not looking forward to it. I was filled with dread. There was going to be all that food there and I was going to have to eat as I would be in front of other people. Not only that, but my biggest worry was I would eat uncontrollably. I wholeheartedly did not want to eat anything, but I feared, when faced with all that delicious food, in the ravenous state I was in, I'd end up stuffing my face as I wouldn't be able to resist. It was a nightmare I didn't want to have to go through. The hatred for myself was growing even before I'd been to the ball and eaten anything!

Rather than enjoying the day and the experience of getting my hair and make-up done with my friends, I spent it agonising over the food, what I was going to eat, the weight I was going to gain and the sheer disgust for myself. The ball started early evening, so after taking lots of photos of ourselves we headed over to the marquee.

Now my memory from here is a bit vague. I can't remember the fine details of the evening as I think I was so ill, so close to my body completely shutting down, that my mind was not all there. I can remember getting a plate full of food from the buffet. I had tried to pick the healthy salad items. We all sat down together and started eating.

"It's nice to see you eating, Bec. I'm glad you've got some food," Kate remarked, seemingly innocently.

I couldn't reply to this. I felt like I had been punched in the stomach. 'Oh my God, she thinks I am eating a lot,' I thought, 'how could I possibly be this greedy? I can't eat this food if she thinks I am eating a lot and if it looks like I am eating normally. I cannot be thought of as someone who eats a lot. This is the worst type of person.' These thoughts raced through my mind, anorexia having manipulated a friend expressing care and relief that I was eating into a reason to beat myself up further, to hate myself even more and to eat less food. I slowly ate tiny mouthfuls of food from my plate while everyone else was eating, placing my knife and fork down as they did, my plate still largely untouched.

"I'm full, I can't eat anymore," I explained as Kate looked at me with worry. I felt incredible shame and guilt for eating what I had, for daring to fill my plate up, for thinking I could eat that food. I felt like I had sinned, that I had done a terrible thing. I'd had the intention of eating that plate of food. I was the lowest of the low. And I felt like this even though I had barely actually eaten any of it.

After the meal was music and dancing and, as I said, I don't remember much of this. I just remember feeling so incredibly cold. Cold to the core of my bones. It had been a warm day – it was early summer – and the other girls were more than comfortable in their sleeveless dresses. But I was frozen to the point where I couldn't move. I can remember sitting on a chair while my friends brought me coat after coat to wrap round me to try and keep me warm. I couldn't participate in any of the dancing or any of the fun; I couldn't physically move from that chair. I was numb with cold and my body felt incredibly weak. I had no energy to move. I don't think I had the energy for my body to function. It was on its very last legs; it was shutting down.

I somehow managed to walk home with Kate at about midnight, her propping me up along the way. I curled into my bed; shivering, numb, and blue. I was desperate to sleep, to have an escape from the mental and physical pain. Waking on the Sunday morning, I had a resurgence to get back to my plan, to get back to losing weight. Yes, I had felt dreadful last night (I couldn't remember ever feeling that bad before; that physically ill) but now I had to get back to exercising, burning calories and losing weight. My first task was to go for a walk. I had a letter to post and there was a post box 150 metres down the road, so I would head there first and continue from there. But I knew it was going to be difficult as I could now only manage a few steps without stopping.

I snuck out before anyone else was up to head to the post box, as difficult as it was going to be. I felt like my body hadn't recovered from the coldness the night before. My core still felt icy, unable to return to normal temperature. I headed out dressed for the middle of winter, despite the fact it was nearly June. I managed to get my shaking, weak legs to stumble me towards the post box. It took me over ten minutes to walk that short distance, but I was determined to carry on. My letter was posted and now I had to continue with my walking.

But, when I'd taken only a few steps away from the post box, a car pulled up alongside me. I didn't look properly at the car as I didn't want to be talked to by a stranger. As the car stopped and I took a glance towards it, I realised I recognised the bright blue Skoda. It wasn't a stranger at all. It was my parents.

I walked up to the car where they had wound the window down.

"I'm surprised to see you. What are you doing here?" I said with a slight angry tone. I was happy to see them, but I didn't want them interfering with my final few weeks of weight loss. I needed to be left well alone, so I could dedicate everything to losing weight with no interruptions.

"We're surprised to see you," my dad replied. This was a stupid thing to say. Of course he wasn't surprised to see me: they had come to see me. There was no surprise about it.

"We need to have a chat with you," he said, a serious look on his face; not a look I was very familiar with. "Come in the car a minute."

I pulled open the back door and got inside, relieved to be off my feet but also annoyed that I wasn't burning calories. As I sat in the back of the car, my parents drove round to my hall's car park, parked up and turned around to face me. There was horror in their eyes as they looked at me, their once athletic daughter now a mere, barely walking, skeleton.

"You need to come home with us," my mum said straight away. "Look at you. What has happened?" she exclaimed with sheer angst in her voice.

"I'm not coming home, I'm staying here. I've got an exam on

Thursday!" I could feel myself getting angrier. How dare they come here and try and take me home, take me away from my weight loss bubble? I would not have them ruin this for me.

"Your friends rang us last night," my mum explained. "They are incredibly worried about you and don't know what to do. We need to take you home."

I could not believe my friends had gone behind my back and rung my parents! I was fuming. How could they deceive me like this? To tell my parents they needed to come for me and stop me before my mission had ended. Hell no, I was not going to stand for this.

"There's nothing wrong with me, I'm fine," I replied angrily. "They shouldn't have rung you. I'm absolutely fine and I'm NOT coming home. I need to stay to do my exams."

My exams were actually the last thing on my mind. The only significance of my exams was that they signalled the end of term when my weight loss mission would culminate and I would see how low I had been able to get. But the exams per se were of no importance to me.

"You can't stay here," my mum was now getting angry, "it is not fair on your friends to have the responsibility of you on their hands. They are worried sick about you, we are worried sick about you, you need to come home."

We continued arguing for a good ten minutes, me refusing to come home, testifying to my wellness, and my parents trying to persuade me otherwise.

Dad suggested, "If you come home now, we will bring you back on Tuesday, ready for your exam on Thursday, how's that?" That seemed like an ok deal. I didn't want to go home at all, but I could tell by now that my parents were not going to let me refuse. At least this way I would only be home for a few days and then I could go back and re-start my diet.

"Only if you promise I can come back on Tuesday," I answered. They both promised, so I went up to my room, collected my revision and said bye to my friends. I didn't tell them that I knew they had contacted my parents. I didn't want them to think they had won so I pretended it was my choice to go home. However, I think we were all well aware of the real reason. I got back into the car and headed for home.

Although I was incredibly angry with my parents and friends at the time, now I see how terribly difficult it must have been for them and how much worry I must have been causing them. It turns out on that Saturday night at the ball when I felt so ill, so cold, and barely conscious, when I sat there huddled under layer after layer of coats, my friends were not able to enjoy themselves either. I ruined the evening for them as they could see me slipping away and were at loss as what to do about it or how to help me. But it wasn't only that evening I ruined for them, as it wasn't that evening that their worries started. They had been riddled with worry over my rapidly deteriorating state on a daily basis for weeks, feeling helpless and culminating in complete despair that Saturday evening.

I cannot imagine how difficult it must have been for them, to be trying to focus on their studies, experience university life, and have their previously fun, jokey housemate literally dying in front of them. They could see the damage I was doing to myself, but they couldn't stop me. I couldn't participate with them in anything anymore; my speech was slurred and slowed, I couldn't walk – how awful it must have been for them to have to live with this. At the time, I was angry with them for ringing my parents but, as it turns out, they saved my life. And for that, I am truly thankful. And sorry for everything I put them through.

Chapter 9
A Dying Shell

My parents wanted me to go to the doctor's when I went home. I was far from happy about it, but I agreed. I didn't think the doctor would be able to do anything anyway. I would tell them I was fine, that I was eating normally, that I had just lost a tiny bit of weight and that would be it. They could tell me I needed to gain weight and eat more, but they couldn't actually make me. I would pretend to agree to their suggestions and then go back to Loughborough and start the extreme end to my diet. That had been my plan.

But I hadn't realised Monday was a bank holiday and that I couldn't see the doctor until Tuesday. So, after initially thinking that I would return to Loughborough on Tuesday morning, I was now told this was not going to happen and I must see the doctor. I was not given any choice in the matter. I couldn't get myself back to university, so what option did I have other than to go along with it? I continued with what exercise I could get my body to do and I maintained a very restricted food intake.

I tried to continue with my studying and revision at home but now, even sitting down and note-taking was proving to be too difficult. I couldn't keep my eyes open for very long, my body did not have the energy to keep awake. Everything was shutting down and my body was giving up. 'I just need to rest my head and shut my eyes for a few minutes,' I thought as I looked at the computer screen, trying to make notes from an academic journal.

I would fall asleep with my head on the desk for ten minutes, before forcing my head up to write another sentence before shutting my eyes again. I wasn't a living person anymore, I was a dying shell. My heart was slowly beating but that was the limit to my bodily functions. I was nothing but skin and bone. I was dead in every sense, except for my slowly beating heart.

First thing Tuesday morning I had my appointment at the doctor's. I wasn't actually registered there, but I had been for an appointment when I was last at home at Easter because my parents insisted. That time I had been able to fob the doctor off with all my excuses and lies, and that had been the end of it. I didn't think this time would be any different.

I insisted on walking to the surgery. It is only about a three-minute walk from our house; however, in the physical state I was in, I found it incredibly difficult. It was particularly hard because I was walking there with my parents and I could not, under any circumstances, let them see I was struggling. I needed to continue to portray that I was fine. I needed them to believe I was ok, so I could go back to university and finish off my plan. But who was I kidding? No one would look at me and think I was well. My parents were well aware my body was deteriorating: all you needed to do was look at me.

On top of that, I was doing everything in slow motion. From my speech to my actions to my thinking, everything was painfully laborious and slow. But I couldn't recognise it myself. Yes, I knew I was struggling to walk and stay awake, but I didn't realise everything else about me was affected as well, and that it was clear for everyone to see. To me, I didn't look thin, I still had a lot of weight to lose and because I was so certain on this, I was oblivious to the fact that my 'secret' was not hidden, but staring everyone in the face.

The three of us sat down in the doctor's room. "We are extremely worried about Rebecca," my dad explained to the doctor.

"Yes, I can see," the doctor replied. "You've lost a lot of weight since the last time I saw you, Rebecca, and that wasn't very long ago."

"There's nothing wrong with me, I'm fine," I said. This

55

sentence seemed to be one I was playing on repeat at the moment. "There's loads of people at university who are this weight. It's not a problem."

"But Rebecca, you are tall. These other people will not be as tall as you." But I didn't care for this answer. Height measurements were insignificant to me. All that mattered were the numbers on the scales, and these needed to be as low as possible. "Let me weigh you," the doctor insisted.

I agreed to this. I did actually want to see what the numbers would say. I was terrified of an increase and hoping for a drop. First, she measured my height, although I already knew I was 1.77m tall. Then the weight. The scales read 6st 0lb (38kg).

"You have to realise, Rebecca," the doctor responded with seriousness. "You are dying."

To be told you are dying is not something most would ignore. It is possibly one of the worst, most terrifying sentences that anyone has to hear, invoking feelings of shock, fear and sadness. But I reacted as if I had just been asked to pass the salt and pepper. I heard the words 'You are dying' loud and clear but they were just that: words. They didn't mean anything, and I didn't believe them. There was no way I was dying. There was nothing wrong with me (words on repeat again). All I was doing was losing a bit of weight and that was not going to kill me. I was strong and I couldn't be beaten. I was certainly not going to die, and it was stupid to suggest this. Those were my thoughts at the time, and I was not going to be persuaded otherwise. I responded with my usual answer, "I'm fine, there's nothing wrong. I'm not dying." I didn't care about this, I was focusing on the scales. I had got down to six stone! That was brilliant. That was all that mattered. I had just been told I was dying but I was overjoyed; I had lost weight.

The doctor said I needed to have some blood tests which would be arranged for later that day. I left the room feeling happy I had lost weight and thinking I had got out of it again. I thought I would be going back to university the next day to finish my plan, now determined to get into the five stones. But my parents were ghost-like; pale, shaken and sick with worry. They weren't living in my world. They'd heard the reality, they'd understood the reality: their daughter was dying.

At around lunchtime the doctor turned up at our house to do the blood test. Later that afternoon, we had a phone call from her.

My mum answered the phone. It was a short conversation.

"Hello, Mrs Quinlan. Rebecca's blood results have come back as a matter of urgency. She needs to go immediately to hospital. Her heart, liver, and kidneys are failing. Don't go to A and E, I have arranged for her to be seen immediately in the intensive care unit. It is very serious, she needs to be treated straight away."

With that, my parents rushed to get ready to take me to hospital. I begrudgingly got into the back of the car. 'For God's sake,' I thought, 'Why do they have to make such a fuss? What is wrong with these people?! There's nothing wrong with my heart, liver, and kidneys. I'm fine, why can't they just leave me alone?' I had never been to hospital before and I had no idea what to expect. I hoped to be in and out within a few hours. After all, I was sure they were making a fuss over nothing and wouldn't find anything wrong with me.

We headed straight to the intensive care unit where I was taken away by a doctor for examination. My two pedometers, which I wore religiously and had done for the past few years to ensure I clocked up the minimum 10,000 steps, were given to my parents. After examination, I was transferred to the unit which dealt with livers, where I had my own room with an en-suite. I was mortified. I could not believe I was being made to stay overnight. What could possibly be that wrong with me that I needed to stay?

They explained to me that my liver and kidneys were seriously ill, that imminent failure was very likely. And that would mean death. Again, I heard the doctor's words, I saw the grave look on their faces, I saw my parents unable to speak, unable to move. But I didn't believe them, and I didn't care. I was angry for being made to stay in hospital and for not being allowed to continue with my weight loss. I blamed everyone for this; doctors, my parents, my uni friends. They were all to blame for me ending up there when I felt I should be back at uni, finally getting to the good part of my diet and losing any remaining weight I had left. They wanted to attach me to a drip which I refused. However, it was the drip or death and they weren't allowing me to risk the latter. My concern with having the drip was that it was going to contain calories, but the nurse reassured me it didn't, so I agreed. I was naïve to 'the system' at the time, and I didn't realise this so-called no-calorie glucose drip was actually slowly pumping calories into me. It was late at night, my parents had kissed me goodbye and left, and I was exhausted.

That night was one of broken sleep, with nurses waking me up on an hourly basis to take my observations (obs). This is a term used in hospital to group together a set of measurements such as heart rate, blood pressure, and blood glucose level. I approached the new day with a clearer mind and a set plan. The staff came round offering breakfast – cereal or toast. I politely declined, saying I didn't want anything, and off they went. It was easier than I thought.

But my mind was riddled with anxiety over my state of immobility. I was terrified by the amount of weight I must be gaining through lack of exercise. I was still attached to several drips and I was going out of my mind just sitting there. I paced up and down the room for ten minutes. I knew it wasn't much, but it had to be better than nothing. But I was rarely left alone with much time to walk as there was a constant stream of nurses and doctors doing blood tests, taking obs, telling me my liver was in a condition worse than a chronic alcoholic, telling me I may die.

I didn't care. I wanted to get out of there as quickly as possible to get back to losing weight. While I feared the amount of weight I was gaining and desperately wanted to continue exercising and restricting, I also knew it would probably be best if I did what they wanted me to so I could be discharged quicker and get back to losing weight. But I couldn't match my logical thinking with my actual behaviour.

Wednesday 28th May 2008,

Apparently my liver and kidneys are dangerously ill, but I bet it's nothing… I didn't get to the good part of my diet when I was going to eat nothing! I can't explain my frustration! So here I am in hospital where I can't exercise and burn calories. But I've decided I will eat what I have to while I'm in here so my liver etc get better and then as soon as I get out, I'm going to go back to my normal uni meals of very little, like I had been doing, because I don't want to put on weight. So, I just need to be a bit cleverer than these people. They want me to see a psychologist after my liver is better but I'm not going to. And if I do, I will just say what they want to hear. I will probably be about seven stone when I leave here which is awful so I will need to lose weight straight away to get back down to six stone. I'm going to do fifty sit-ups now.

At the time, it all felt like my choice, my decisions and that I was doing what I wanted. But my mind had been poisoned. I wasn't being spoken to by another voice. Anorexia wasn't saying, "You should do this, you should do that." No, it was "I want to do this, I want to do that." My head wanted to lose weight. But my head was very ill and had been taken over by anorexia. Some sufferers talk of anorexia as a voice in their head. But it wasn't like that for me at that time. Anorexia wasn't a separate entity to me, it *was* me. It wasn't Rebecca and anorexia. It was all encompassed into one. Rebecca had become anorexic and this had become too powerful.

The doctors were concerned with my heart rate, amongst all the other complications. My pulse was down to 25 bpm and I was immediately hooked up to a heart monitor. They feared that at any minute my heart was going to stop, especially as I was continuing to eat very little, my blood tests were not improving, and my skin was breaking out in terrible sores (which is common in anorexia when you are critically ill). It was touch and go as to whether I would be alive to see in the next hour. But I could think of nothing but my weight.

Thursday 29th May 2008,
Another boring and pointless day in hospital. Not been able to burn calories but I've been able to restrict quite well. I know I probably should be trying to put on weight as, when I get out of here, I am going to end up putting it on anyway, but I just can't help it. I got weighed today at 6st 0 and I want to lose more. I'm in a dilemma about what to have for food

tomorrow because I know I need to eat but I don't want to put on weight if I'm able to lose it. Today I had an apple at lunch, and half a salmon fillet and a little bit of veg for dinner, but I don't know what to do about tomorrow. I know I get hungry, but I just want to lose weight! And I know there's nothing wrong with me.

I would order the hospital meals but not eat them; the fear of the unknown calories and weight gain was too great. I had also started to exercise more. I was detached from all my machinery in the mornings to have a shower but instead of washing, I ran up and the down the bathroom, trying to burn any calories I could. I was also now getting up earlier to walk in my bedroom, trying to avoid getting tangled up in all the wires attached to me and avoid being sighted by the nurses who were now very closely monitoring my movement.

Because I was refusing the hospital food during the day, they wanted me to drink two 'energy drinks' of 250 calories each. I was horror-struck by this. 250 calories in one bottle of drink! I had never known of such a thing, not realising these 'energy drinks' that I had never encountered before were going to form the staple of my diet over the coming years. I pretended to drink the drinks, taking a few sips and then pouring the rest down the sink. There was no way on Gods Earth I was going to consume 500 calories, especially when I hadn't been exercising.

Four days after I arrived in the general hospital at the end of May 2008, I received a visit from an eating disorder nurse. She asked me lots of questions about what had happened when I was at university, what I ate, what exercise I did, what I thought of my size etc. I was unsure whether I should be telling her the truth and that I still wanted to continue losing weight. I was very honest about what I had been eating and the exercising and, following our hour-long talk, she said she thought I had anorexia nervosa. But I was adamant I didn't.

"There is no way I can be anorexic. Anorexics do not eat and are far thinner than I am. Also, they have a lot more serious health problems than I do and are near death. I am not," I forcibly tried to tell the nurse. I was also insistent that I must be allowed back to university until the end of term. I repeatedly explained how I was only trying to lose as much weight as I could until the end of term and then I would stop, and I needed to go back to complete my exams. I had to finish the year. There was nothing wrong with me and I *had* to go back, I *had* to finish the term.

The nurse who came to see me that Friday afternoon continues to be my nurse to this day. She says that, when she first met me, she was taken aback by my forcefulness, determination, and fixed way of thinking. Not only was she surprised by this, but by the fact I was still alive. She wondered how, in my current physical condition with my starved organs, fading heart and septic skin, I hadn't died. This reflects how my mind was completely under the control of anorexia.

I found it so infuriating speaking to these people who would not believe me when I told them I was fine. The nurse explained that she wanted me to go to an eating disorder hospital on Tuesday and stay there for four weeks. The decision for this was going to be made on Monday. I didn't even know places like that existed! I never imagined there were designated places for people with eating disorders to go. I thought if you were anorexic you were left to live your life as you wanted, being thin. The idea of having to go to an eating disorder hospital was horrific!

Friday 30th May 2008,
There's no way I'm going to an eating disorder hospital. On Monday I'm going to convince them that if they let me out I will eat normally and be absolutely fine because I was before. I wish they could have left me alone until after my exams because then I would have started eating normally again anyway. Because I do love food and I have to try really hard not to eat it. Therefore, there's clearly nothing wrong! I will tell them about Ma's amazing puddings and how I will ensure I eat one every day (but I will figure out a way to cut back). And I will tell them I won't exercise as much (which is actually true because I can't physically do it anymore).

I had it all planned out – how I was going to convince them to let me home. I hoped this would be possible as it all seemed so rational and logical in my mind. But I also knew that if I had any chance of convincing them, I had to appear to be eating over the weekend. So, with my constant refusal of hospital food, they agreed to let my mum bring in my dinner. I reluctantly agreed to eat it – a bowl of tomato soup or a small portion of chicken with some veg.

With knowing I was going to eat more, I tried to up the exercise. I got up at 5.30am to start walking in my bedroom. But the nurses were aware of what I was doing and, during the day, they stopped me from getting off my bed except to go to the toilet. My anxiety levels were heightened and the closer we got to Monday the more I worried about whether I was going to be sent to an eating disorder hospital. I received the news I didn't want to hear on the Monday.

Monday 2nd June 2008,

Well, the worst possible result happened. I have to go to the eating disorder hospital ASAP. It's so unfair because there is nothing wrong with me! Apparently, if I had carried on until my exams then I would have died. I don't believe that though. I was functioning just fine. I weighed 36.2kg (5st 9lb) today which is amazing – I made it into the five stones! How good is that?! But I want to stay at this weight, I want people to look at me and think I am thin and think I am anorexic. I don't know why I do but, to me, being anorexic is a good thing. It shows your strength and willpower. But I am not and never have been anorexic. And the weight loss has ended now and I'm absolutely gutted.

I'm not allowed to leave the eating disorder hospital until I'm a BMI 16 which is about eight stone! That is so much! But I will do everything they ask – even the bed rest (I'm not going to have a choice). I'm not ready to put on weight yet though, it's so annoying. At least I managed to achieve quite a low weight in the end. And as soon as I've convinced them I am no longer anorexic and that I've recognised the error of my ways and am at eight stone, I will be allowed out. I'm not going to put on any more weight than that. I bared all my feelings today as well, how being skinny makes you something different – it makes you stand out. I like being thought of as the skinny one. It's going to be so horrible putting on weight, I'm going to get so fat and fleshy. But I will try and turn it into muscle when l leave.

I told them all how I'd planned on losing as much weight as possible until the end of term and then I was going to go back to normal – that's not being anorexic in my opinion. And also, I said how I have to try really hard not to have unhealthy food because it tempts me. But I don't want unhealthy food and I want to be able to stop eating when I am full, but I just don't! If they give me lots of unhealthy food there I will like it too much. That's the difference between me and anorexics – I like food and they don't! I hate being me. I was able to control my eating before and now I'm not going to be able to. I don't want to put on weight. I don't want to be happy to eat normally – I like being different. And I don't want to leave Ma and Pa. I love them and I want them near me.

I genuinely did think it would be easy to go into the eating disorder hospital and do exactly as they said. I would eat everything, do no exercise, gain the necessary weight and be discharged. I truly went in there with that attitude, to get on and do it, leave at eight stone and get back to normal life. I hadn't realised how difficult it was going to be; that I was suffering from anorexia and it was incredibly strong, and I was powerless against it.

I also had a big issue with feeling full. Feeling full made me feel dirty and I liked feeling empty and clean. I also liked being thin. It was something I had aspired to for years, having spent my teenage years longing to lose weight. I had always been a nobody, fading into the background – the boring one, the one without friends or a boyfriend, the one not invited to things, the one always on the periphery. But now I had something. I had something that would make me stand out amongst all these other people that had so much going for them. In a crowd, I could be the thin one which made me happy. Having had nothing and feeling rejected for so long, I finally had something I valued and something that gave me a sense of worth. I could not give it up.

Chapter 10
The Start of St Ann's

Tuesday 3rd June 2008 was the day I was to be transferred to the eating disorder hospital, St Ann's, in London. I was terrified. I was taken out of my room in a wheelchair to an ambulance. I had to lie on a stretcher in the ambulance with my mum sitting on the seat next to me, a paramedic beside her. I had no idea where I was heading or what was in store for me. All I knew was that I felt exhausted. I held my mum's hand and she looked at me, trying to comfort me, but she too had a look of exhaustion. Her daughter had nearly died and was far from safe now. She too had no idea what I was entering, and she never imagined the sickening worry was to continue and that a new life was to follow for all of us, full of lies, arguments, fear, and anorexia.

I couldn't keep my eyes open in the ambulance and, to be honest, sleep was the nicest place to be at that moment. It meant I could escape the fear, worry, and bullying in my brain. Constant thoughts of needing to exercise, needing to restrict food, worrying about weight gain, hating myself for eating; it was exhausting. I wanted a break from it. Sleep was the only escape. The journey seemed to take forever but I didn't mind. It meant more time before I entered the terrifying unknown, and more time with my mum. But the ambulance eventually came to a stop and the paramedic announced that we had arrived. I stumbled out, my legs shaking beneath me, both through nervousness and lack of strength.

"It's just up there," the paramedic said, pointing. I looked up. There was a steep flight of twenty concrete steps leading up to a big blue door with 'Phoenix Wing' written across it. I edged my way towards the steps, my legs feeling like they were about to give way beneath me. I stepped onto the first step and it felt like I had run a marathon. I was a walking skeleton, nothing but skin and bone, and making each step was exhausting. Many people find walking upstairs difficult and it can be tiring, but never before have I experienced such utter weakness, such sheer difficulty at carrying out an everyday task. It took me well over five minutes to reach the top of the stairs. It's hard to explain the feeling in my legs. It is not that they felt tired, they didn't possess any muscle, so a feeling of tiredness wasn't relevant. You don't realise you can't do it until you try. As soon as you take a step you just physically cannot. Your legs feel numb to the point where you can't feel them.

On entering, I was met by a nurse who led me down a long corridor. I was very aware that I was in my long, red, fleecy, Winnie the Pooh dressing gown. Walking through a small lounge area with a TV and sofas, I could feel the eyes of the other patients on me. I kept my head down and carried on walking. I finally reached what was to be my bedroom, where I was taken inside with my parents and we were given a brief explanation of how the unit operated. I was to be kept in my room for the first week. Meals and washing were at designated times and had to be supervised, and I was to have half-portion meals and snacks, of which I must eat and drink everything. The dietician told me I was allowed three food dislikes which I wouldn't have to eat, and I instantly said tomatoes and cheese. These were genuine dislikes to which my mum confirmed. I couldn't think of a third dislike at the time, so I just left it at two. My parents were told the visiting times and we were left alone to say our goodbyes.

In the room opposite mine, I had seen a patient who was walking continuously up and down her bedroom.

"I don't understand it," I said to my parents, "why is she doing that? Why doesn't she just get on and do what she has to do and then she can leave? It's ridiculous, it doesn't make sense, there's no point to it." I really couldn't understand why this girl was walking like she was, even though I had been doing the same when I was in the general hospital. I didn't recognise it in my own behaviour, but I could totally see how pointless it was in relation to this other girl. I couldn't understand why she wasn't simply doing exactly as they wanted and trying to get out of there as quickly as possible.

"There's no way I will do that," I said. "I'm going to gain the weight and get out of here asap," I explained to my parents, who seemed reassured by this, agreeing with me that this girl was achieving nothing by pacing her bedroom. We hugged, kissed and said goodbye. I was alone, I was terrified and I cried.

Wednesday 4ᵗʰ June 2008,

Well here I am having spent my first full day in this mental hospital. It's such a surreal experience, I can't explain it properly. Physically I feel awful. It's starting to sink in actually how ill I was… I was near death. My liver was eating itself, my heart is flickering; clearly not a good sign especially as it's averaging 20-30 bpm. And there's problems with my kidneys. I'm finding it really difficult to remember things, too. I can't believe I've done this to my body. I can't even walk properly or do anything, and yet I carried on trying to lose weight. Even this past week being in the general hospital when they said bed rest and not to walk, I couldn't resist. And the longer I was in there, the longer I was walking for. Until I physically can't walk anymore, I think I will always want to. But if I reach that point when I can't put one foot in front of the other, I will probably be dead. I know I need to control it, but that's far easier said than done.

They aren't going to let me out of here until I get a lot bigger. Originally, they said BMI 16 which is approximately eight stone which is ok, I accepted that. But then it went up to BMI 20 which is just huge, nearly ten stone, and they also want me to get my periods back but that's ridiculous. In the year I had my periods I was overweight and desperately unhappy with my body.

I'm finding the portion sizes a real struggle to deal with and they are causing a lot of fear in me. Even though I'm on half portions, they are ridiculously huge! And now I don't have control over my fullness so I will just stuff and I hate the feeling of bloatedness and the hatred of myself when I do it. Why do I do it? It's so unnecessary… you should stop when you're full. That is what I had learnt to do, but now they are going to change all that because I have to stuff myself in here. The portions are stressing me out big time. I need to learn to stop eating when I am full as that is what I battle with, but this is just adding to my fear. I am so stressed.

And then there are all the other problems I explained to Ma about. About being the 'skinny' one – that's what I want. It makes me stand out from the rest of my friends and that is who I want to be referred to as. There are two issues in my mind:

1) The body/self image and confidence

2) Food/calories/bloating.

At the moment my biggest worry is the portion size but then I guess that's linked to the body image and everything else, as I could eat the big portions but I can't because it will make me not have the body image I want. Ma reckons I have body dysmorphia, but I don't think I do. It is a fact that everyone does have a better figure than me and is prettier than me.

I feel ashamed that I have been able to come into this hospital and eat all the food when I know other people wouldn't have been able to, and it makes me feel less adequate. I fear putting on weight as a concept in itself. And as a result of putting on weight, I won't stand out, I will blend into the background and be a nobody. But I don't want to be a nobody. I don't want to go back to Loughborough/life and just be normal again like I always have been, merely blending in… never the fastest or most muscly or prettiest or slimmest. At least now I can officially be someone.

I don't think I have the mental side of anorexia that badly either. Like I said to the psychiatrist today – I ate and have always eaten and have always liked and wanted food, and it took so much control to not eat food, whereas anorexics hate food and don't eat. I don't want to like cakes and biscuits and unhealthy food and I don't want to want to eat them. But I know I can eat them and will eat them, and this place is going to make me do it more because we have to eat to the point of bloatedness. AND I HATE THAT FEELING!!!!

Ma and Pa make it sound so easy: I've just got to eat the food, talk to the staff, put the weight on and get out. And that is genuinely what I thought I would do. But I didn't realise it was going to be this difficult. I don't want to eat the food, but I want to get out of here. I don't feel like me anymore. When I speak to people, I feel different to how I used to, but I can't explain it… I am a different person now. It all feels very strange.

I can't help but feel lazy for not exercising. There's nothing I can physically do, but I'd still feel better knowing I had burnt calories. And that is something I don't want them to change about me… I enjoy exercising and I want to be as healthy as possible. I am scared of this place changing me… I don't want to grow up and I don't want this place to make me more mature. And the thought of having to continue eating so much is actually making me hate food.

This was the start of what was to be a very long, tortured journey. My innocence, my naivety, and my attitude to food soon changed. On that Wednesday, the day after arriving, I weighed 35.4kg, making my BMI 11.5. The next day (Thursday) I had gone up half a kilo. I was mortified. I stood and looked at myself in the mirror. I saw a fat, fleshy lump with a protruding stomach, chubby cheeks and thunderous thighs. I hated this place for making me eat, for making me sit in my room all day every day, eating meal after meal, snack after snack.

For the first few days I had to eat and spend most of my time in my room, so I didn't have much contact with other patients. But I could see them walking past my bedroom, all looking very sad (often crying) and in my eyes, all looking far thinner than I did. They all had anorexia. I didn't. I didn't struggle to eat like I knew they did. When my meals were presented to me in my bedroom, I got on and ate them, every last bit of them. I hated myself for it, but I did it. I wasn't crying and agonising over every mouthful like I imagined those other girls were. I was convinced those other girls all knew they had anorexia and that they wanted to get better. I thought I must be evil and possessed because, I didn't want to get better, I didn't want to put on weight. I wanted to stay thin and I wanted to be anorexic. Being left to stew in my room alone all day didn't help either. I felt I needed someone to talk to but the only contact I had with staff was when I was eating my meals and that was normally a healthcare assistant who didn't have much understanding at all of the mental illness and mental battles of anorexia.

As I went to sleep that Thursday evening, two days after my arrival, I experienced something like never before. I was standing at my childhood nanny Jenny's wooden back gate, knocking and waiting for her to open it. As she opened the door, inside was a room that shone brighter than the sun. I stepped into the room and found myself sliding down, passing through the room in my red dressing gown. I was very confused. Jenny and her girls were all sitting in front of me and I was slowly getting close to them. I didn't know how I had got to where I was. The last thing I remembered was being in the eating disorder hospital and now I was here. My grandparents then walked in through a door in front of me, with other people from school and university. They gathered on either side of the bright, shiny room and I slowly moved past them all. "I'm dying, aren't I?" I said aloud as I continued to pass these people from my life. I could feel the presence of people behind me. It was my parents, walking behind me as I progressed through the room. They were whispering something which started to get louder and louder. "You're dying," they kept repeating. I knew this was it, I was reaching the end. I was moving further away from everyone else and closer to the bright light at the end of the passage, which was now all I could see, just incredible white light. "This is it. I am actually dying," I thought with terror. I was sliding further and further away, and closer to this bright light. I felt helpless. I accepted this was the end, that I was going to die.

Chapter 11
The Dining Room

With a jolt I sat bolt upright in my bed. It had been a dream. My heart was racing ten to the dozen, I was sweating, and I did believe in that moment, I was going to die. I was terrified, and I could not go back to sleep for fear that I may never wake up. Yet, even acknowledging that I had literally been seconds from death and from never waking up, I couldn't give up my desire to be anorexic, to be thin, and to not gain weight.

I was mentally exhausted. The constant worry of the food I had to eat, the calories, the lack of exercise, whether I was or was not anorexic, the hatred of myself for eating, for wanting to be anorexic, for not wanting to put on weight; I couldn't bear living in that state. All I wanted to do was sleep; it was the only escape. But with sleep comes reduced metabolism and I could not allow that. So, I had to battle every waking minute of the day, counting down the time to the next meal or snack. I dreaded its arrival and wished for it not to come but in such a miserable, stressful, and boring existence, meal times were also a significant way of passing the time.

My mind would torture me and I was offered no professional help to ease it or to try and help me rationalise my thoughts. My mum did try, but this was a completely new experience to her as well. She encouraged me to distract myself during the day to help take my mind off my thoughts. But to me, distracting my mind was a betrayal and a sign of losing anorexia. 'If I am not thinking about it, it means anorexia is going away, and I do not want it to go away. I must think about it all the time to make sure I hold on to it. The more I let more normal things happen, the more it means I am returning to normal,' I would think.

The hospital's focus, as they continued to tell me and parents, was on their weight-gaining programme. The psychological side of the illness was of little significance to them, or so it appeared. And it was the lack of psychological support that lead me down the path I ended up following.

Saturday 7th June 2008,
I hate me, I hate me,
I want to be a tall, skinny tree,
Standing out from the crowd,
Everyone feeling proud,
Of perfect little anorexic me.

But my head felt confused. One minute I thought I hated food and couldn't bear the thought of it, the next I worried I was hungry and wanted to eat everything in sight. One minute I felt so incredibly full, the next I was thinking I could eat chocolate. One thought that was always consistent – I despised myself. And with the limited support from the staff, I turned to the other patients for reassurance. It was that which fed my anorexia. If it wasn't strong before, it was soon to grow into Hercules.

My first conversation was with a lady called Molly who was in her early thirties. We immediately got on and developed a friendship. I had never encountered anorexia or anorexia sufferers before and now here I was in a room with ten of them. Of all of them, I was instantaneously drawn to Molly. She was so nice, so kind, so reassuring. She definitely had anorexia and was not a fake like I thought I was. When she told me that sometimes she felt like she wanted to eat, it eased my own concerns. And seeing everyone else eating their evening snack, I felt relieved that I only had a glass of milk.

My disgust for food was growing stronger. I was aware a new patient had arrived who was refusing to eat anything. 'That shows she is a real anorexic because she has got the willpower to refuse the food,' I thought. 'I am just a fat greedy pig because I eat everything'. My first weekend in hospital, four days after my arrival, I left my first bit of food. The meal was broccoli mornay, which consisted of broccoli and butter beans covered in a cheese sauce. I was sure I shouldn't have been given the meal because cheese was one of my dislikes and there was no way I was going to put all that fat-laden cheese into my already fat and ever-increasing body. I didn't leave much, but enough to make me feel a little bit better. That was the start of things to come. Now I'd refused a bit, I knew I could do it.

That same weekend, on the Sunday, I was told I had to start eating my meals with the other patients in the supervised dining room. Eight patients sat along a long wooden table, with a member of staff at either end watching our every move. One girl, Jane, didn't eat, she just drank supplement drinks, the staff constantly reminding her that she must not spill it. Other girls questioned the portion sizes. "There's far too many bran flakes in this bowl", and "there's too much butter on this toast". I could see some of them physically shaking as they brought the spoons to their mouths. Some cried. Molly refused to eat her breakfast, saying the butter hadn't melted and she was not going to eat it as it was. It was a completely new world to me. It is hard to put into words the terror in some anorexia sufferers' eyes when they are presented with a tray of normal food. How can something so normal as eating breakfast cause so much fear? But it does. And sitting round this table really brought home to me how terrified of food I actually was. Seeing other patients refuse to eat, reinforced to me that I could now start refusing. It felt like I had been handed a 'get out of jail free' card.

Lunchtime on Sunday, my second meal in the dining room, I was presented with a roast dinner. I looked at it – two huge, greasy roast potatoes, the butter-filled apple and blackberry pie – I felt repulsed. There was no way on Earth I was going to put all that food inside of me. I couldn't do it. And I knew now I didn't have to. I ate the vegetables and a small bit of chicken – I had to appear to be doing something. But I could not put anything else into my mouth. And I most certainly was not going to drink the meal replacement drink, *Ensure*, they provided when you didn't complete a meal. Having eaten virtually everything in my bedroom, I was now refusing ninety percent of only my second meal in the dining room.

My parents and Nicola came to visit me that afternoon for the first time since my arrival. They tried desperately to be upbeat, making general chit-chat, asking me questions and telling me about their week. But I was annoyed, angry, and moody, and I didn't have the energy to talk to them. My concern was with what food I was going to be presented with next, what calories I was consuming, and what weight I was gaining. At 5pm I asked them to leave. Then I felt guilty. They had made all that effort to come and see me, they had been out of their mind with worry for weeks that I might die, and there I was telling them to go, to leave me to my miserable self. The hardest thing was that I did actually want them to stay, to be near me and comfort me, but the reality was, I knew no one could comfort me. No one was capable of making my situation any better. No one could ease my suffering or my mental battle. So I was best left alone.

Sunday 8th June 2008,
My mind doesn't understand today,
What's been going on,
A physical and mental battle,
That's left me feeling wrong,
I don't know how to feel,
Or what to say or do,
I thought things were meant to get easier,
But the dining room is something new.

I was collected on Monday morning at 5.30am for weigh-in, six days after my arrival. I dreaded standing on the scales and seeing what gargantuan weight I was. The scales read 38.9kg (6st 1lb). I was mortified.

'That's three f***ing kilos since Thursday,' I wailed to myself as I got back to my room, sobbing. I was utterly horrified and panic-stricken. I responded in the only way I knew how to cope with things: I stopped eating. That was the only way I could stop the ridiculous weight gain. The hospital had outlined that patients are expected to gain between 0.5-1kg per week and there I was, having gained 3kg in four days. Not one member of staff came to reassure me, to explain that I was suffering from re-feeding syndrome (where you are fed too much too quickly following a period of starvation, causing fluid retention) and severe oedema in my feet. All I could think of was *3 kilos*. And I was not going to eat any more. My concerns – am I hungry? do I want food? do I like eating? – had vanished and I was now full of hatred for everything and everyone (except my family). I hated food, I hated the staff, and I most certainly was not going to put another meal inside me. The fear and horror of weight gain and food was so great, I could not continue to eat.

So that is how the week continued. Me sitting down for every meal in the dining room and barely touching any of it, never more than a few mouthfuls. I wasn't alone in leaving food. I was now really good friends with Molly and another girl, Sophie, and they too occasionally left food. There was one girl on the ward, Helen, who hated me with a passion and I have to say the feeling was mutual. From the moment I arrived on the ward she had been 'off' with me. When I tried to make conversation or smile at her she was always very aloof, self-obsessed. Our relationship worsened when I joined the dining room and proceeded to not eat my meals. She always made a dramatic scene about how I was putting her off, how it wasn't fair, how I wasn't even trying and how selfish I was. She would cry, wail, and wave her arms. The difference between Helen and I was that she was complying, and I wasn't. I wasn't aware of actually how difficult it is to eat when other patients are restricting; that is something I came to learn over the coming months and years. But at that time, when trying to cope with my apparently massive weight gain, I was physically and mentally incapable of eating. I did not have the strength to fight my head and put food into my mouth.

Friday 13th June 2008 really did live up to its unlucky expectations. It was a week and a half after I had arrived and I was told I had to eat my next meal, otherwise I would be sectioned. I didn't really know what sectioning was or what it entailed. I knew it was a bad thing, but nothing could make me start to eat again; I just couldn't do it. After refusing my fish and chips at lunchtime, I was assessed by two doctors, with the resulting decision that I was to be placed under Section 3. I was immediately put on bed rest (I'd had a couple of electrocardiograms (ECGs) the day before and the results suggested my heart was in danger) and had a nasogastric (NG) tube inserted which I would be fed through. I tried to resist but I was weak, tired and the little common sense I had left was enough to tell me there was no point; they were going to do it anyway, they were going to win.

I had the tube inserted up my nose and it went down the back of my throat and into my stomach. It was a very uncomfortable process, but the worst thing was that I was now completely out of control. They could do what they liked and pump as many calories into me as they wanted, and I couldn't do anything about it. I wasn't given the choice of eating anymore. Food was removed from my meal plan and replaced with 500 calories of *Ensure* which was to be fed via the tube. Because I was suffering from re-feeding syndrome, 500 calories a day was the maximum my body could safely tolerate but even 500 calories felt like far too much to me.

My parents came to visit me the following day. I felt embarrassed to see them with the tube up my nose. I didn't want them to know I'd been refusing the food. I didn't want to upset them, make them angry, worried, and disappointed. But obviously, with the sectioning, they had to be informed of everything. I felt like a freak sitting in front of them with a tube. They'd never imagined their daughter would reach such a point, where she had to be fed through a tube because she simply could not eat. I had gone away to university less than a year ago; how did it all go so terribly wrong? But university had been the final flame to an already burning fire. I didn't have the energy to talk to my parents. They again tried to be positive and talkative, but I could see the look in their eyes. One of worry, sadness and helplessness.

Monday 16th June 2008,
They are upping my calories to 800! That's ridiculous, especially as I've had absolutely no exercise today (normally I force myself to do a bit of

walking). In this hamster cage prison cell, every calorie counts, and I can't do anything but think about how to reduce the amount of calories entering me. They are watching me all the time, especially now I have moved to this medical room which has a window to the office so they can watch me all the time! I hate it! I hate it so much it is unreal. I can't express how much I hate it, it makes me want to cry. They, and the whole situation, drive me mad. Madder than I've ever been in my whole life. I know the only way to get out of this situation is to put on weight but they don't seem to understand... I DON'T WANT TO PUT ON WEIGHT! The only thing I could do would be to put on weight just to get out of here and then lose it when I leave but that is so much easier to say than to do. The ability to face putting on weight is so traumatic I actually can't do it. I can't face putting on weight.

My parents came and visited me again mid-week, despite me telling them not to. Mid-week visits were not usually allowed but my consultant had called them in for a meeting and allowed a short visit afterwards.

"We want to come and see you," they explained over the phone. But I didn't want them to waste their efforts on me. All I wanted was to be at home, having a cuddle with my ma and pa and for them to make everything better. But they couldn't. I had to face the hell hole alone. It was easier for me not to see them, that way I could just focus on surviving that place, rather than also having to deal with loving and missing my parents desperately.

Chapter 12
Fighting the System

My friendship with Molly and Sophie was growing stronger. The three of us would sit on my bed in the evening and watch DVDs, chatting about our lives, how much we hated the hospital and how the staff were never going to take anorexia away from us. We had our own Pro-ana community and our hatred of the staff, and their regimental treatment increased our desires to show everyone they could not beat us. The more contact I was having with the other patients, the stronger my anorexic mind was growing. I had entered the hospital innocent and naïve. I don't blame the other patients for making my anorexia stronger. My mind was already incredibly taken over by anorexia in its thinking, and I was looking for reassurance and support. They were magnets attracted by my anorexic mind. And when you are in hospital with such severe and chronic cases of anorexia, it is very easy to find the defiant, treatment-resistant, anorexic-willed patients. Patients actually wanting recovery in this setting are few and far between. The staff were rarely there to talk to you, to rationalise your thoughts, to support you in trying to do the right thing, so talking to my fellow patients was my only option, and they supported my anorexia.

The visits from my parents also started turning to arguments.

"I don't want to gain weight," I tried to explain to my mum, telling her how fat I felt, how horrible gaining weight and consuming calories was.

"Well you have to," she said in a matter-of-fact way. "Are you going to try?"

"I don't want to try because trying would mean gaining weight and that's not what I want. I can't do it, I can't put on weight, I can't bear it."

My mum's voice was now raised and angry. "You are so selfish. You are thinking of no one but yourself. It's not just you involved in this, who is affected by everything. We have been out of our minds with worry. You have to put on weight."

But conversations and arguments like that only added to my anger and hatred of everything. I was well aware that I was being selfish, but I couldn't help how I felt. My fear of gaining weight, my desire to be thin, it was all-encompassing and nothing and no one could change that, no matter how much I loved my parents or felt guilty for putting them through it. I was resentful and this resentment fed anorexia.

After a week of being fed through the tube, I returned to the dining room to drink my calories orally. Jane and I would sit at the table with our drinks while the other patients had their trays of food. 'I cannot bear the thought of eating', I would think to myself, 'thank God I haven't got to do that. I wish I never had to eat again'. I knew if I didn't drink the *Ensures* and the milk then it would go via the tube. Either way, the calories were going to get inside me, so it seemed pointless refusing. I sat at the table and quietly drank my drinks, feeling relieved I was not eating. But I found being back at the table an infuriating and stressful experience. I could now see why Helen had found it so difficult eating while I was refusing. I could see all the other patients getting up to their little tricks – spilling, scraping, hiding food – with Molly and Sophie still often continuing to refuse to eat their meals. It felt so unjust and unfair. Everyone else was getting away with having less; disguising the fact they hadn't eaten or flatly refusing to eat and nothing happening as a consequence. They could be told off and given the punishment *Ensure*, but they couldn't be made to have it. Because I was sectioned, I could be forced to have everything via the tube. I could have calories pumped into me no matter what. There was no getting away with it for me and I hated it. I hated the fact I *had* to have calories and they didn't, and the dining room just highlighted this.

The next few times I was weighed I'd lost weight due to a combination of reduced oedema in my feet, reduced calorie intake due to re-feeding, and because I had started secretly exercising. But all I could see was a fat lump, with everyone else around me looking far thinner and getting more of what they asked for. Once a week, patients made written requests to the staff which were discussed in ward round between doctors, psychiatrists and nurses. For weeks I was not granted any of my requests, which ranged from being allowed to go home, to being allowed on the daily trip to 'the bench' where you could sit outside for ten minutes, to being given a little, pink present. It seemed so unfair that everyone else got their requests and I didn't get any. They suggested that my at-risk heart, low BMI and abnormal blood results were too risky to allow me out. 'This is a one-way street', I told myself, 'they expect me to do everything they want and say but give nothing back. Well f*** them, I *hate* them.'

I was starting to secretly exercise more and more. I would try and get a few hours of walking in throughout the day, getting up at 6.30am to start. I would pace up and down my bedroom while nobody was around and would sneak into the bathroom to run up and down in five-to-ten-minute intervals. As it was quite a small space, I could only run about five strides before I had to turn around, and the floor could sometimes be a bit slippery, so I occasionally found myself falling over. My hips, bottom and knees were covered in bruises. But I just couldn't sit there all day doing nothing, consuming calories, with nothing else to do but sit, eat and think. My mind was driving me mad, I was getting angry and stressed with myself; my own thoughts sending me into states of panic and confusion. Without the option of restriction, the only way I knew how to ease the stress was to exercise. However, it wasn't long before the ward manager unlocked the bathroom mid-run and caught what I was doing, insisting that from then on, I was not allowed into the bathroom unsupervised.

Saturday 21ˢᵗ June 2008,

I just got caught running in the toilet. They are on to me now and making me go to the toilet supervised. I hate the ward manager so much, she's permanently on my back. They all are – it pisses me off so much! I hate it here, I absolutely 100% hate it with the whole of my heart. I hate every single one of them. I wish they would rot in hell and stay away from me.

F***ing nurses I hate them
I'll kick and shout and spit at them with phlegm
Always sticking their noses in
Interfering in my life
If only I could be given
A human hand carving knife
I'd remove them from my existence
So they would never interfere again
I hate the f***ing nurses
They deserve the witch's curses

The nurses started to threaten me with a one-to-one because of my exercising. This had to be the most horrific punishment they could give. Jane was on a one-to-one, so I knew what it involved, and I could not allow that to happen to me. A one-to-one involved a member of staff (normally a healthcare assistant rather than a trained nurse) staying with you 24/7, watching everything you did and following you everywhere you went. Even at night they would sit there while you slept. There was no escape on a one-to-one; no privacy, no time to just be alone or talk to your friends. You couldn't even have a conversation on the phone to your parents without them sitting there listening. I could not think of anything worse, especially as being on one would mean the end of my now not so secret exercising. And if I couldn't exercise, I couldn't cope. I could not be put on a one-to-one, I just couldn't. I had to be extra careful, but my mind was again in conflict. I knew I needed to reduce my exercising to avoid being put on a one-to-one, but I felt that with the amount of calories I had to consume I couldn't afford to limit the exercise. I didn't know how I would survive if I had a one-to-one.

I was in a constant battle with the nurses and health care assistants. Because my behaviour wasn't compliant, I felt that, whatever I did, they nagged. 'Sit down,' 'stop walking around,' 'why aren't you eating?' 'you're not helping yourself,' 'what do you think you're doing?' They did have what appeared to be their favourites who they regularly praised and encouraged, telling them how well they were doing and that they were doing the right thing and getting their lives back. They told these patients I was making life worse for myself and that they must ignore me and my defiance and focus on themselves. At an already very low ebb, the staff were doing very well at making me feel even worse. I felt picked on by them and this resulted in my hatred, anger and resentment growing to greater heights. They were driving me closer to my like-minded friends, and closer to anorexia. Yes, my behaviour wasn't following the rules of the unit, I wasn't as 'compliant' as I was meant to be, but this was surely evidence that I was struggling severely mentally, that I could not fight anorexia. In retrospect, I can see these other patients needed support from the staff so that they weren't negatively affected by my behaviour, but I also needed the staff's support and help, ideally through calm, kind and soft words rather than what seemed to be constant punishment, tellings off and being made an example of.

Because I was constantly at odds with the staff, feeling hatred in every ounce of my body and desperate to lose weight, I was turning into a hardened, tough anorexic. My parents still visited me on the weekend but, by now, I really didn't want to see them. Less than a few weeks before, all I had wanted was my parents there to give me a cuddle and ease my suffering, but not anymore. The hospital regime was brutal, and I was becoming brutal with it. Now, a visit from my parents merely meant sitting on my backside for a few hours, which I most certainly did not want to do. I didn't want them there. I wanted to be left alone to get on with my exercise. My parents were a nuisance, an interference and a hindrance in my attempts to avoid gaining weight. I was full of hatred and I didn't care who I hurt along the way during my battle with the hospital and their regime.

Chapter 13
Secrets and Struggles

On Monday 23rd June 2008, after ten days of being tube fed and drinking *Ensures* and milk, I was reintroduced to solid food at breakfast. I was terrified. The idea of food and eating was now one that I greatly feared. Trying to battle my way through a meal required energy and strength that I didn't have. My half a portion breakfast consisted of one slice of toast with *Flora*, a bowl of cornflakes, 100ml of full-fat milk and 200ml of orange squash. But as daunted by this prospect as I was, I told myself I must eat it, I would go into the dining room and do what I hadn't done for several weeks – eat a complete meal.

When I decide on something, that is it, I do it no matter what, reflecting my innate stubbornness and strong-willed personality. My parents did warn staff of this and maybe if they had listened, recognising that when I say I will do something I will go to hell and back to do it, that when I say I know my limits, I do know my exact limits and there is no pushing that, then maybe things would have turned out differently. Rather than them dismissing everything I said as something all anorexics say, if they had only listened to me, treated me as an individual, maybe my life could have taken a completely different path. I might not have ended up wasting years as a revolving-door patient going in and out of hospital, my life passing me by.

So that Monday morning I was determined to eat my breakfast. But what I didn't anticipate was the complete lack of compassion or understanding from the nurses supervising the table. I was trying my very best, slowly but surely putting food in my mouth. Following ten days of not eating, it was a struggle. It felt alien, it felt wrong, but I was doing it. However, I was struggling and I was eating slowly and, when the half an hour allotted breakfast time was up, I had eaten only half my toast and three quarters of my cereal. All I needed was an extra ten minutes to finish it off. After all, this was my first time of eating again and I was making an effort.

But my tray was swiped away from me and replaced with the punishment *Ensure*. They said I hadn't completed my meal and had to drink the *Ensure* or it would go down the tube. I couldn't believe they would do this to me. I was trying so hard to eat my breakfast and all the acknowledgement I got was that I had yet again failed to comply with their rules and would be punished.

I had sat in the dining room on numerous occasions the past few days when patients were struggling to eat but, because they were trying, they were given extra time and received constant praise and encouragement. But not me. They had all the power over me, and I was helpless. Molly, who wasn't sectioned, also hadn't eaten all of her breakfast and refused to drink the replacement *Ensure* as well. But I had the replacement *Ensure* forced down the tube. This happened several times, me having my breakfast tray taken away after the thirty minutes, but the nurse's favourites being told they could keep theirs for an extra ten minutes to complete. I felt so penalised and unfairly treated. I would shout at the nurses in my anger and frustration. It felt like they hated me, and I sure as hell hated them. My hatred for them and drive for anorexia was growing stronger by the second.

Because I was becoming more and more anxious about the calories I was consuming and lack of exercise I was getting, I started self-harming. I would scratch myself with my nails, carving words like 'fat' and 'hate' into my arms until they were red raw and bleeding. The scratches and scars soon became visible (it was a very hot summer and anything but a short-sleeved t-shirt was too much) so in response, the staff conducted a room search and went through all my personal belongings to look for sharp objects that I might be cutting myself with. They didn't ask me how or why I was self-harming. I was actually screaming out for help. 'Help' was one of the words I scratched into myself, like in *The Exorcist*, when the girl's stomach appears to read 'help me' because the girl is possessed by the Devil and trapped inside. I was possessed by the Devil and I was trapped inside. And no one came to help. So the Devil continued to take over.

I was also learning tricks at the table to get away with consuming less. I was regularly spilling *Ensure*, wiping it with my fingers and onto my clothes. The nurses in the dining room were constantly looking out for Jane and me spilling our drinks and we were sometimes caught out and punished with extra millilitres down the tube. But more often than not, we were one step ahead and continued to spill, pour and wipe our drinks into our clothes.

My clothes were constantly covered in sticky drink, feeling crusty and smelling of vanilla, chocolate, coffee, or whatever flavour *Ensure* I had been given. I was now only wearing dark clothes as they were best at disguising the stains, and I would often have to change outfit during the day. But we were only allowed one washing machine day a week, so I often had to ask Jane, my bedroom neighbour who I had become very good friends with, if I could put a load in when it was her day, and I would repay the favour.

When I started eating food again, I became quite adept at removing food from my plate and placing it in my pockets. My pockets would be filled with grease from roast potatoes, chips, anything I could get off my plate. I would even hide pieces of apple as I thought any calories were too many. I was like a walking dustbin. Every meal time was a source of contention. If I wasn't hiding food, I was trying to squeeze and scrape any fat out of it. The nurses knew most of the tricks. They stopped allowing me to walk into the dining room with my own tray because I would spill and hide as I walked, and I most certainly was not allowed a napkin like the other patients. Each meal time they would repeat the same things: "you must hold your bread by the corner," "you mustn't turn your toast over," "don't squeeze the mayonnaise out of the tuna," "don't smear your cereal round the bowl". Meals were battlefields and it felt like a triumph if I was able to get away with my antics.

From my experience of eating disorder inpatient units, jealously and competitiveness are rife amongst the patients. From the moment you arrive, you are silently analysed by the others as to how skinny you are. Everyone wants to be the skinniest, everyone wants everyone else to put on weight and, if they can see you playing tricks, they sure as hell won't let it go quietly. So occasionally, when I had outwitted the staff at the table, I would be approached later by a nurse and asked to empty my pockets because one of the patients had told them what I had done. I wanted the ground to swallow me up, terrified of what punishment was going to follow. Sometimes it would be a telling off, other times it would be *Ensure* forced down the tube. I hated the nurses and I hated the patients for dobbing me in, and I knew exactly which ones were responsible.

Tuesday 1st July 2008 was the group trip to Brighton, for all the patients with some of the staff. I desperately wanted to go, mainly because it would have been an ideal opportunity to do lots of exercise and not consume many calories. But I was told I was too much of a health risk and had to stay on the ward with the remaining members of staff and two other patients who chose not to go. I was gutted. I felt like a teenager being told they were grounded and couldn't go to the party. All the other patients arrived back about 9pm, exhilarated by their trip out; chatting, laughing, and reminiscing. Molly, Jane, and Sophie brought me back a present – a very tall, pink and blue Tinkerbell mug which was absolutely beautiful. But it was instantly confiscated because the nurses said it was too big, so it got locked away in the office.

Listening to the gossip there seemed to have been a few antics on the trip, and one patient returned completely and utterly drunk, unable to walk properly and with slurred speech… she had to go straight to bed. As staff were well aware, some anorexia sufferers prefer to drink alcohol rather than eat any food, so how this happened on a supervised trip is unclear. Listening to them all talk about the trip only made me feel more left out. But recently I had started isolating myself anyway and was spending less time with Molly and Sophie. This wasn't because I didn't want to see them, I did. But spending time with them meant time not exercising and I couldn't afford this. Every opportunity now had to be spent exercising, even if it was for only one minute. If I wasn't in the bathroom running, I was pacing in my bedroom and doing squats, star jumps, sprints on the spot – anything to burn calories. It was a bit like playing musical chairs, but instead of every time the music stopping you having to sit down, every time a member of staff walked past it was a quick slide on to my bed to give the impression I hadn't been exercising. But the staff knew what I was doing and actually, the more exercising I was having to do, the more miserable I was becoming.

Thursday 3rd July 2008,

I feel so depressed. I absolutely hate eating. It makes me feel so full, disgusting, fat, and guilty and I hate it. I just don't want to eat. If I'm not eating, I'm spending the rest of the day waiting for opportunities to exercise. But the more food I'm eating, the less energy I feel I have, and doing exercise feels more like a chore. I dread waking up every day. I know it's going to be a miserable day, I know I'm going to have to eat, and I know the exercise I have to try and do, but I get to the point that I can't be bothered. But I have to do it. I have to burn the calories. And I should have so much energy because of all the calories I'm consuming but I just don't. It's so frustrating. I hate me so much.

At the start of July 2008, my weight was showing no signs of increasing. I was glad not to be gaining weight, but it resulted in them increasing my meal plan. So one month after arriving, I was moved on to full portion breakfast – two slices of toast with *Flora*, a big bowl of cornflakes, 200ml of full-fat milk and 200ml of orange squash. It seemed colossal. In supervision times after meals and snacks, where you were made to sit down for half an hour as a group under supervision, I had researched calories on the internet. That, coupled with my nutritional knowledge as an athlete and sport scientist, meant I had become a walking calorie counter. Each meal time I calculated whether what I was presented with on my tray was more or less than the *Ensure* punishment which, in my case, had been doubled. I would then decide whether to eat the food or opt for the double *Ensure* based on calories.

Thursday 10th July 2008,
I've eaten everything. Every f***ing thing put in front of me like a fat, greedy pig. I really, really hate myself. I wish my Ensure *punishments were the same as everyone else's because then the calories would be less and I'd be able to not eat and have the* Ensure *instead, which would prove I was anorexic. Helen didn't eat her lunch or tea earlier which I wish I could have done. It shows she's a more worthy anorexic than I am. But her* Ensure *option is much smaller than mine which seems so unfair. If I had her* Ensure *penalty, I would pick it every time. And then I would feel much better about myself.*

It wasn't long after being placed on full portion breakfast I was also moved onto full portion tea. The food was never ending. Just as I was getting my head around eating again, they were doubling the quantities of my meals. But the more food they kept giving me, the more I felt I *had* to exercise. The oedema in my feet had started to reduce but during the day, because I was exercising, my feet would swell to quadruple the size. This gave it away to the staff what I was up to. My feet and ankles were incredibly sore. They had become cracked and bloody because the skin had stretched so much with the oedema, but if I was going to be pumped full of calories I had to try and burn them off. They also started checking my heart rate and blood pressure on an hourly basis. They were concerned about my irregular, slow heart beat but regular checking also enabled them to see if I had been exercising. Plus, I was still being caught occasionally running in the bathroom.

So I was trapped in a vicious cycle – I didn't want to gain weight so I exercised, but the more I exercised and didn't gain much weight, the more calories they gave me. I hated having to exercise and wanted to be able to stop but couldn't because I knew I would put on a lot of weight given the amount of calories I was having. I longed to have that feeling of skinniness again and to actually be physically incapable of exercising because I was too weak and ill. That would be an achievement. But not here.

Here I was moving away from 'ill' and closer to 'normal', and I hated it.

Chapter 14
The One-to-One

"Rebecca, it's your turn for your status sheet," the ward manager called from the lounge area.

Status sheet was what we received every Wednesday afternoon following ward round to find out the outcome of our requests. I walked into the room and sat at the long, plastic table opposite the ward manager and my other most hated nurse. I had been hoping to get some of my requests granted this week. I had been complying with all my meals and I had gained a bit of weight, so I thought it must be time for them to allow me on the daily trip to the bench.

"Right, Rebecca. We know you have been exercising. You have been caught in the bathroom several times and the other nurses and health care assistants are noting that you are constantly pacing in your bedroom and getting up early to exercise," the ward manager said in a serious tone. "I'm afraid we have no other choice. We are going to put you on a one-to-one."

I couldn't believe what I was hearing.

"You can't!" I screamed, having taken a gasp of breath after feeling punched in the stomach. "You can't do this to me!" I cried hysterically. "Please don't. I will be good, I won't do it anymore. Please, you can't put me on a one-to-one."

"I'm sorry, Rebecca," the other nurse took over, "we have to stop you exercising. Your one-to-one is waiting for you outside." And with that, I was led out of the room sobbing and trembling and taken to the healthcare assistant sitting in the lounge. I walked back to my room and flung myself on my bed in hysterics.

I cried continuously for the next two hours. I had visits from Jane, Molly, and Sophie, all trying to console me, but I was beyond help. I was utterly distraught. When called to snack time at 3pm, I stumbled out of my room, my one-to-one following behind, and I had a panic attack. I threw myself on the sofa, screaming, crying, shaking and gasping for air. I couldn't breathe... I couldn't cope... I wanted to die. I didn't eat or drink anything for the rest of the day; it all had to go via the tube. Not only was I too upset to fight the battle of eating, but I also wanted to prove a point to them that they shouldn't have put me on a one-to-one. What was I going to do now I couldn't exercise? I was dependent on that exercise to burn the calories of my ever-increasing meal plan. I needed to exercise. It was the only thing keeping me sane. But now I had someone following me twenty-four hours a day. My hatred and anorexic determination grew ever stronger.

Two days after being placed on the one-to-one, I had the NG tube removed. I was told they would use it as and when they needed to, i.e. when I refused to comply with my meals or *Ensure*. They would insert it for each occasion, rather than leave it permanently in. Without the tube in, the desire to stop eating and restrict was overwhelming, even though I knew they would still use the tube. The first main meal I faced without the tube was the dreaded Friday fish and chips. A fillet of chunky fish in breadcrumbs with greasy chips and a spoonful of peas. I hated this meal so much and it was always a real battle to get through it.

On this occasion, the breadcrumbs coating the fish were quite burnt. But there are no excuses for leaving food in eating disorder units. You have to eat everything on the plate regardless of how it is cooked and served. So, knowing I was going to have to eat it anyway, I ploughed through the burnt breadcrumbs and the rest of the meal, Molly and Sophie doing the same alongside me. As I finished my main meal and moved on to start my fruit and yoghurt, I looked up to see that, opposite me, Helen had removed her fish from the breadcrumbs which she had pushed to the side of the plate.

"It's far too burnt," she explained, stabbing at the sheet of breadcrumbs with her knife, "I can't eat that. I've tried, but I just can't eat it." With that, the supervising nurse told her it was fine and she didn't have to eat it.

I was furious. Molly, Sophie, and I had eaten all of ours in that same burnt condition because we thought we had to, and now they were letting Helen leave hers. This was the one time I was not going to mind my own business.

"That's not fair," I said, trying to hold back tears. "We have managed to eat all of ours, she shouldn't be allowed to leave it." But I was dismissed by the nurse as interfering and told I should focus on myself. Angrily, I carried on eating, trying to keep my blood from boiling over. I finished my yoghurt and got up to walk away from the table.

"Rebecca," the nurse stopped me, "you have a few breadcrumbs left on your plate. You need to finish them up."

Seriously?! I had a few measly specks of breadcrumbs on my otherwise spotless plate and was being told I hadn't finished properly and had to scrape the remains, whereas Helen had the entire fish coating of breadcrumbs on the side of her plate and was being allowed to leave it unpunished! I had been teetering on the edge and this well and truly tipped me over. I picked up my empty bowl and threw it across the room. Molly, Sophie, and Jane all looked at me in shock as the bowl flew past their heads and bounced off the wall. But I wasn't finished there. I was livid. I picked up my dinner plate and threw that across the room. It shattered as it hit the wall. I repeated the same with my cutlery and cup until everything on my tray had been flung at the wall and smashed onto the floor.

With that, I burst into tears, ran back to my room and threw myself on my bed. But then panic surged over me. I shot up from my bed and made a desperate attempt to run. I just wanted to run: run away, run anywhere. I had to get that fish and chips out of my body. I wanted to rip my stomach out. I tried to get out of my room but my one-to-one, with help from several other nurses, blocked my exit. I had lost all control of my body. I was screaming, kicking and punching as I tried to get out. The staff managed to lock me in my room where I collapsed onto the floor, shaking, kicking and rolling around, screaming to be let out, begging to get this food out of me. My head was banging against the hard lino floor, the staff trying to cushion my blows. Eventually I started to regain control of my thoughts and my body, which flopped into an exhausted, sobbing heap on the floor.

Because of the scene I had caused in the dining room, the staff decided I needed to be moved back to my bedroom to eat my meals. I was not happy about it, not only because eating in my room in a one-to-one situation provided far less opportunity to hide food, but also because Jane, Molly, and Sophie were all together in the dining room and that horribly familiar feeling of being left out took over. After only a few days of eating in my room, as I sat down at my table to face my expected half-portion lunch, I was presented with a full portion. It was huge. There was absolutely no way on Earth I was going to put all that food inside my body. Not now, not ever. Half-portion lunch made me feel full in itself, I was not going to eat double. It was simply not going to happen. So, I sat there for forty-five minutes staring at my plate as the stodge turned cold and solidified. I was then presented with my double *Ensure* punishment of 660 calories which, if I didn't drink it, would be put down an NG feeding tube.

At the same time as the introduction of full portion lunches, my dietician also introduced a *Scandishake* into my meal plan as a snack. A *Scandishake* is like a milkshake, made from a powder with full-fat milk. It comprises 600 calories. I was horrified. How the hell could she be adding 600 calories to my meal plan, especially now I was having full portions at breakfast and tea and more than double the amount of calories at lunch? I couldn't believe the amount of calories they were making me have. It felt a ridiculous and unnecessarily large amount, made worse by the fact it was so much more than anyone else on the ward was given. I could not bring myself to drink the *Scandishake*. I could not put 600 calories inside me. I was able to refuse the drink without consequence for the first few days because I didn't have the tube in and, for some reason, they didn't want to insert it just for that. But after several days of constant refusal, they reinserted the tube on a permanent basis. There was now no escaping the calories.

With the increased meal plan, and the one-to-one making it harder to exercise, I started to gain more weight and by the end of July 2008, my weight had crept up to 40kg and my BMI was nearly 13.

Thursday 31ˢᵗ July 2008,
My thighs and stomach are absolutely foul beyond belief. My thighs bulge, my stomach sticks out, my face is fleshy. I look like a dumpling!

I was repulsed by myself and how I looked. But one of the positives with gaining weight was that I was allowed a daily trip to the bench. I also tried to tell myself that the more weight I gained, the closer I was to leaving. With my weight slowly going up, there was less confrontation between me and the nurses. I was still on a one-to-one which I hated, but I was given my first 'timeout' at the weekend. I was allowed to go to the park opposite the hospital for one hour when my parents and Jenny came to visit. I was so happy, it was my first time being in the outside world in nine weeks, and I loved it. It was great to see Jenny and hear about her girls, and I had a go on the swings and a stroll round the park. I loved that I was able to get more exercise, I loved being with my parents and Jenny, and I loved feeling free. But the little taster I had of being back in the real world only increased my desire to get back out there so I could start losing weight again... and lots of it.

Chapter 15
Fighting and Secrets

I was looking at the photos in my bedroom of my college prom from the previous summer. There I was, in the beautiful pink halter-neck dress and all I could see was a fat lump, surrounded by beautiful, skinny people.

"Look at you in that photo," one of the few nice healthcare assistants said, "what were you? A size 6? What's so good about that? What's in a size 6?" she asked.

'Too much,' I thought, 'that's what's in a size 6... far too much flesh.' I kept my thoughts to myself and shrugged my shoulders.

"You have to be willing to try, Rebecca," she said. "Try to do the right thing, gain the weight, do it to get out there and get back to normal. You need to stop fighting."

There was not one part of me that wanted to get back to a normal size, or back to the size I was in that photo. I didn't want to be bigger, I didn't want to gain weight and I was going to fight with every inch of my being, every step along the way, to prevent it. 'She thinks a size 6 is too small. Wait until I get to size zero and below,' I thought. 'I'll show them'. But by now I realised that I couldn't keep voicing these thoughts and feelings aloud if I wanted to leave. I had to play the game, I had to pretend I wanted to get better otherwise they would never let me leave. But as much as I tried to play the game, I always found it so difficult to pretend that I wanted to get better. Saying the words felt like a betrayal even though I knew I didn't mean what I was saying. Anorexia was my god and I was devout, and I couldn't pretend otherwise.

I was still trying to exercise when I could, despite the one-to-one. Some of my one-to-ones were there for an easy job and we reached an unspoken agreement. They would allow me to pace up and down my bedroom but, when a nurse or doctor was approaching, they would give the secret signal and I would sit down. I got to do the exercise I wanted, they got an easy job, and neither of us got any bother from the nurses. This way I could still exercise during the day but at times when I had stricter healthcare assistants and nurses, I was made to sit down and I hated it.

Also, although I didn't like having the tube reinserted because of my refusal to drink my snack of the *Scandishake*, I did try to use it to my advantage. Every evening when I had a shower, I would turn my back on the one-to-one supervising me, unscrew the cap off the tube and suck the end, drawing some of the contents from my stomach up through the tube and into my mouth. I would then spit out. I was pleased with myself for discovering this new way of getting rid of calories. I have never been able to make myself sick, I have always lost weight through restriction and exercise, but with hospital preventing me doing these I found this alternative method. It worked well for a while, every evening sucking out as much as I could. But then I got caught so from then on, the staff had extra eagle eyes on me.

After one month of being on a one-to-one 24/7 and gaining over 3kg in that time, I had my one-to-one reduced to between 9am and 5pm. With the reduced hours, I instantly started exercising more. Then began a long, troubled journey of water-loading to disguise the fact that I wasn't gaining any weight. It started with only a small amount, about 300ml, to get my BMI to 14. I felt horrific at the weight I was and I was convinced I looked like the biggest patient on the ward. I was also worried they were going to keep me sectioned for as long as possible, making me gain more and more weight. So, if that was going to be their plan, I had to be smarter. I had to make my weight gain as slow as possible, otherwise I would be back to a normal weight before they removed the section. But I couldn't let them know I wasn't gaining weight, hence the introduction of water-loading.

With each weigh-in I was gradually drinking more and within two weeks, I was drinking nearly two litres and not going to the toilet after 5pm on evenings before weigh-in. The fullness of my bladder was incredibly uncomfortable and kept me awake during the night. If I found myself drifting off, I would occasionally wake up having wet myself, requiring me to drink more all over again. Once, as I sat waiting on my bed for 5.30am weigh-in to come round, holding my privates, it all just started coming out and I had to climb over the sink in my bedroom as all the water I had drunk eleven hours ago came flooding out.

But the staff were on to me and, within those first two weeks of starting water-loading, they spot-weighed me (asking to weigh me at random times during the day). I had managed to retain a lot of the water and my spot-weight was only a few hundred grams below what I had been weighed at on weigh-in. They knew I was water-loading, but they didn't quite know to what extent. Despite their knowledge of the water-loading, after three weeks of being on the reduced one-to-one, they removed it completely. One might consider this a strange move on their part – giving someone they know is exercising and water-loading more freedom to do just that. But for me, this was great news.

With the complete removal of the one-to-one, my exercise regime became all-encompassing. I was exercising continuously from 5am to 11pm, with the only rest periods being meal times and supervision. I hated every minute of it. I was permanently exhausted, wishing to escape the constant torture of my mind. All I wanted to do was sleep, to sleep away the pain, sleep away the anxiety, sleep away the stress, sleep to escape this hell that I was living. But sleep wasn't an option. I could not bear the feelings of guilt, laziness, and shame that came with not making myself exercise. The only option was to exercise, hide food at every opportunity and commit myself wholeheartedly to anorexia. I was fighting a war.

Alongside the removal of the one-to-one came increased timeout. This provided ideal opportunities to exercise to help me prevent weight gain. I started having two hours out on both Saturdays and Sundays which my parents took in turn. But I didn't care about seeing my parents, I just used them to do exercise. We would go to Finsbury Park and I would march us round. My parents had come to see me, to spend time with me because they loved and cared for me, and all I wanted to do was exercise. I couldn't have cared less if they were there or not, as long as I was exercising. I was possessed and I was nasty and heartless. My mum in particular found it difficult. As I stormed around the park, she would try to make me slow down or stop. Once, she took me shopping on the high street, buying me presents; lots of pretty stationery, pink flowery photo albums, beautiful hand-decorated paper. And I re-paid her with my vicious tongue, giving her a barrage of moans and spiteful words. I did feel bad afterwards when I knew I had been mean to her (and my dad), but at the time I couldn't help it. I *had* to exercise and I was possessed. There was only one thing on my mind and nothing and no one was going to stop me. My mind, body, and life were dictated by anorexia.

I was allowed home for the weekend for the first time for my twentieth birthday on 17th September, 2008. My dad came to pick me up at 9am on the Saturday morning and drove me home. I couldn't keep my eyes open, the motion of the car and the exhaustion from fighting the system coupled with continual exercising made me fall asleep. As I was drifting in and out of sleep states, whizzing down the motorway at seventy miles an hour, I imagined the car skidding, spinning out of control and crashing off the road. I wanted it to happen, I wanted the car to crash and take my life, so I didn't have to endure this hell that I was currently living in. I didn't want anything bad to happen to my dad, but I wanted my life to end to escape the torture. But we made it home safe and sound, everything as I had left it three months before.

I was worried about going home. How was I going to do all the exercise I had been doing in hospital? How was I going to cut down on calories with my mum being so strict and eagle-eyed? But it was all a lot easier than I was expecting.

My main meal in St Ann's was my lunchtime double *Ensure* at

660 calories (because I refused to eat a full portion). But at home I told my mum I would have a salmon fillet with jacket potato and vegetables, telling her it was the right amount of calories but knowing it was less. As my parents had been given no information about my meal plan by the unit, they believed me. And my *Boots* low-calorie sandwich with low-calorie crisps was far less than the high-calorie sandwiches and yoghurts provided at hospital for teatime. I reduced breakfast as well, opting for an English muffin instead of two slices of toast and butter, saving calories. I also told my mum that I didn't have food snacks in the morning and afternoon, so I was able to avoid having a *KitKat* and cereal bar. And the big 600 calorie *Scandishake* for morning snack I made using less milk.

'Result!' I thought. I had cut down on calories and this was what I wanted, though I was still angry with myself for eating what I had. But this had been my first trip home and I had to test the water. Now I knew I could do it and, with the trips home that followed, I cut out more and more. I felt like I was living on the edge, constantly worrying I was going to get caught, riddled with anxiety for eating anything, and sneaking around trying to hide bits of food and shave calories at every opportunity without my mum noticing.

There was all the exercise to fit in at home as well. I knew I would be able to do some as we had been doing a fair amount of walking in previous timeouts in London. But how was I going to fit in the other eleven hours that I had been doing in hospital? I got up at home at the same time, 5am, and jogged up and down the kitchen for one hour, trying not to make any noise, listening out for any footsteps. Then followed my usual circuit training exercises. During the day, my parents did try to stop me exercising but I was like a caged animal who had been set free, trying to make the most of the little opportunity before being locked up again. I did love my parents and I did feel bad for lying to them and treating them as badly as I did, but they were not my priority. They had to come second to exercise and restriction and, ultimately, anorexia. They were an obstacle to me, my weight loss, and my dedication to anorexia... and I was going to trample over them to get what I wanted. I knew I would hurt them, but I couldn't help it. I was so entrenched in anorexia that I could not think or behave in any other way. And having the weekend at home didn't change my mind about not wanting to get better, as the hospital had been hoping it would. They had hoped that I would see 'life' again and become motivated to try and get better. But the opposite happened. I now couldn't wait to get out of hospital to lose weight again and do all the exercise I wanted. It wasn't a question of if, but a question of when. I only had to bide my time.

Now, looking back, I hate myself for how I treated my parents. They showed me nothing but love and care and I trampled all over them. Yes, I know I was 'ill' and my behaviour was not really within my control, but I will never forgive myself for how I treated them and I *never ever* want to go back to that. At the time I could not see it, but anorexia is pure evil and makes you the same; careless of anyone and everything. My parents mean too much to me to put them through that again. I will not go back to being a slave to a demon that causes nothing but misery and pain.

Chapter 16
Water-loading

Friday 3rd October 2008,

    I love bone… and I need bone. Hopefully we will be reunited in the not-too-distant future. Flesh and fat are the Devil, bone is God. I will return to the God and I will never ever give up on it. God will wrap his arms around me and take me to heaven. It's only a matter of time and a temporary stay in hell.

The more often I was going home, restricting and exercising, the more my parents became suspicious of what I was doing; questioning me and checking up on me. This made me angry. They were getting in my way, they were a nuisance and an interference and my weekend trips home were full of arguments. Sitting down to my lunch of a low-calorie tuna sandwich, my mum sprung a packet of *Skips* on me, which I had managed to cut out the past couple of trips home.

    "I'm not eating them," I said angrily. "They aren't part of my meal plan and I don't need to eat them."

    "You are going to eat them," my mum said sternly.

    "No, I'm not. I didn't eat them last week and I'm certainly not eating them now," I shouted.

    Mum was now shouting back. "We know what you're doing. You're constantly trying to cut out, trying to lose weight. I won't put up with it. You will eat the crisps or we are taking you back to hospital."

The argument carried on like this for several minutes, until I ran off to my bedroom, slamming the door behind me and slumping onto the floor, crying. I couldn't stop the tears. A 94-calorie bag of crisps had put me in that state and caused yet another horrible, full-blown argument between me and my mum. Yet again, I felt exhausted.

Eventually my mum persuaded me to open the door.

"I can't do it anymore," I sobbed. "I can't bear it. It's all the time, non-stop, constant worrying and torture in my mind." I was beginning to let my guard down as my mum listened to me, her arm wrapped around me as we sat on my bed. "I am so fed up with always worrying about food; it's all the time. And I always feel I have to exercise and I so wish I didn't. I wish it would all just go away," I cried.

This was the first time I had said how I was really feeling, that actually I hated my head and what it made me do and how it made me feel. I was trapped in my body and a slave to my anorexic mind, although I didn't realise it at the time. Yes, I was tired of it and hated it, but to me, it was simply my mind. They were my thoughts and the thoughts were clear. I wanted to lose weight and be thin and I definitely didn't want to gain weight. So I had to do everything I could to achieve this, no matter how exhausting and painful it was. I had to keep fighting. And letting slip to my mum how I truly felt led to yet another battering by my mind. I felt guilty, ashamed, and sinful, so I made a vow to myself to be stronger than ever, fight harder than ever, and to never let go of anorexia.

My parents had been attending the carers' support group, held once a fortnight in the evening, as often as they could. They didn't find it particularly helpful, constantly being reminded by the nurses who were running it that the regime was a weight-gaining programme; that was the main focus. But my parents were worried about my mind; my psychological state. Yes, the hospital could fatten me up and make me gain weight, but what about helping me psychologically? After all, anorexia nervosa is a mental illness. But their concerns were always dismissed, being reminded the priority was weight gain.

But my parents knew me better than anyone and they could

see my behaviour when I went home on weekends, exercising like a dervish and lying about restricting. They could see I was subordinate to my own mind, that I was mentally struggling and taken over by anorexia. They were worried about what would happen when I was discharged, knowing anorexia was going to run riot. They also knew how strong-willed and determined I was and had tried to explain this to my consultant. When I told everyone (and I repeatedly did so) that I could only cope going to a BMI of 16, I meant it, and my parents knew I meant it. But my consultant would tell my parents that I was just another anorexic and all anorexics say things like this, and he knew the best way anorexics like me needed to be treated. So again, their fears and concerns were ignored. This was a completely new situation to them, they didn't know any different, and they felt they had no choice than to trust and go along with what the consultant said.

I was on about 3000 calories a day, the most of anyone in the unit. But I was also exercising for eleven hours a day. My consultant told my parents that he would keep giving me more and more calories to counteract the exercising. My parents questioned this approach, suggesting that maybe it would be preferable to try and combat the exercising, rather than simply piling on more and more calories. Again, they were dismissed, my consultant knowing best how to treat 'just another anorexic.' But they knew the more and more calories I was having was forcing me to do more and more exercise which deep down I didn't want to be doing.

As the weeks rolled by, with exercising non-stop in hospital and weekend visits home becoming a regular thing, I became increasingly successful at preventing any weight gain and I was having to drink more and more water to disguise the fact I wasn't gaining weight. I built up to drinking three litres of water before weigh-in and it made me feel so ill. I would feel light-headed and would have a pounding headache for the rest of the day, coupled with crippling stomach-ache and nausea. In anticipation of being spot-weighed, I was having to drink like this on a daily basis and not only for the normal twice-weekly weigh-ins. I was living in a permanent state of stress and anxiety over the food, calories, fear of getting caught exercising, and fear of spot-weighing.

Although I was trying to prepare for spot-weighs, occasionally I would get caught out weighing less than my official weigh-in. My consultant came to tell me that he knew I was exercising madly and water-loading and, if I was to have any chance of being 'un-sectioned', he needed to know my real weight. I was constantly waiting for them to put me back on a one-to-one and cut my timeout. This to me seemed like the logical thing for them to do. If they knew I was exercising all hours of the day and drinking water before weigh-ins, surely they would want to stop this and put me on a one-to-one to do so? I lived in fear that this was going to happen and that I was going to have someone stuck by my side all day every day, stopping me exercising and drinking water before weigh-ins. But it never did. And until it did, I was going to carry on doing exactly what I had been, exercising ferociously and drinking more and more water to disguise my lack of weight gain to prevent them increasing my meal plan.

At the time, water-loading had felt like my only option to avoid gaining weight. Every time I got caught out I was relieved that a one-to-one was not reintroduced. However, looking back, I really wish the staff had put me on a one-to-one after the very first sign I was water-loading. I needed them to take the responsibility away from me. I couldn't stop myself from doing it, but they could have. And I so wish they had. Anorexia had convinced me that water-loading was the answer to my problems.

To anyone reading this who has been convinced in that same way – anorexia is wrong. Anorexia is deceitful and malicious, and water-loading does not solve anything. Anorexia makes you believe you can't cope with weight gain. But you can. That is not to say it isn't bloody hard… but you *can* do it. Life is so much better for fighting the anorexic voice than letting it completely destroy everything and everyone around you. So, if you are water-loading or considering doing it, *please don't*. It doesn't get you anywhere and it wraps you up in a web of lies which takes you further and further away from a life worth living. You deserve to be happy and you deserve to have a life – water-loading and anorexia do not bring this.

Remember: to succeed in anorexia is to fail in life.

Chapter 17
Target Weight

"Sit down, Rebecca, I want to have a chat," my consultant said as he entered my room in the afternoon, interrupting my pacing. It was Wednesday 29th October, 2008, and I had now been in the unit for nearly five months. I sat on my bed as he sat on the only chair in the room.

"I know you have been asking about discharge, and target weights, and un-sectioning, and I have decided you won't be able to leave until your BMI is 17. That will be your target weight and then we will lift the section," he said, speaking at me rather than to me.

"Please, no," I said, starting to cry. "I can't get to a BMI of 17, I can't. I can get to a BMI of 16 and I will try and maintain that when I leave, but if you push me to a BMI of 17 I won't. I will lose it straight away when I leave." I had tried explaining this to him on many occasions, but I was always dismissed as being the same as all those other anorexics who all say the same thing.

"No, my decision is final," he said. "You will get to a BMI of 17. That is still within the anorexic diagnosis, which is anything under 17.5. It is lower than we would normally agree to."

"No, it's not," I said angrily. "You let most other people leave here at much lower BMIs."

"Yes, but Rebecca," he said calmly, "a lot of the other patients here have had many hospital admissions and have been anorexic for years and are chronic. This is your first admission and normally on first admissions we would pursue your weight gain back to a healthy BMI of between eighteen-point-five and twenty."

"So you are punishing me for not being anorexic as long," I said with hatred.

"Well, you may see it that way, but to us it is not punishment. And if you agree to stay until you are a BMI of 17 then I will consider lifting the section sooner."

"No. There's no way I'm agreeing to it. It's not fair. I do not want to get to a BMI of 17. It's pointless and I won't maintain it. I won't do it." I was now crying.

"Your water-loading, constant exercising and your frequent hiding of food gives me no choice but to keep the section in place. And I will keep it going until you reach a BMI of 17 if you do not agree to this," his voice still very calm.

"Get out," I screamed. "I don't want to talk to you anymore. Leave me alone!"

With that, my consultant stood and walked out the room, leaving me crying hysterically on my bed. I was absolutely devastated. I could not believe he was going to do this to me. 'BMI 17! That's horrific,' I thought. 'My BMI is barely 14 at the moment and I already feel obese. There's no way I can get to 17.'

I cried for hours and refused to eat anything. My tube had recently been removed but the nurses reinserted it as a one-off to force the calories (in the form of *Ensure*) into me. I decided I needed to prolong the weight gain process for as long as possible, gaining as little as I could, so that when my section was due to run out after the six-month period, I would be as low a weight as possible. Then I would be allowed to leave because I was convinced there was no way he would be justified in renewing the section. So, I had to carry on with the exercising, water-loading, and food-hiding.

Molly, who had recently been discharged but quickly readmitted, tried to console me, reminding me that the weight gain is temporary and that we had to endure the pain to be able to lose weight when we left. And by God were we going to do this. We would talk about it all the time, reassuring each other that we were still very much anorexic and were going to lose all the weight they were making us gain in hospital, and more. We would concoct our plans of weight loss, remind ourselves of our anorexic abilities, and vow to each other that we would put two fingers up to everyone in that place when we left and lost more weight than they could ever imagine. We had our own anorexic club.

However, there was a girl in the room next to mine, Kim, who I didn't get on with. She wasn't a compliant patient either and I think there was a competitive air between us. She told staff I was exercising continuously, pacing from the early hours of the morning to the late hours of night, and she also told on me whenever I hid food. I really hated her. One of the nurses I hated came into my room early November 2008.

"We know you are pacing all day," she said. "The staff that work in the offices below have told us they hear you continuously walking up and down your bedroom all day. They can hear it through the floor boards."

My heart was now beating ten to the dozen. I couldn't work out whether I had been well and truly caught out, or if she was lying to me to try and make me admit it. I remained silent.

"And we have also had complaints from other patients on the ward about your continual pacing and getting up at 5am to do so," she said.

I knew this was coming from Kim. But I still remained silent. I knew that she knew what I was up to, but I was not going to admit to it. She then moved on to talk about my water-loading.

"I know you are drinking every morning in case you are spot-weighed," she said trying to tempt me to open up to her. I hated that she knew what I was doing. I thought I was being clever by drinking every morning. But she had sussed me out. And the only thing I knew to do was to deny it.

"I'm not," I replied sheepishly.

"Oh, come on, Rebecca," she said, "we know what you're doing. You need to stop pacing and you need to stop water-loading." And with that she walked out my room. So I started pacing again. I wasn't going to stop if they weren't going to make me. I was going to continue with my plans until they stopped me with a one-to-one.

Monday 10th November 2008,

I hate feeling that I have to exercise all the time and being so tired and miserable and fed up. But I know I'm going to feel even worse when I get bigger. Luckily at the moment, I'm still managing to prevent any weight gain. I feel so sad and lonely. I want to be at home, but I don't want to be bigger. I know I'm going to get spot-weighed tomorrow so I've got to get up extra early and drink three litres of water. I'm dreading it but I can't let them find out my real weight.

My real weight was found out in a spot-weigh-in mid-November 2008 but, again, there was no consequence to this and I was immediately back to exercising and water-loading. A week later I had a CPA. A CPA is a big meeting with everyone involved in your care. My consultant discussed my progress so far and plans for the future with my parents, nurses and a member from my community team – the nurse who I had met in the general hospital at home. My consultant made me explain to my parents that I had been water-loading. I wanted the ground to swallow me up as my parents had been unaware of this. I don't think they even knew what the concept of water-loading was and it certainly hadn't occurred to them that this was something I was doing. I had never heard of it before myself until I entered the depths of the eating disorder hospital. I had entered as a novice but quickly become a hardened professional and I was up to every trick in the book. I had not wanted my parents to know. I knew it would hurt, upset and disappoint them and I hated doing that to them. I really did care for them and I could not bear the feeling of upsetting them. But anorexia was too strong and my quest to be faithful to anorexia meant I hurt my parents along the way. I hated my consultant for making me tell them and making me hurt them. They looked devastated… and it was me that caused it. I felt like the devil-child, bringing them nothing but hell and misery.

'I feel so guilty for putting them through this', I thought, 'but I wish they didn't care. I wish they would leave me alone. I don't want to be mean to them, but they are ruining my life. Everyone here is ruining my life.'

Later that evening I had a text from my mum:

> 'I'm sorry you are so ill that you have to lie to me all
> the time. I can't believe anything you say I'm afraid
> as you have told so many lies.'

I felt sick to the stomach as I read it. All I had ever wanted to do was please my mum and now the hospital had made me admit to her my bad behaviour. 'I might as well not live anymore,' I thought. 'I cannot live with my mum feeling like that towards me.'

With my mum's disappointment and the hospital forcing me to a BMI of 17 and continual spot-weighing, I felt I was left with no choice. I had to run away.

Chapter 18
Run Away

On Tuesday 9th December 2008, the ward manager came into my room and told me I had to pack my things up and move bedrooms. Kim found being next door to my pacing too stressful and the ward manager said I had to be closer to the office so they could keep a better eye on my exercising. This was now the third time I had been made to move bedrooms, and it was the straw that broke the camel's back. It pushed me over the edge. My plans of running away had to be put into action, because I simply couldn't cope anymore. I was helpless and desperate.

Wednesday 10th December 2008 was the day. I got up at 5am, same as normal, to do my pacing and exercising. But I also had adrenaline surging through my body. I knew that within a few hours I was going to be out of there. Every day, morning snack was from ten until ten-thirty and then we had free time until lunch at midday. In that free time, despite still being under section, I was allowed out with some of the other patients for an unsupervised, fifteen-minute walk around the hospital grounds and I knew this would provide me with an ideal opportunity to sneak out.

Morning snack time arrived and I drank my 600-calorie *Scandishake* and ate my *KitKat* faster than I ever had before. Usually it took me the full half an hour to finish, but not that day. I knew it was the last thing I was going to consume for a while and the anticipation of restriction felt good. I couldn't wait to feel empty again. I was so nervous – my heart was pounding, butterflies flickering, palms sweating. I quickly went to my room to get ready, ensuring I had my debit card, phone, charger, passport, and some cash. I wrapped up in several layers and was ready. I rounded everyone up for our walk at 11am. There was seven of us allowed on the unsupervised walk and the cleaner opened the door to let us out. Stage one – getting out of the building unnoticed – complete.

Every time we went for a walk, I sang the Beyoncé song 'Irreplaceable' with my good friend Alistair. Someone in the group would always ask "What way shall we go, left or right?" Alistair and I would respond with "To the left, to the left." But this day was different. I had told Alistair my plan and we stayed at the back of the pack. He was the only one who knew and I knew I could trust him. The first part of the walk takes you right past the entrance to the hospital and with everyone walking ahead chatting away together, I said goodbye to Alistair and walked casually out of the car park and onto the street. That was it: I was free!

I knew exactly where I was going as I had walked around the area a lot in my previous timeouts with my parents. I ran up the road, nerves and adrenaline surging through my body. I hadn't run like this for months and it felt incredible. I just kept running and running for what must have been five minutes, never tiring, my legs going round and round. I knew I had to keep going until I got to the bus stop on Green Lane. Every minute was precious. Lunch was at midday, so that would be when they realised I wasn't there. I had to get as far away as possible before then.

The number 29 bus came along straight away. 'Brilliant,' I thought, 'That's the bus I need'.

"Single to Manor House, please," I asked the bus driver politely.

"You have to buy your ticket beforehand," the bus driver replied shortly. "You can't buy your ticket on the bus, you have to use the machine."

I stepped off the bus and it instantly drove away. I was so frustrated with myself, I was losing valuable time. I walked over to the machine and tried to figure out what to do. It was £2 for a ticket and it only accepted coins. I counted the scraps of change in my pocket. £1.70. Bugger, I was 30p short. 'What shall I do?' I thought. 'I need to get away ASAP'. I looked around and saw a lady standing nearby.

"Do you have 30p I could have, please?" I asked the lady quietly. She started looking through her bag and finally pulled out three ten pence coins and handed them to me. "Thank you so much," I said and walked back to the machine to buy my £2 ticket.

Clutching my ticket, I kept looking at my watch as I waited for the next bus to arrive. 'Come on!' I thought. 'There's only half an hour until lunch now. Hurry up!' I kept looking round, worrying someone was going to approach me and stop me. I was like a prisoner on the run, and I was sure people knew what I was doing and that someone was going to ruin my plans. After what felt like an eternity, but was in fact only of matter minutes, the next bus came along and I jumped on.

As the bus pulled to a stop at Manor House underground station, I ran to the ticket booth to buy a ticket to St Pancras. I knew I needed the Piccadilly Line and it was, to my surprise, incredibly easy to follow. All the while, I kept looking at my watch and scanning round, waiting for midday to strike and them to realise I was gone. I was sure I was going to get a tap on the shoulder from someone ready to take me back to hospital.

I arrived at St Pancras and ran through the station, following the signs to St Pancras International. I had been through the station before when I came home on the train from Loughborough, but it seemed like a completely different station to me now; I didn't recognise any of it. I found the Eurostar ticket office and was relieved to see there was barely any queue; only one person in front of me. But this one person seemed to be taking forever. I checked my watch, it was now just gone 12pm. The penny would have dropped that I was missing.

The next Eurostar train to leave would be at 1.10pm to Paris. 'Perfect,' I thought. My plan was to get to Paris and then make my way to Spain to stay with my sister, who was living there. I hadn't thought any further than that, or what she might do when I turned up. All I cared about was that I was out of that hell hole… and I wasn't going back. I showed the man at the counter my passport and bought my single ticket to France. 'There's no way I'm going to need a return,' I thought. I paid the £178 with my debit card and headed straight for the check-in and departure lounge.

I wandered around the small lounge, waiting for 12.50pm to arrive so I could board the train. 'They must be out looking for me now,' I thought. 'They can probably trace where I used my debit card.' I panicked, my anxiety growing stronger by the second. I was second in line in the queue to board the train and, as soon as boarding opened, I headed straight to my seat – Platform 6, Coach 5, Seat 66. I took my seat next to the window, watching the seconds tick by on my watch. I needed the train to depart before I got caught. I felt like I was sitting on a knife edge. I now knew what it felt like to be on the run. After what seemed like a lifetime, my watch read 13.10pm. The train started moving. I was away.

As I sat there, the green English countryside whizzing past my window, I got out my phone. I wanted to let people know I was safe as my absence would be noted by now and, now I was on the train, I couldn't be caught. It was exhilarating. Alistair, Jane, and a couple of other friends from the unit had already rung and texted me, saying they were worried about me. I replied to them all, explaining I was ok.

I had several answer-phone messages between 12.30pm and 12.45pm from the ward manager and one of the other nurses, saying that I needed to come back or they would have to call the police. I had been missing since 11am and it wasn't until 12.30pm that it was noticed, or any contact was made.

While I had been waiting for the train to depart at 13.10pm, my parents back at home were contacted by the police at 1pm. My mum was at work, so their first contact was with my dad.

"Your daughter has gone missing," they explained. "Is this of worry to you?"

What an idiotic question. "Yes it is of great concern," my dad replied.

The police explained they would go to the hospital to talk to staff and patients about my potential whereabouts. As soon as my dad got off the phone to the police, he rang my mum who, panic-stricken, came home immediately.

My phone was constantly ringing with calls and texts from my mum and dad, the ward manager and other nurses, the police and fellow patients. I didn't answer any calls. I didn't want to talk to anyone, I only wanted to get away. But I replied to text messages from my parents, letting them know I was ok. I received a text back from my mum saying:

'Please just come home so we can give you a cuddle. I'm worried you're going to die and if you do, I will kill myself because there will be no point in me living'.

I was making them worry and I did feel guilty for this, but I felt like I had been left with no alternative. The hospital had pushed me over the edge, and I couldn't cope anymore. Escaping had been my only choice.

The police were in regular contact with my parents and, having spoken to some of the patients, they told my dad they thought I was going to my grandparents who lived in Barking. But my mum knew this wasn't likely. She knew I wouldn't to go somewhere I could be easily found. She knew this was far more serious than simply running to a safe place to escape a few meals.

As the train entered the Channel Tunnel my phone lost signal which was a relief; it gave me a break from the constant ringing, texts and answer-phone messages. It was painful listening to my mum and dad on the answer-phone, hearing how worried and upset they sounded. I didn't want them to worry about me; I was going to be fine. But any parent would be the same with their child missing: worried they did not have the resources to survive. It was a bitterly cold day and my mum's greatest fear, with me being so underweight, was that I would die from the low temperature, especially as she knew I wouldn't be eating or drinking.

On leaving the Channel Tunnel, when the messages and calls started coming in again, I knew I had to put my parents' minds at rest. I told my mum to ring me in half an hour, when I knew I would be off the train. Three hours after departure, the train finally pulled into the Gare du Nord. I had made it to Paris. Relieved to stand up, I got off the train and followed the hordes of people heading to what I presumed must be the exit.

It was a huge station and it was mind-numbingly cold. I was overwhelmed by my arrival in a foreign country. I was terrified. I tried reading the signs and information boards but couldn't understand any of it. 'Come on, Rebecca,' I told myself, 'you did GCSE French. Think! You must know some of this.' But the enormity of the situation was overpowering. As I approached the exit, there were masses of people waiting, like at the airport when arrivals come in. But unlike other passengers who were greeted with hugs and kisses from their loved ones, I was stranded, alone and petrified.

I could see taxi drivers holding up signs with people's names on and then I caught a glimpse of a board with the word 'Airport'. 'Brilliant,' I thought, 'that's what I want. I need to make my way to the airport and then I can get on a plane to Spain.' I wandered around the station looking for a clue of when and where to get the train to the airport, but I couldn't find one. There were so many people and so many boards and signs everywhere, I didn't know what to do. I made my way out of the station and onto the busy road.

It was now a pitch-black night sky, but the street was glowing bright, filled with Christmas lights, lights from cars and buses; everything was lit up and colourful. On the other side of the old, cobbled road was a row of restaurants, including a *McDonalds*. As I turned to look to my left, I saw a hotel. 'I suppose I could stay there for the night,' I thought. But I was reluctant to have to use my debit card as I feared the police would trace me and then I would be taken back. As I stood in the middle of the bustling street – people, cars, bikes, buses all going about their business – I felt like a rabbit caught in headlights, not knowing what to do. In that moment the phone rang: Ma.

I answered and broke down in tears. Hearing my mums voice on the phone, I just wanted her to cuddle me and make everything better. My mum, relieved to hear my voice, relieved to hear I was ok, kept telling me I needed to come home and asking me where I was.

"I can't come home," I cried. "I never ever want to go back to that hospital."

The conversation continued like this for at least half an hour until I eventually told her where I was and that I was planning to go to Nicola. I could hear she was sick with worry and, after more conversation, she persuaded me to come home, promising me I wouldn't have to go back to the hospital. I naively believed her and, feeling completely out of my depth, I bought a ticket home, desperate to be in the arms of my parents. My train wasn't for another forty-five minutes, so I went into a few shops to buy souvenirs – a Paris snow globe, and an Eiffel Tower teddy and keyring. I spent the three-hour train journey back to St Pancras walking up and down one of the corridors near a mini bar, listening to music on my phone, angry with myself for not following through with my plan, but desperate to see my parents.

In the meantime, my mum rang the police to tell them what was happening. They told her they wanted to meet me at the station to take me straight back to the hospital. My mum told them no. She did not want them there, waiting for me in uniform and carting me off back to the hospital that had been so careless in letting me get out. She wanted me home safe and sound. She was terrified of what I might do if I returned to find policemen waiting for me. The police agreed to her demand; as long as I was safe, they didn't mind me being at home, realising being with my parents was probably the best place for me after my ordeal.

As I got off the train at about 11pm and made my way through the station to the exit, I could see masses of people standing there waiting. As I approached the crowd, I was desperately trying to spot my mum and dad. There he was – my dad in his giant blue and red mountain coat and woolly hat. I marched straight to him, flung my arms round him and cried. My mum appeared moments later, shivering with cold and anxiety, and I hugged her tighter than ever before. We headed back to the car, a good ten minutes away, and had a silent journey home, all of us exhausted from the experience and relieved to be with each other. When we got home, I hugged them again and went to bed exhausted.

First thing in the morning, though, I was back to my normal exercise regime. I didn't know what my fate was going to be or where I was going to end up, but my exercise was a constant and I had to do it no matter what. In all the uncertainty, that at least was certain. I sat with my parents in the morning as I reluctantly ate my breakfast and we decided I would not go back to St Ann's until we had all had a meeting with my consultant. But my consultant rang not long after, telling my mum she had to bring me back immediately.

She was furious. "Why in God's name would I want to bring my daughter back to a hospital that has allowed her to escape all the way to Paris?" she asked rhetorically.

My consultant replied in his usual, socially awkward manner, "Well, we have had people escape to places further than that."

This response only angered my mum further. "Do you really think that is an acceptable answer as to why Rebecca was able to get to France? It was over an hour before anyone noticed she was gone, and she was let out by the cleaner!"

"Yes," my consultant replied. "We do have to take responsibility for that."

"And why," my mum was getting angrier by the second, "did you do nothing about Rebecca water-loading, even though you have known about it for weeks?"

"Yes, I am sorry about that," he replied. "We did know, and we should have done something, but we didn't."

"So why, with all these failings, am I expected to bring her straight back to your care, when your care seems to be negligent?"

They talked on the phone for a good hour and then he asked to speak to me.

"Why did you run away, Rebecca?" he asked. "Did you think that by running away I would change my mind about you having to get to a BMI of 17? Because I haven't."

I started crying, unable to talk to him properly, I handed the phone back to my mum. 'How could he be so cruel?' I thought. 'I am at my wits' end and he brings up my ultimate fear and rubs it in.' I sincerely hated him with every bone of my being.

"Why doesn't she like me?" he asked my mum.

"Because," my mum explained, "you never treat her as an individual. When you talk to her, you dismiss everything she says or feels as being typically anorexic. You don't listen to anything *she* has to say. And this makes her feel even more insignificant and worthless."

My mum did understand me. She knew I needed to be listened to as a person, that I did know my own mind and I meant what I said. Anorexia gave me a significance, and continuing to dismiss me heightened my feelings of insignificance.

After hours of phone calls, it was agreed I would return to St Ann's at 5pm. My mum had tried her best but was given no other option because I was sectioned. I was devastated.

When I returned to the ward, I walked back down the corridor to my room, leaving my parents at the entrance, tears dripping down my face. My consultant came to speak to me, asking me lots of questions, telling me I wasn't going to be allowed any timeout, that I wasn't allowed on the Christmas shopping trip scheduled for all the patients in a few days' time, that I wasn't going to get as much time at home over Christmas. He also told me he was going to start me on antidepressants. I felt ashamed with myself for coming back from France, for not going through with my plan, for not having the courage to run away properly; for failing.

Chapter 19
Giving In and Gaining Weight

I wished I could have complied with the hospital regime, stopped exercising and eaten everything, but I couldn't bring myself to. It didn't help that they were still trying to make me eat a full portion for lunch which I simply could not do. I was still opting for the double *Ensure* replacement which had now been increased to 800 calories. I knew this was far more than the food, but I simply could not eat a full portion. They thought that increasing the calories of the drink replacement would encourage me to eat but I told them – "I cannot eat a full portion." They didn't try to help me find a manageable solution whereby I could bear to eat food. They only wanted to get the calories into me. They were more than happy for me to become further detached from food and normal eating, as long as I was gaining weight.

Wednesday 17th December 2008,
There's no way I'm ever going to do full-portion lunch. I wholeheartedly refuse to. I can't do it. Eating full-portion would be like an anorexic surrender. And I most certainly am not going to give up and surrender. The white flag may be above my door at the moment but its only temporary and I will always have control in my mind. I must never allow it to slip. They can and they will physically destroy me but the moment I leave here I will be able to do what I want again… and I want thinness.

January 2009 started as 2008 had ended; exercising and water-loading. It was now a real physical struggle to consume the amount of water I needed to cover the fact I wasn't gaining weight and I would gag and vomit up water, my body unable to cope with the load. I knew I had reached my limit. There was no way I could continue adding to this amount of water. I could not keep drinking more and more.

After lunch on Wednesday 7th January 2009, the ward manager called me into the medical room.

"We need to weigh you," she said.

I hadn't anticipated this and I wasn't prepared. I tried to refuse, but she told me I would not have any timeout if I didn't. If I didn't have timeout, my parents would know something was wrong. I stood on the scales – four kilos down. In the seven months I had been there, I had gained about 8kgs, which was much less than the expected weight gain of 1kg per week. I knew that was it. I couldn't carry on fighting and I couldn't carry on water-loading. I was going to have to gain weight. I told the ward manager how much I didn't want to get to a BMI of 17, how if my consultant would allow me to leave at 16, I would be able to do it (which I genuinely did believe). Her response? She told me I could lose it when I left – probably not the most appropriate answer.

As I knew I was not going to be able to drink my way out of hospital, I decided I had to cut down on the exercise and gain weight as it was my only way out. I kept telling myself that I had to gain weight in order to lose it, and I most certainly was going to lose it when I left… and more. I was still exercising a lot, but less than I had been and I found it incredibly difficult.

Following the spot-weigh, my meal plan was increased and I was put on a one-to-one at night to try and stop me water-loading. I had been water-loading for months, which they had known about, and now they decided to put me on a one-to-one. 'A bit late,' I thought. Although I knew I couldn't drink my way out of hospital, because I had been water-loading for so long, I couldn't give it up completely and even the one-to-one couldn't stop me. During the day I would go to the toilet and fill up with water, my empty nail varnish remover bottles and any other implement I could find that could store water. I hid these under my pillow so that in the morning of the weigh-ins, despite my one-to-one sitting in my doorway, I would put my head under the duvet and drink. I was helped by the fact that a lot of the time the one-to-one had fallen asleep! But I made sure I only drank a small amount as I knew I would get caught out otherwise.

My decision to finally stop resisting weight gain didn't come easily and I found the process of weight gain horrendous. I hated feeling and seeing myself gain weight and I despised every minute of every day, looking at myself in the mirror and seeing my stomach getting rounder, and looking at my thighs when I sat down and seeing them bulge more. It was unbearable and I was in constant worry that I was losing anorexia, that I was hungry, and that I wouldn't be able to lose the weight when I left. I was riddled with guilt for every moment I wasn't exercising. Apart from meal and snack times, a one-hour therapy session each week and an occasional group session, we were left to our own devices to stew in our own stress. The sole focus was food and weight gain.

Thursday 22nd January 2009,

The ward manager said to me yesterday that my anorexia seems to be getting the better of me. I'm glad she said it. It reassures me that it's still there and I will never lose it. NEVER. The only thing I am going to lose is weight. There's no doubt that I won't be able to do it. No doubt whatsoever. I will lose every last pound and more. They will never take anorexia away from me. Anorexia is God and thin is in. This is just a temporary fat shell that has to be endured for a short time but I will shed the shell the moment I leave here. And love every minute of it. Putting two fingers up to this place and everyone in it involved in making me fat. I'll show them. I'll prove that pushing my BMI up so high is just giving me more desire to lose it and making the anorexia stronger. I will never let go of it. NEVER. It is all I need in this life. Skin and bone - it will be all I own.

One evening, I had been in a new patient's bedroom having a chat. She had only arrived that day and she was incredibly underweight. She was very nice, and she didn't seem poisonous like some of the other girls on the ward. We spent the evening chatting about normal things with Alistair. As I left her room to go to bed she said, "Come and have a chat whenever you want, you know where I am." The following morning she wasn't there. She had been rushed to hospital in the night. Five days later we were informed that she had died. I was shocked and upset. I could not believe her life was gone, ripped cruelly from her. I felt so very sorry for her. But despite this, anorexia had me gripped so tightly that even death happening right in front of me was not enough to stop me in my determination to lose weight and give myself to anorexia.

By the start of March 2009, I was only 3.5kg away from my target. My consultant told me he would lift the section when I got to my target BMI of 17. So, I had to get there asap. The hiding of food, the persistent exercising… it had all been reduced. I told my mum not to let me exercise as much when I went home on weekends as well. It was painful, but it was temporary. And it was necessary if I wanted to leave. I was still water-loading a small amount, but my mind was now focused, set and determined on gaining weight to get out. I was on Mission Weight Gain. I would write in my diary every day, committing myself to anorexia. It became like a legally binding document: setting out my plans for weight loss when I left, reminding myself I was wholeheartedly 100% anorexic and would never lose it.

I hit my target weight of 52.3kg on Tuesday 14th April 2009, ten months after arriving. The band within which my weight was allowed to range was 51.3-53.3kg. I was relieved to have reached my target with no more need for further weight gain. I just had to maintain my weight until my CPA (the big meeting with everyone involved in my care) on June 4th June 2009, when my consultant, he had told me, would discharge me. I was put on a weight-maintenance diet which was still incredibly high-calorie. I was allowed to remove the *Scandishake* but everything else had to remain. I was still on nearly 3000 calories a day, and I was still having *Ensure* drinks and not solid food at lunchtime. They didn't care that I wasn't eating a proper main meal – I had reached my target and that was all that mattered.

My meal plan consisted of:

Breakfast – two slices of white toast with *Flora*. Two *Weetabix* with 200ml of full-fat milk. Squash.

Snack (three times a day) - *KitKat* or *Frusli* bar with squash.

Lunch – 800-calorie *Ensure*.

Dinner – High-calorie sandwich, apple, a full-fat yoghurt. Squash.

Tuesday 14th April 2009,

I have come off the final bend and hit the home straight. I may have a few more hurdles left to jump but I can do it and I will cross the finish line. I will finish this torture of weight gain and start a new everlasting pathway of weight loss and thinness. I hate eating, I hate food, I hate my size and I hate my life. I've actually got nothing to live for other than being thin. That's why I'm 100% going to be thin again when I leave here.

I was registered to sit my first-year university exams, which I had missed the previous summer, at the start of summer 2009 while I was still in St Ann's. It meant I could start back at university in September which I was hoping would be my golden opportunity to lose all the weight I had gained. I was trying to revise, but it was very difficult to concentrate. My mind was persistently thinking about weight, food, calories, and exercise. I was still exercising a fair amount which, to me, had to take priority over revising. But I had to ensure that I passed my exams to enable me to go back to university where I could start hard and fast on weight loss.

I was allowed to go home from Friday 29th May 2009 until my CPA on 4th June. I went up to Loughborough on 3rd June to complete my first exam. I briefly saw my old friends, Kate and Selin, before the exam and as nice as it was to see them, it felt like we had all moved on and I was not a part of things anymore. They had spent another year together in Loughborough which I had not been involved in. They had carried on living, whereas my life had been stagnant. But I didn't care that they had moved on. I had anorexia and that was all that mattered. They had carried on with their lives and all I wanted in mine was anorexia. I didn't want to be a part of anything, I only wanted to lose weight. One of the questions in the exam asked me to calculate someone's

BMI. If there was one question I knew I could get right, it was this.

Chapter 20
Weight Loss Free for All

On the 4th June 2009, exactly one year since being admitted, I was removed from Section 3 and discharged with a weight of 51.9kg. As the hospital door shut behind me and we drove away, I felt euphoric. Finally, I was free of that place. Now I could start exercising, restricting, and losing weight. I couldn't wait. But at the same time as feeling relieved to be leaving, I was scared and daunted by going back into 'normal' life. I had become completely institutionalised. The hospital had become my home and I had my own little life within the hospital walls. Although I hated being in there, being made to eat and gain weight, it had a sense of safety and familiarity. I had formed good friendships, I had my daily routine, and I was protected from the outside world which seemed terrifying. The uncertainty over university, how I would fit back into normal life, whether I was going to be able to lose weight, the fear of upsetting my parents – those were scary thoughts and staying in hospital had protected me from having to deal with them.

I had to go back for follow-ups at St Ann's once a week for four weeks. I instantly started losing weight so, on the train journey up to London, I would buy bottles of water to drink. But as well as weighing me when I was there, I also had to have blood tests. I knew with the amount of water I was drinking that my sodium levels would be low, and this would indicate to them that I was water-loading. So, on arrival at Liverpool Street, I would go to the *Burger King* booth and grab handfuls of salt sachets which I would eat on the tube. It tasted disgusting and just added to my feelings of nausea, but it was essential if I wanted to get away with my weight loss and not be readmitted.

I would walk for a good hour round the local area before going into the hospital. I hated those follow-up days as it meant reduced exercise and more calories. Having spent all my time during my hospital admission in the supervised dining room with staff there to monitor my eating and drinking, as I was now discharged and living at home, I was moved into the unsupervised dining room where there were no members of staff, only other patients deemed responsible enough to eat without supervision.

When presented with my 800-calorie *Ensure* at lunchtime, there was no way I was going to drink it all. So, coupled with my old tricks of spilling and wiping, I also took off my trainers and poured most of the chocolate liquid into them, watching the blue soles absorb it all. 'What a genius!' I thought. However, what I hadn't anticipated was the other patients in the unsupervised dining room telling on me. My shoe trick worked for the first two weeks of follow-up but, as I was leaving the dining room on the third week, the ward manager called me over and made me take off my shoes. She could see the sole was soaking wet and discoloured brown. So, for the final week of follow-up, I was moved back into the supervised dining room. It is a wonder how, when the staff were aware I was behaving in this way and had done similar things throughout my whole admission, I was deemed ready to be discharged. I know you cannot keep patients in forever, but my behaviour continued to be dictated by anorexia. Nothing had changed during my hospital admission, yet they were more than happy to discharge me when I was at an appropriate weight, leaving my parents to try and cope with my out-of-control behaviour. The hospital couldn't cope with it and frankly, they didn't care. I was heavy enough and they wanted to wash their hands of me. If the trained hospital staff couldn't deal with me, what hope did my parents, complete novices to the situation, have? They didn't stand a cat in hell's chance.

For the first four weeks following my discharge, as well as

attending the weekly follow-up sessions at St Ann's, I also saw my local community nurse once a week. But after the first month, this became once a fortnight or even once every three weeks. This was brilliant for me. With infrequent weigh-ins it meant I could go on a weight loss free for all. And that is certainly what I did.

My mum worked full-time Monday to Friday and with her not there to monitor my exercise or eating, anorexia became ever more powerful. My dad worked part-time and had to go to help my grandparents twice a week. He would take me for a daily two-hour walk. My parents thought this was the total exercise I was doing for the day and therefore believed they were keeping it under control. But I was like a caged animal let loose. I could not control myself. Every waking moment had to be spent exercising.

I was instantly back to getting up at 5am to secretly exercise and, once my mum and dad had gone out, I would take to the streets to walk for hour after hour, making sure I was back in time for when my dad would return home to take me for our walk. When he headed back out later in the afternoon, I too would return to pounding the streets. I would tell him I had eaten lunch when I hadn't. He didn't question it. I don't think he thought I would lie outright like that. I had lied to my mum about what my maintenance diet was as well, making it a good 400 calories less than it should have been and, even with what I did eat, I would try to hide a lot of it in my pockets.

I had been terrified I wasn't going to be able to lose weight when I went home, but I had become so adept at lying, so manipulative – I had become a professional anorexic and I knew every trick in the book. So, my intention had been to lose weight slowly and subtly, biding my time until I went back to university, but I couldn't stop myself. Everything was devoted to losing weight. But I had to try and disguise the fact I was losing weight rapidly.

I would drink litre after litre before I saw my community nurse and when I could no longer drink any more, I bought ankle weights to wear under my clothes. The infrequency of her visits made it easier for me to get away with this, and the numbers on the scales showed that my weight was staying stable, so she would leave satisfied. I barely spoke to her when she visited; I would just sit there in silence, nodding and saying the occasional yes or no. She did all the talking and that suited me. I could keep my innermost thoughts and anorexia private.

I would tell my mum that my weight was remaining stable, but she could see me shrinking in front of her. We were constantly arguing, and she was always accusing me of lying. I would always deny it... I didn't want her stopping my weight loss. She could see I was losing weight rapidly, but she felt helpless. What could she do? Even my dad had noticed I was losing weight and my dad is one of the most unobservant people ever. I told my mum she could speak to my community nurse. I knew I was successful at disguising my weight loss from my community nurse, so I thought this would get my mum off my back. My mum approached my community nurse on one of her visits to me and expressed her concerns about my seeming weight loss.

"No, Rebecca isn't losing weight," my nurse replied. "She is maintaining her BMI at 17." And that was that. My mum was left with no option but to believe what I and my nurse were saying. Lying had become second nature to me; I did it without a blink of an eye.

But within a few months, I was really struggling mentally. For my twenty-first birthday on 17th September 2009, my dad took me for a long walk by one of the local rivers. I enjoyed the walk, but I didn't enjoy the occasion. Most people spend their twenty-firsts celebrating, having parties, seeing friends and family, getting drunk. I didn't have a single celebration. There wasn't anything to celebrate. I was plagued by anorexia, and my mum and dad could see it. I wasn't their daughter, I was merely a shell. I didn't enjoy anything, I didn't care for anything, I didn't talk to anyone, and my birthday was no exception. It wasn't a happy occasion. None of us were happy, quite the opposite. Anorexia was ticking away, destroying everything and everyone in its path. My life was dedicated to and dictated by anorexia and I didn't care about anyone else. I had lost touch with all my old school and uni friends and I felt incredibly lonely. But I told myself it didn't matter that I did not have any friends because I had anorexia instead, and I was sure that was the best friend I could ever have. I was getting my revenge on all those who had made me gain weight in hospital, pushing my weight up to a BMI of 17 when I told them it wouldn't work. It was their fault and I hated them… and I was going to show them.

But I was exhausted. Although I thought anorexia was my best friend, it was really wearing me down. I was completely subordinate to my mind and had no control over my own behaviour. When I got up early in the morning to exercise, I would often be running up and down the kitchen crying, wishing I could stop and curl into a ball on the sofa and go to sleep. But I couldn't, and my mind made me feel sick with guilt for even contemplating the idea. Anorexia enveloped my whole mind and I was completely at its mercy.

Within three months, I had lost over 10kg. My mum was at her wits' end but, with the numbers on the scales falsely showing my weight was stable, there was nothing she could do. Then, one morning at the end of September 2009, before my community nurse was due to arrive, I had drunk the necessary water from the stash of water bottles in my bedroom and was strapping the weights round my ankles, as I had been doing for weeks. But in that exact moment, my mum walked into the room.

"What are you doing?" she snapped.

"Nothing," I replied, as I casually tried to pull my trousers over the weights so she wouldn't see.

"What's that?" She questioned as she started towards me. She looked directly at the weights. "What the hell are you doing?" she shouted. "How long has this been going on?"

I started crying; upset that I had been caught, but also exhausted. Living with my mind had been exhausting and torturous. All the exercise, all the lying, all the secrets: I hadn't enjoyed any of it. Anorexia still did not exist as a separate voice in my head, it was my head. And my head had made my life hell. I recognised this but I couldn't stop it, I couldn't change how I thought. I just had to lose weight and go to any means to achieve it. But getting caught by my mum was actually a huge relief. She could take responsibility for my actions now, rather than me being slave-driven by anorexia.

I told my community nurse about the weights and the water-loading. The scales revealed that I was over 10kgs less than I had been portraying; my BMI was 13, not 17. Obviously, this was a huge difference and my community nurse, on finding out my real weight, said she was going to apply for funding for me to become a day patient at the local Priory Hospital. I could cope with that prospect. Being a day patient was far better than being an inpatient. Also, anorexia had completely worn me down and I felt utterly trapped. I knew I needed something to help me.

My appointment for The Priory came through quite quickly and I was due to see the eating disorder consultant, Dr Williams, on 8th October 2009. My nurse and I had agreed that I would get my BMI back up to 14 and maintain it there. My life had been so taken over by anorexia and I was tired. A BMI of 14 felt, to me, manageable. I did not want to lose anorexia and I knew I couldn't cope with a higher weight. My nurse agreed, acknowledging it was better to have me agree to maintain a weight than force me higher and have me lose it again. My nurse explained to Dr Williams over the phone that this was our agreement and that she was happy to manage me in the community at this weight. Dr Williams agreed to this, provided I was medically stable at that point.

My mum drove us to The Priory and waited in the car as I went in for my appointment. A short, stocky man opened a door and called me inside. He introduced himself as Dr Williams and the lady in the room as the lead therapist. After talking about my history, my experience at St Ann's, how The Priory could help me and what it would involve, he asked to weigh me and take my pulse and blood pressure. I hadn't been expecting that. I was still a novice to these types of situations. I had never had an appointment with a consultant before and I didn't know how it worked. I just thought we were going to make arrangements for me to become a day patient, and I did not realise being weighed was going to be involved. I knew I had lost slightly more weight since last seeing my nurse.

My weight was just under 40kg, making my BMI under 13 and my pulse was reading below 40 bpm. With that, Dr Williams explained he was very concerned and would like to speak to my mum. With my mum and I both in the room, he said that with my weight lower than expected and my pulse dangerously low, I would not be allowed to be an outpatient. I had to be admitted as an inpatient. He said my health was at serious risk and instantly referred me to the general hospital, saying that The Priory was not medically equipped to deal with my at-risk condition.

I could not believe this was happening again. We got back in the car and my mum drove us straight to the general hospital where they were expecting me. After several tests, I was hooked up to a heart monitor and moved into a cubicle on a busy ward. We sat there for several hours, my mum expressing concern to the nurses and doctors that I was missing meal and snack times. I hadn't eaten since breakfast that morning and it was now gone 5pm. They did then offer me some food, but I declined. There was no way I was going to eat now if I had to go into hospital.

I explained to every doctor and nurse that walked past that my low pulse rate was not unusual for me. Eventually they agreed that I was safe to go into The Priory in the morning. We went home and I had a bowl of soup for my dinner, my mum just relieved that I had agreed to eat anything. I went to bed, fearful of what was going to be in store for me over the following days and weeks.

Chapter 21
The Priory

I arrived at The Priory the following morning with my parents and my suitcase full of carefully chosen clothes. My mum had bought me several tracksuits while I was in St Ann's and these were the clothes I took to The Priory. If you walk into any eating disorder unit you will find that a lot of patients wear baggy tracksuits, not wanting to wear tight, fashionable clothes that reveal their body shape, and many not wanting to take care in their appearance. The tracksuits for me had the added bonus at being good at disguising spilt drink and having pockets to hide food. I had also packed lots of beads and coloured string for jewellery-making, as I had become interested in this in St Ann's. Anorexic patients in hospital tend to do one of three things (or all three). Card-making, jewellery-making, and crochet. As Molly once said to me, that really made me laugh, "This girl sent me a card. Why do all anorexics make bloody cards?"

I had a meeting with Dr Williams on arrival and he confirmed that, providing I was physically stable, we would stick to the plan of me being discharged at BMI 14. My weight was 37.8kg, making my BMI 12.5. However, they had recorded my height wrongly, at 1.73m instead of 1.77m, but I didn't tell them. He explained that, for health and safety reasons, I would be kept in my room on bed rest and put on a one-to-one. The idea of the one-to-one didn't bother me that much anymore. I had got used to it in St Ann's where I had always pretty much been able to do what I wanted with them there anyway.

But the regime at The Priory was different to St Ann's. Rather than being left to do what you want during the day as it was in St Ann's, at The Priory they ran compulsory group therapy sessions every day. However, because I was on bed rest, I didn't attend these to start with, which I was pleased about. I didn't want to attend groups where I would be made to sit down, but, most importantly, I didn't want them to try and change me and my mind. Although I had agreed to get to a BMI of 14, and I did actually believe this was possible and manageable to live with in the community, I still wanted to remain completely anorexic. I would tolerate my weight at a BMI of 14, but I was determined that everything else in my life had to stay committed to anorexia. I didn't want my mind to change its way of thinking and for them to take anorexia away from me and encourage me to want to get better.

The first day at The Priory I refused to eat or drink anything. The nurses and healthcare assistants sat with me for hours in my bedroom, trying to encourage me to eat, but I had made up my mind. The thought of putting on weight terrified me, even though I knew it was only to a BMI of 14. I knew if I had to gain weight, I wanted to get as low as possible before that happened. And I wasn't low enough yet. To any normal person this probably doesn't make sense. You know you will have to put on weight, you have a target to get to before you can leave, yet you are still trying everything in your power to lose a bit more weight. Anorexia was so strong in my mind, and it doesn't reason logically. Anorexia stops for nothing. And if there is any opportunity to lose weight, you will take it, powerless to do anything else.

The next morning, after my first day of not eating, the healthcare assistant who was my one-to-one, Nicola, asked me what cereal I wanted for breakfast. I was allowed cornflakes or *Rice Krispies*.

"I don't eat them," I replied. "I don't want anything thank you. I only eat *Weetabix*."

With that, Nicola, trying to be helpful and kind and to encourage me to eat, went to get me *Weetabix*.

"There you go," she said kindly, "try eating these." But there was no way I was going to eat them.

"I only drink soya milk," I replied. I had converted to soya milk at home when leaving St Ann's because it was a good way of cutting calories from the full-fat milk I was meant to have.

"That's ok," Nicola replied, "you're not meant to have it but I can get you some if it means you will eat."

I felt guilty because she was being so nice when I had absolutely no intention of eating or drinking anything.

"There's no point," I answered honestly. "I'm not going to eat anything."

She sat with me for the next half an hour trying to get to me eat, but I just sat there quietly. The breakfast was taken away and I went to stand against the radiator. I knew pacing wasn't an option initially: I had to get to know the system first. Every time I stood up the staff were instantly telling me to sit down. I would sit down for a few minutes and then stand up again for several more. In the short time I had been there, I could already tell the staff at The Priory were much stricter than St Ann's with standing up and exercising. The staff also had to write notes on their clipboard of what I was doing every five minutes (because I was put into the 'red category' which meant 'serious risk') so everything was documented on my file. They had a strict policy of no standing or exercising and they were trying to enforce it on me.

In the afternoon of my second day, when I was still refusing to eat or drink anything and still trying to stand up at every opportunity, Dr Williams came to visit me in my room. He told me they were going to section me as my health was too much at risk. I couldn't believe it. 'How the hell did I let myself get into this situation again?' I thought, 'I could have complied, gained the weight and been out of here in a matter of weeks. How could I have been so stupid? They are going to have all the power over me again.' I was so angry with myself, and also scared of how my parents were going to react. My parents were called to come into the hospital and it was decided that I should once again be placed under Section 3.

I told myself that I had to eat now, I had no choice in the

matter. I just had to eat, gain weight, leave, and then maintain and manage in the community. But when presented with the plates of food, I wasn't capable of putting it into my mouth. I couldn't voluntarily put food inside me and make myself gain weight. I couldn't do it. I was told they would have to put an NG tube in and feed me via that. As much as I hated being fed through a tube and wished I didn't have to be fed at all, at least it took the responsibility away from me. I could not be responsible for feeding myself: that was the ultimate sin.

Within a week of arriving at The Priory, my weight had fallen to 35.8kg (BMI 11.4). They had not been able to feed me many calories because of the risk of re-feeding syndrome, so my weight had continued to fall before starting to slowly pick up. However, after only a short period of complete tube-feeding, I soon began eating again, only requiring the tube when I wasn't able to eat a particular meal. My meal plan now comprised of:

Breakfast – two *Weetabix*, 200ml of semi-skimmed milk, 200ml of fruit juice.

Snack – 200ml of juice.

Lunch – custard or yoghurt and tinned fruit. 200ml of fruit juice.

Dinner – half a portion of fish, vegetables and new potatoes.

For lunch and dinner, all patients had to choose from the hospital restaurant's menu which provided three options – meat, fish, or vegetarian. I explained to Dr Williams that the only way I was able to eat dinner was if I could have plain fish. So, with a focus on actually engaging me with food and encouraging me to eat, he agreed that, for my dinners, I would not pick from the menu. I had a standard meal of half a portion of fish with vegetables and new potatoes. I was being treated by Dr Williams, the nurses and healthcare assistants at The Priory, in a way that was very different to my experience in St Ann's. All the staff at The Priory were kind and caring and, above all, they listened to how I was feeling and what I said I could cope with and what my limits were. They treated me as an individual and developed an individualised treatment programme.

After starting off with tube-feeding and meals in my bedroom, after a few months I joined the other eating disorder patients in the hospital's restaurant, where patients from other wards also ate. The eating disorder unit would sit on one table, with members of staff dotted between us. Unlike St Ann's, there was no designated supervised and unsupervised dining room and it was a much more relaxed environment. Staff still monitored and kept an eye on us, encouraging us when we were struggling and pulling us up if we were doing something wrong, but the atmosphere was much more like a normal restaurant than a battleground between patients and staff.

Because I felt more valued at The Priory, I behaved in a completely different way than I had in St Ann's. I was generally compliant and a lot calmer. I still, very occasionally, had an outburst but this was only on the odd occasion when dinner was served and I felt the portion was too big. My dinner always came with two new potatoes and sometimes these would vary greatly in size. When I perceived them as being too big, I couldn't eat them, and the potatoes did sometimes find themselves being thrown across the room. But generally, I didn't have the same anger and hatred as I had in St Ann's. I didn't feel the staff were forcing everything upon me against my will. No, I was being involved in decisions and I was working with them, rather than against them.

I also made the conscious decision to keep myself to myself. I didn't want a repeat of St Ann's, where I went in and made friends and we developed our own little lives in hospital. I didn't want that again. I was still in touch with Molly, Jane, and Alistair from St Ann's as they had become my friends more than my old school and university friends now were. I was grateful for the friends I had made in St Ann's, but I was still careful not to make my Priory admission my new life. So generally, I was very quiet. I didn't speak much to anyone and I certainly didn't say anything in the group sessions. I was no longer raging for revenge, but I was still protective of my anorexia and did not want anyone to shift it. In a world where I felt like I didn't have anything, anorexia was very important to me. I was certain I couldn't live life without it; I needed it. Having anorexia was the only way I could cope with the disappointment of life. So while I didn't want it to completely take over and send me into a life as a revolving-door patient, I most certainly was not willing to give it up. BMI 14 was my target and I could manage that. That would enable me to keep my anorexia and live in the community at a weight I could cope with.

revolving-door patient, I most certainly was not willing to give it
up. BMI 14 was my target and I could manage that. That would
enable me to keep my anorexia and live in the community at a
weight I could cope with.

Chapter 22
No Focus or Goals

Three months after arriving, at the start of January 2010, I
reached my target weight of 42kg, having gained just over 6kg
(although this target was based on my wrong height of 1.73m
and not my real height of 1.77m). At the start of March 2010, I
had maintained my weight for several months and I wasn't over-
exercising. Together with Dr Williams, my community nurse, and
my parents, I deemed myself ready to be discharged. I still found
eating a struggle and never ate unsupervised as, if left to my own
devices, I would not be able to resist the temptation to restrict. I
didn't want to restrict, but the guilt for not doing so was
overwhelming. Feeding myself so that I wouldn't lose weight felt
sinful and I hated myself for doing it. So eating with my parents
made the battle slightly easier as I could tell myself that I *had* to
eat because they were there, that it wasn't me choosing to eat. It
helped to ease the guilt I would feel for putting food into my
mouth.

My behaviour wasn't out of control like it had been when I
was discharged from St Ann's. I wasn't exercising like a dervish,
and my parents knew exactly what I was meant to be eating,
having been regularly involved in meetings with The Priory staff.
This had made it much easier for them to deal with me and to
know how best to cope. My parents felt The Priory had been a
completely different experience, not only for me but for them
too, and it seemed it had actually helped me.

My dad had rang me every day when I was in The Priory, having to ring through to the office for them to connect me in my room. One of the nurses commented how lovely it was that he rang me every day. We only ever had a brief chat, him telling me what he had done that day before passing me over to my mum. As much as I missed them and wanted to be with them, I was scared of returning to my real life. Being in The Priory had felt safe and I was apprehensive about entering normal life again. As much as I wanted to avoid making my hospital admission become my life again, I had become slightly enclosed in a bubble. And stepping outside of this bubble alone felt daunting. I had my parents, but this wasn't the same as having staff around you 24/7, with structure to every day. I knew what I was capable of with anorexia, that I could easily go free-falling back into weight loss, and this scared me.

On the day I was discharged, my parents came to collect me. They were chirpy and happy; pleased to be having me home. But I couldn't help feeling sad, depressed, and anxious. My world was going to change – again – and I did not know what the future had in store. When I got home, my dad gave me a *Boofle* teddy bear he had bought for me that day, with a heart round its neck saying, 'I love you very very much'. I have always loved teddy bears; my bedroom is full of them. And this one was extra special. But it made me feel guilty. Guilty for everything I had put my parents through over the past few years, guilty for them showing me so much love and care when, deep down, all I could really care about was anorexia. I felt guilty for them being happy to have me home, when I thought that maybe I didn't want to be. Thinking that I may actually have preferred to be in hospital sat very uneasily with me. I couldn't understand how I could possibly rather be in hospital than be at home with my parents. I would berate myself for this. But it wasn't being at home with my parents that I didn't want; rather, being in hospital brought with it safety, regularity and familiarity.

I had to attend The Priory once a week for four weeks after my discharge. It is very difficult transitioning from hospital, where everything is regulated and structured, to 'normal life' where, without a job, studying or friends, you have no structure.

I felt I had been thrown in at the deep end and I was having to kick furiously to stay afloat. I had spent the best part of the last two years living purely for anorexia. Now I was faced with trying to manage it in the real world and I was terrified. I didn't know how to live in 'normal life.'

I was just about managing to keep my head above the water during my four weeks of follow-up. During that time, I signed myself up for voluntary work as a kitchen helper in a homeless shelter. Since being admitted to St Ann's, I had developed a keen interest in cooking and reading recipes (a common trait of many anorexia sufferers) and I decided that I wanted a career in the catering industry. I imagined that my ideal job would be working in a tearoom. Volunteering to work in the kitchen of the homeless shelter seemed an ideal way to get some experience.

However, it was when I started my volunteering job every Friday, when I was no longer attending follow-ups at The Priory, that things started to slide. I was weighing myself twice a week (following the routine from hospital) and while I had been attending follow-ups, my weight had been stable. But when the follow-ups stopped and I didn't really have anything in my life (except for the one day a week volunteering which I didn't enjoy because I struggled with social interaction), my weight became my focus again. When I weighed myself and saw the numbers stay the same, I felt a sense of inadequacy. I had no purpose in life and I hated it. I had no goals, no drive, nothing. I was merely drifting along, and I felt at a loss with life. Then, one morning near the beginning of April 2010, when I weighed myself, the numbers had gone down slightly. It felt incredible. I had forgotten how good it felt. Now I had tasted it again, that was it, I had fallen back into anorexia's clutches. With a complete lack of direction in my life, losing weight gave me a purpose and a reason to get up in the morning. It gave me something to focus on amidst the dark and gloomy clouds hanging over me.

The volunteering gave me the opportunity to start restricting and exercising more. I was there from around ten in the morning to two in the afternoon and this meant I had to change my eating routine. I began to have lower calorie yoghurts for lunch, at half the calories of my normal ones, as well as a lower calorie breakfast. And because my mum was still working full-time and my dad doesn't know the first thing about calories, this was easy to get away with. I took advantage of him. He would see me eating a yoghurt and think I was having what I was meant to, not realising that I was having far fewer calories. And once I had started introducing it on the one day a week I was volunteering, I then had to have it every week day, only eating what I was meant to on weekends when my mum was there. That is the thing with anorexia: once you start making changes and slipping back, you can't stop. My mind had once again been overtaken by anorexia. It still wasn't a case of having a separate voice in my head: no, it was my head – I was completely and utterly possessed by anorexia.

I started exercising a lot more when my parents weren't around. And the same as with food restriction and weight loss, once you start exercising more, that becomes your new baseline which you have to exceed. If I walked for two hours one day, that was it: I could no longer walk for less than two hours. And because I had walked for two hours one day, the next day I would try and do a little bit more until I was exercising to the extreme again, getting up early to exercise and walking as much as I could throughout the day, taking advantage of the lengthy time my dad spent at work or at my grandparents.

My afternoon snack of *Ensure* and my evening meal and snack were always the same and always eaten. My dad made sure he was home at 4pm for me to have my *Ensure*, and I continued to eat dinner with my parents. But with restriction earlier in the day coupled with more exercise, my weight continued to fall, albeit slowly. My nurse was weighing me once a fortnight, but I had started to water-load again to disguise that I was losing weight.

By the start of May 2010, I was down to 38.6kg, a loss of 3kg since my discharge two months earlier. My BMI was down to 12.4 but, with water-loading, my nurse thought I was stable at BMI 14. With my weight already too low, any weight loss was putting my body at severe risk. By the middle of June 2010, my weight had fallen to 37.1kg. I was greatly struggling in all aspects of life. I was being eaten alive by anorexia. My mind had worn me down and I just wanted everything to end. I felt incredibly lonely and trapped in my own mind.

I struggled to walk, climb stairs, or do any daily activities. I would sit on the edge of my bed every morning, telling my legs to work, to muster up the energy to complete the necessary exercise for the day. But even standing up was a challenge to my weak and wobbly legs. I felt light-headed and dizzy most of the time, and I would often lose my hearing with my ears blocking up. There was a lack of blood flow to my head and unless I tipped my head upside down to increase the blood flow, I struggled with my vision and hearing.

I was very depressed, and I hated life. I knew I couldn't keep on going. I was trapped alone in my prison cell of anorexia and I was helpless. My body ached with pain. Not physical pain, but sheer sadness. I felt so trapped in anorexia and I could not see a way out. My world was in blackness. I was desperate for my mum to just give me a hug and take away all the pain. I didn't want to be living like this, but I could not see an alternative. I had to do what my mind, what anorexia, wanted. It was also that same summer I found out the devastating news that my good friend, Alistair, who I had kept in touch with from St Ann's, had died. Anorexia had taken his life. I remembered one of our many conversations when he said, "I will either fully recover from anorexia, or it will kill me." It killed him. And I could feel it was killing me, too.

My body was giving up on me and I couldn't drink enough water to falsify my weight anymore, so I told my nurse that I was water-loading. On finding out my real weight, alarm bells rang. My nurse told me and my mum that she was going to have to admit me to hospital unless I gained weight immediately. She explained she would try and get me back to The Priory for a top up to get back to BMI 14. I could cope with that. I had been to fourteen before and I knew I could do it again. It was manageable and I desperately wanted it to work. I did not want to carry on living the way I was. But there were issues with funding and after weeks of negotiations, I was told I was not allowed back to The Priory. I was gutted. That was the one place I trusted, the one place I knew could give me the treatment I needed and that I could comply with.

My nurse said she did not want me to go back to St Ann's because of how badly I had got on there, so she was applying for other places. I did not know what was going to happen to me or where I was going to end up. As all this was going on and I knew I was going to end up in hospital somewhere, I saw my final opportunity to lose as much weight as possible. By the end of June 2010, my weight was 35kg, making my BMI 11.3, and my fate was sealed. I was to be sent to Avalon ward, the eating disorder unit in St George's hospital, Tooting. My nurse explained it was the best place for the worst cases of anorexia, so I needed to go there. She reassured me they would listen to me and take account of my views. So, I was not prepared to enter the most horrific experience of my life.

Chapter 23
Too Ill to Stay

It was a boiling hot summer's day when I was due to be admitted to St George's. I had got up early to exercise, but my body was on the brink of shutting down. I managed to do twenty minutes of pacing before feeling utterly dreadful and exhausted. Having refused dinner the night before, I also refused to eat breakfast. I still had to lose the last few pounds of weight that I could. I finished packing my suitcase, and found my parents waiting for me at the bottom of the stairs to try to get me to eat something. I adamantly refused and, as I stepped off the last step, I fainted, my dad catching me as I fell.

He carried me to the sofa and they called an ambulance, terrified I was dying in front of their eyes. The ambulance arrived and the first thing the paramedic did was check my pulse. He looked up to his assistant arriving with equipment and passed her a look of danger. They explained they were very concerned about my pulse, having never seen one so low at just twenty beats per minute. They checked my blood glucose and blood pressure, both of which were dangerously low. The male paramedic tried to get me to eat a glucose gel. Did he really think I was going to put all those calories into my body? I had worked hard to get to this weight and I wasn't having him ruin it for me. The paramedics explained they were extremely concerned about my physical condition and they wanted to call a doctor. As the doctor arrived and the paramedics showed them my notes, he walked up to me as I lay half-conscious on the sofa.

"You know what you need?" he said. "A jam sandwich."

My dad's head fell with despair. It highlights the complete lack of understanding of eating disorders by many medical doctors. The medics explained they could not possibly leave me in the state I was in and would have to take me to my local general hospital unless I ate something.

I had to quickly weigh up what I thought was the better option. Should I eat something and go to St George's, or eat nothing and go to the general? My experience of the general before was that I'd ended up in St Ann's and getting to a weight I could not cope with. I certainly did not want that happening to me again. My parents encouraged me to eat something, telling me St George's would be the better option. My nurse had explained to my parents that St George's had the best, most renowned eating disorder psychiatrist in Britain and that it was *the* place to go, there being no better eating disorder unit in the country. So, obviously they wanted me to go there, to get the expert specialist help that I needed. I told them I would eat one *Weetabix* with 100ml of milk. The paramedics and doctor left, reassured by my parents that they were taking me straight to St George's.

I sat in the back of the car in thirty degree heat but wrapped up in several layers. I was cold and my parents were dripping in sweat. The car journey took nearly three hours as we mazed our way across London. I could not keep my eyes open and I slept for most of it. At least that was some light relief from my mind. We arrived at this huge hospital that didn't look like a hospital at all, more like a boarding school. I felt sick to the bottom of my stomach, terrified of what was going to be in store.

We found our way to the right building, my dad carrying my suitcase. We were greeted. Well I say greeted but it wasn't exactly a greeting but more of a moody grunt from a woman who showed us the stairs up to the ward. I looked up at the stairs and felt my legs weaken beneath me. There was not a hope in hell of me making it up those stairs. It seemed a nonsensical thing for the staff to suggest. When you are admitted as an inpatient you have your exercise restricted to virtually nothing. So why, on arrival, encourage someone to take the stairs?

My mum, knowing my current state, flat out refused. "There

is no way she is going to be able to walk up those stairs," she said with anger. "Is there not a lift we can use?"

With that, the woman pointed over to the corner of the corridor to where there was a lift and made a noise which I vaguely made out to say, "over there". The lift took us up to the first floor where we found the locked doors for Avalon ward, the eating disorder unit. We were taken inside, and shown to a small barren room with three wooden chairs, and told to wait for the doctor who would come to collect me to go through the initial assessment.

We waited for hour after hour. There were no windows in the room and the temperature was in the mid-thirties. My parents had taken every layer off possible, but I was still there wrapped up in all of mine. My body was so thin I had no natural insulation and even the boiling summer heat was not enough to make me feel warm. My mum had discussed over the phone with the ward manager the best time to arrive and was told after lunch about 1pm. That is what we had done. But it was gone 3pm and we were still waiting to see someone, being told the doctor had to go to an emergency elsewhere in the hospital.

Eventually, the doctor arrived about 4pm and took me into a small medical room to do my assessment, which consisted of an ECG and taking my weight and height. I was then sent back into that small room where my parents had continued waiting. A few minutes later the doctor came in to talk to us.

"I'm afraid we cannot keep Rebecca here," she explained. "She is too physically ill for us to care for her here. She needs to go to A and E at the general hospital. We have called for an ambulance."

Before the ambulance arrived, I met with the dietician for her to explain the meal plan. She said all meals would be half portions with snacks of banana and milk to start with. I explained to her my fears and that I doubted my ability to actually start eating. From my previous admissions, I knew how hard I had found putting food into my mouth in the initial stages and I knew now that I wouldn't voluntarily be able to do it. I knew I could not eat for myself. But I also knew I wanted to avoid being sectioned. If there was one thing I had to do, it was to ensure that didn't happen. So I asked her if I could have the tube inserted and be fed through that if I wasn't able to eat. I wouldn't be refusing to comply, but I needed them to assume responsibility for putting calories into my body. She agreed, explaining I could have the tube voluntarily without the need for sectioning. This came as a huge relief. As much as I didn't want to have any calories inside me or to gain weight, I knew it was unavoidable. But I needed them to take the responsibility away from me.

The ambulance took us to A and E where we were immediately taken to a bed within the resuscitation unit. I was hooked up to a saline drip and a heart machine and had a battery of blood tests and injections. I was exhausted and I felt seriously ill. I was still lying in all my layers but had become incredibly hot. I wanted to take my coat and jumper off but was prevented from doing so, instead being given an electric heated blanket to put over myself.

"I don't want that," I said angrily to the nurse trying to enclose me in heat, "I'm boiling hot, I need to cool down." I pushed the duvets away from me.

"You have severe hypothermia," the nurse began. "Your body temperature is critically low. Your whole body is shutting down. We need to raise your temperature as soon as possible or your heart will stop."

I wanted to cry. How could this woman be telling me I was hypothermic when I felt so hot? I could not possibly add more heat to the heat I was already feeling. I looked desperately to my parents who had stood by my bedside since we arrived.

"Honestly," I said to them, "I'm not cold. I am really boiling hot. I'm not making it up."

My dad explained that with hypothermia that is what happens – the sufferer can begin to feel very hot when in fact their body temperature is dropping. But I could not believe him. I could not understand how I could possibly feel so hot when I was actually cold. My parents had, in some ways, got used to me being quite ill; they had experienced it before. They hadn't realised this time, though, how ill I actually was until I arrived at the A and E unit. I had been bad before, but never this bad. My pulse was averaging below 20bpm and I was drifting in and out of consciousness. They were terrified that this time was going to be the end. The doctors certainly weren't giving me much hope of pulling through.

Every time I drifted off, I would awake to find the heated blanket over me. Angrily, I would push it back off me, only to drift off again and the scenario would repeat itself. It was now gone 9pm and my parents were seated by my bed, shattered and fearful. A man who'd had a motorbike accident arrived on a stretcher, one of his legs smashed to pieces, blood everywhere. "How is our daughter so critically ill she is being treated like these other patients?" my parents thought. Resuscitation units are where deaths occur, and they were terrified I was going to add to the total.

I was wheeled on my bed to a cubicle round the corner as the doctor told me she needed to do an internal physical examination. As I lay there waiting for her to prepare what she needed, I said to my mum, "This is like being in *Casualty*. All I need now is Charlie Fairhead."

My mum forced a smile through the sheer look of terror on her face. I was not completely 'with it' and I certainly didn't realise the seriousness of the situation. To me, everyone was making a fuss and there was nothing wrong. But my mum knew I was on the brink of death.

My parents were told that I was going to be moved to a ward and it would probably be best for them to go home and get some sleep. It was now 10pm and it had felt like an eternity of a day. Looking back to the start of the day, my parents, knowing now what they did, wished they had allowed the paramedics to take me to the general hospital straight from home. If it was a general hospital I needed, the one ten minutes from my house would have been most practical and probably safest. I wouldn't have had to endure such a long car journey and waiting for hours in a cramped room. But hindsight is a wonderful thing, isn't it? It turned out that a bit of hindsight before this admission would have been very helpful. As hell was to come.

Chapter 24
Trapped

I was moved to a ward in the early hours of the morning and I spent the majority of the next day asleep. At lunchtime, a lady came to my bed to ask if I wanted fish and chips. I politely declined and she carried on serving it to the rest of the patients. 'This is brilliant,' I thought. 'They aren't making me eat anything.' I was a bit confused about what was actually happening food-wise. I had expected to be presented with my 'meal plan' that the dietician had told me about in Avalon, but no one mentioned it to me. I had also prepared myself to ask for the tube. But with not being asked to eat anything, I didn't mention it.

That evening, I woke up in the night to a nurse trying to inject me with something.

"What are you doing?" I murmured sleepily, pulling my arm away from her.

"Your blood glucose levels have dropped dangerously low," she said. "We need to inject you with this to get them up."

I knew what 'this' was. 'This' was a glucose injection with calories. There was no way I was letting them inject that into me.

"No. I won't agree to it," I replied. "I won't let you."

With that, the nurse walked away but came back minutes later saying that if I didn't have it I would be sectioned. So I agreed. About an hour later, the nurse came back to inject me with more glucose. I said I didn't want any more and the nurse went away. This time she didn't come back. Then, at approximately 1am, I was woken up by a doctor.

"We are going to section you," he said. "We have arranged for you to be assessed. They will be here in a minute."

I could not believe what I was hearing. How could they possibly be sectioning me? I'd literally slept all day. I couldn't understand how this could conceivably warrant sectioning.

"No, please don't," I begged. "I will have the glucose injection, I will do anything. Please don't section me."

"We are applying for a Section 2," he explained. "We cannot risk you not agreeing to treatment. Your health is in a state of emergency."

I was then taken to a room and sat before three people (I don't know what their status was). It was 2am, I was tired, I hadn't eaten anything for over twenty-four hours and my body was giving up on me. I told the people I would agree to all treatment and I hadn't been thinking right in refusing the glucose injection. But they decided I was to be put on a Section 2, which was different to the Section 3 I had been on previously. A Section 2 only lasts for four weeks and is meant to be used when you are not sure what someone's illness is, and need time to assess and treat. A Section 3, on the other hand, lasts for six months (and can be renewed) and is put in place when someone is refusing treatment that they need, and you know what their illness is and what treatment is needed. So, it seemed strange that they were putting me on a Section 2.

I went back to bed sobbing and cried myself to sleep. I was alone, it was the middle of the night, my parents were miles away and I had just been sectioned. 'How is this happening to me again?' I thought. It was the worst possible thing that could have happened. I knew it, and my parents would know it when they were told. I was well and truly trapped.

My parents were told in the morning over the phone and immediately came to the hospital, though it took them three hours. We were met at my bedside by an eminent consultant endocrinologist who informed us that he worked closely with the lead consultant at the eating disorder unit. The endocrinologist explained to my parents that 'she' (meaning me) was critically ill; that they always receive anorexic patients when they are at their lowest ever, 'she' being no exception; and that they knew the best way to treat me, the section being essential. He continued to explain that 'she' would be kept in the general hospital and fed through a tube for several weeks until 'her' weight had risen considerably so that 'she' could be returned to the eating disorder unit. At this point, my mum pointed out that my name was 'Rebecca'.

The nurses inserted an NG tube so they could start feeding me. My weight was 33kg, making my BMI 10.6, so they had to be very careful to avoid re-feeding, resulting in me being placed on only 200 calories a day. I was moved to my own room on another ward and told I was on complete bed rest. Avalon ward would send members of staff so I could be placed on a one-to-one. This was when I started to really experience hell on Earth.

The one-to-ones that were sent to me were all agency staff who had no interest in helping me or, come to that, any interest in me at all. They would sit on a chair at the end of my bed, read their magazines, talk on their mobiles — they would even go to sleep. I was baffled at the unprofessionalism and complete stupidity and carelessness of these staff. I was on a one-to-one because I was a serious health risk. They were meant to be keeping a close eye on me, not shutting their eyes and nodding off, even snoring occasionally. Their behaviour was completely inappropriate, and I found them very frustrating.

Adding to this frustration was that caused by being on complete bed rest. By complete bed rest I do literally mean *complete* bed rest. I appreciate this was necessary for health reasons but, for someone who was addicted to exercise, this was excruciatingly difficult and I wasn't given any support. I had to sit all day, every day, on my bed, with my legs up. My legs were not allowed to even dangle over the side of the bed which seemed unnecessarily restrictive. If I did try to sit up, they would pull the barriers up on the side of my bed and lock me in like a caged animal. The only time I was allowed to move was when I had to go to the toilet. In that instance, a commode would be brought to my bedside and I would stand up from my bed and sit immediately on the commode before returning immediately back to bed.

Not only was it mentally tormenting, but it also caused physical side effects. I developed bed sores, infections, and was in constant pain from pressure on my bottom. My mum asked them to provide a cushion for me to sit on to help alleviate the pain, but this was denied. I sometimes tried to roll onto one side for a few minutes and then back onto the other to give my bottom some respite but even that was forbidden and they told me I wasn't allowed to move like that.

The senior endocrinologist explained to my parents a few days after my arrival in this new room, that "anorexics are deviant, manipulative, and malicious" and this is the only treatment to "stop their bad behaviour." He said I could not be trusted and that I would be kept on this ward, in this room, on this bed, until I had reached an appropriate weight to return to Avalon. My parents could not believe what they were hearing. They knew I had been deceptive in the past, but they also knew this was the result of the anorexia — a mental illness. I wasn't being malicious and intentionally deviant. I wasn't a naughty child who needed telling off; I was ill. But he and all the other staff at St Georges and Avalon refused to accept this. Their belief seemed to be that anorexia is about lying and getting your own way which needed to be punished and stopped.

I was devastated and utterly hopeless. Even though the journey to the hospital was so long-winded, and my mum was still in full-time work and my dad still had to care for my grandparents, my parents came to visit me six times a week, sharing the visits between them. They could see for themselves this was no place for anyone to be treated. My treatment was shocking and there was no way I was going to get better in there.

My mum wanted me to speak to an independent mental health advocate which the Mental Health Act gives patients under section the right to do. My mum had spoken to the local advocate and explained my position and he said he would visit me on the ward to discuss my situation. However, the ward staff tried to prevent him gaining access to, only allowing it after legal action was threatened. Myself, my parents, and the advocate decided I should appeal the section and I met with a solicitor to put together my case. The solicitor also advised that I could ask the tribunal for a transfer to another hospital nearer home. While the tribunal was being organised, my parents and I decided to try persuade my home care team to get me transferred back to The Priory. However, the staff at Avalon made it quite clear they were going to put up fight. They did not want me off the section and they most certainly did not want me to be transferred. It was the beginning of a war.

Chapter 25
Hell on Earth

Every day was the same in St Georges. I would spend all day lying on my bed, alternating between sleeping, watching TV, and crying. I was hooked up to a heart monitor and was on 'nil by mouth' which meant I was not allowed to consume anything orally. I was fed through my NG tube which dripped into me continuously day and night. I would sit and stare at the feed as it slowly went through the tube and up my nose where it would end up in my stomach. I hated the thought of those calories going into my body and making me put on weight. My medication also went via the tube, but I was not aware of what they were giving me. A lot of the time I felt incredibly tired, sleepy, and spaced out. The only medication I was aware of were the anti-blood-clotting injections I was given due to my immobilisation.

July 2010 had an average temperature of 24°C, with a high of 31°C. Sitting in a stuffy hospital room for weeks on end without any windows to open was painful, made worse by the fact I wasn't even allowed to drink any water to relieve my excruciating thirst and dry mouth. Instead of allowing me to drink water, they hydrated me through a drip. My lips constantly bled because they had become so dry and cracked. It wasn't until after a few weeks, when I was having a visit from my mum and my lips were raw and cracked, that she insisted they regularly dab my lips with water to prevent them drying out so much.

I was also in constant pain from the NG tube. It didn't feel like it had done in St Ann's and The Priory, and I soon developed a throbbing pain in my nose and an immensely painful sore throat which persisted 24/7. I complained about the pain constantly to the staff, and also my parents whenever they visited. It wasn't until one day when I couldn't speak because of the pain in my throat, that my mum insisted the staff have a look at me. The staff quickly discovered they had fitted me with the wrong size tube which was, in fact, far too large. So I had been sitting there for several weeks in pain because of this wrongly fitted tube. I had never felt worse in my whole life, neither physically nor mentally. If animals had been treated this way, it would be considered abuse. But I was mentally ill and needed this treatment to 'correct' me...!

Although I was physically weak, the way in which I was treated did not always seem to be warranted. They would not even let me wash or shower, despite the fact the showers had seats so I could have done so sitting down. For over two weeks, I sat on my bed day after day, week after week, without a wash, without a change in bedding, without a change in my hospital clothes, without a drink... without anything to satisfy basic human needs. The staff's only concern was to fatten me up. I was left on my own with a disinterested one-to-one, all day every day being pumped with calories and medication. I would beg the staff for a shower. I felt so dirty and disgusting, not only in a cleanliness sense but deep inside myself. I wanted a shower to wash away all the horrendous feelings I had inside due to how anorexia had abused me, and how the staff were now making me feel. The staff always responded with "Showers are a reward and privilege that you must earn through good behaviour and compliance." I couldn't believe what I was hearing. And it wasn't even as if I was misbehaving. Anorexia had trampled all over me and I was utterly exhausted. Now it felt as if the staff were adding to the abuse.

One day when my dad came to visit me, a nurse told us he should not be in my room. They said they didn't know who he was and I wasn't allowed to have visitors they didn't know. When he told them who he was they relented, but everything was a battle. And I wasn't even battling with them about my anorexia, I was battling with them for proper care for basic needs. My parents were furious, seeing the way I was being 'treated,' with my physical and mental state deteriorating and not even my physical comfort adequately provided for. I couldn't understand why the staff were being so nasty. My own head had bullied me black and blue. Living a life dedicated to anorexia had not been a choice: I was utterly powerless to fight my mind. I desperately wanted someone to help me. To help lift me out of the black hole anorexia had left me in. Instead I was treated like I had chosen to do all of this, that I really was that evil person my head told me I was. I was in a black hole and I was falling even deeper.

My parents and I were desperate for me to be transferred back to The Priory where the focus had not solely been on weight gain and where I had made some progress and trusted the staff. The treatment approach at St George's, and Avalon, was sending me into sharp mental decline. There was no hope of me making progress with regards to my anorexia and I was becoming suicidal. I genuinely did want to die. I had never felt like this before. I could see no future for myself. I was going to be kept in St George's and Avalon and treated in this way until I reached a BMI of 20 from which I would then relapse, and to me, a life like that was not worth living. I was overwhelmed with feelings of fear and hopelessness. Dying seemed like my only option. I wasn't going to get better in this hospital, not mentally.

Living with my head screaming at me every second of the day had been torture. I had followed my head's rules for years in the desperate hope that, in doing so, I would feel happiness. That I would somehow find a scrap of self-worth that had been missing for a decade. But anorexia had made me feel worse than I ever thought was possible. And now that I knew this hospital wasn't going to help me recover, that it was going to secure my fate of a life in an abusive relationship with never-ending mental torture, I wholeheartedly wanted to die. It was my only escape. My only way out of being in my head. My only way of ever being happy. One evening as I was on the phone crying to my mum I told her, "I'm going to go to sleep now, Ma, and I hope I never wake up. I really do. I just want to die."

My mum, who knew me better than anyone, knew I was

being deadly serious. I can only imagine what it must be like for a parent to hear their daughter tell them they want to die, to be miles away and not be able to put their arms around them, to make everything better. Because my mum and dad were trying. They were trying in every way possible to get me transferred to The Priory, to give me some hope at life. But they were fighting a losing battle against the system. I had given up hope. I could see no way out of the situation.

I felt I was being attacked from every angle. During the first ten days in St George's, my weight had fallen to just over 5st, making my BMI 10.5. This was because of the low total number of calories I was on to avoid re-feeding. However, I was accused of doing something anorexically deviant and manipulative to make myself lose weight. But I hadn't been doing anything. There were no opportunities to be up to 'anorexic tricks' sitting on a bed all day with a tube inserted to continuously drip calories 24/7. Moreover, they had completely destroyed me. I had no fight left in me. I didn't want to fight for anorexia, or for life.

The ward manager from Avalon came to visit me one afternoon when my dad was there. She said they were going to extend the Section 2 to a Section 3 because I hadn't been compliant. I questioned my lack of compliancy, asking when, I was meant to not have been. She said that staff had reported I was regularly exercising around the ward. I could not believe such blatant lies had been fabricated. If I so much as dangled a foot over the edge of the bed I was forced back to a lying position with the barriers put up on the side of the bed. Moreover, I was attached to a heart monitor, so God knows how I was meant to be exercising around the ward carrying this huge monitor as well as pushing all the various stands with drips and feeds attached that were inserted into my body. It would have been impossible, even for Superman.

She also said I would be transferred to Avalon when my weight was appropriate and there made to get to a BMI of 20, and that I would not be allowed to transfer back to The Priory. She said there was no way they would let that happen and nor would my community nurse, and that the only reason I wanted to go there was to have a lower target weight. This had not been my reason for wanting to move to The Priory, as it was possible that The Priory would make me get to the same weight as St George's. My reason for wanting to go back to The Priory was because it was on a different planet to St Georges and Avalon in terms of insight, understanding, care, empathy, and treatment! The Priory offered everything you wanted in terms of treatment to help recovery and Avalon offered nothing.

I burst into tears and shouted at her to get out of my room. My dad tried to console me, but I was hysterical. I didn't feel angry. I wasn't angry the staff were making lies up about me or treating me so badly. I was simply overtaken by fear. Fear of my fate being sealed. Fear of never getting my life back or recovering. I had been locked in my anorexic prison cell for years. And now they had thrown away the key. I was terrified.

My dad left, helpless to do anything, and I cried myself to sleep. He rang my mum as soon as he left the hospital, explaining he had never seen me so upset and that he found it difficult to see me in such a bad way. I had given up hope and resigned myself to whatever Avalon wanted to do to me. But Avalon did not know what they were entering into with my parents. My parents were not going to give up the fight easily.

With the ongoing battle over my transfer to The Priory and the section appeal bubbling in the background, my parents fought for my rights to help my current situation. After two weeks, I was allowed to have a bucket of soap and water brought to my bed in the morning so I could give my body some sort of wash. Every time Avalon tried to stop me seeing the advocate, my mum forcefully informed them of my legal rights. They were messing with the wrong person when it came to my mum and legal issues.

After three weeks stuck on that bed in St Georges, they decided they would transfer me back to Avalon. It was now the end of July 2010. Because I hadn't gained as much weight as they expected, they were convinced I had been up to something, so they wanted the 'expert' and 'specialist' eyes of Avalon to keep a closer watch of me.

Chapter 26
DeathLine

My regime at Avalon was pretty much the same as St Georges general hospital. I was not allowed any interaction with other patients and had to remain in my room, lying on my bed, being fed through the tube and with a one-to-one. If I needed the toilet, I was taken by wheelchair to the toilet at the end of the corridor. There were two sections to Avalon ward. At one end of the corridor were the bedrooms of people like me who received tube-feeding, and the other end in the main corridor was for patients who were eating. I was the only one who wasn't allowed out of my room.

Although I wasn't allowed to talk to the other patients, I could hear conversations in the corridor, and I could hear patients at meal times in the nearby dining room. None of them seemed happy and none of them seemed to be benefitting from the battery farm regime. My weight when I arrived back at Avalon was 34.6kg and they wanted to get me gaining weight as soon as possible. I was now allowed to drink water and the cold, soothing liquid trickling down the back of my coarse, parched throat was wonderful. It took me a while to get used to swallowing again, but I treasured those three cups of water I was allowed per day. It is barbaric to think I had been denied drinking water for the best part of a month, and a hot month at that! What that was meant to achieve, I don't know.

They also allowed me to start taking my medication orally. I still wasn't told what I was taking, except for one drug, which was highlighted as my antidepressant. That was going to be my lifeline, my way out of this hell. Although it was more of a deathline than a lifeline. I would put the pill in my mouth and pretend to swallow. Once the nurse had left and the one-to-one was back paying me no attention, I would spit the pill into my hand and store it in my empty box of tissues. I was building up a collection so I would have enough for an overdose. I did not want to live anymore, and this seemed to be my only way out. It was a relief to know that this torture was going to end. The hospital was not going to help me escape my head and I couldn't help myself, so dying was my only option. It was now just a matter of time, a matter of storing enough pills for this all to end.

I felt desperately guilty for what it would do to my parents and I knew how hard they were trying to get me transferred. I didn't want to leave them, I loved them so much. But I knew I couldn't live with my head anymore. If I stayed in Avalon, I knew that once I was discharged anorexia would take over again. That I would again become powerless to my mind. I didn't have the strength for that and I wanted to give up. I just couldn't fight anymore. In St Ann's I had told myself my body was a fat shell that I had to endure until I was discharged. Now, my body was only a shell and anorexia had killed everything inside. Anorexia had killed my soul so now I needed to kill the shell. But I had to make sure I had enough pills for the overdose to actually work, so I had to endure the hell until I did.

I was still not allowed to shower but continued to be brought a bucket of water in the mornings. My hair was a mesh of grease and my bedding still hadn't been changed. Eventually, with the bed sores and skin infections I had developed getting worse, my mum told them she would not leave until my bedding was replaced with clean, fresh sheets.

I had a TV in my room, one that my dad had brought me from home as the room did not come with one. I kept it on day and night, scared and lonely without the noise to keep me company. Silence at night in that dark bedroom was horrible. I would reflect on how awful my current situation was, how I so desperately wanted my parents near me, how my life was not worth living. Having the TV on helped me sleep and helped me feel not so completely isolated. But particular members of staff weren't happy about it and, when they were working the night shift, they would come into my room and turn it off, telling me I was not allowed it on. I would turn it back on when they left, but my one-to-one would again turn it off. On one occasion, one of the nurses stormed into my room in the early hours of the morning as I tried to sleep and started shouting at me.

"You can't have this on," he forcefully insisted. "You are not allowed."

"I can't sleep without it," I replied honestly.

"You have got to," he said. "When you are an adult living a normal life and going out to work, you cannot lie in bed watching TV all day. You have to earn a living and you get tired and have to sleep. I will not let you keep your TV on." He switched it off and stomped out the room as I lay in bed crying, lonely, and scared.

On the next visit, my dad brought with him his little hand-held TV so that whenever the staff turned my TV off in the night, I could turn this little one on and there would be nothing they could do about it. It wasn't as if I was asking for much, just to have my TV on quietly in the background as I slept. I wasn't interfering with anyone else and, being away from home, it gave me a slight bit of comfort.

My mum was furious when I told her what the nurse had said. She was so angry he had made out like it was my choice to lie in my bed all day, like it was my choice to be suffering from a mental illness, like it was my fault I was not living a 'normal, adult life'. She made a formal complaint, as she had been doing on regular occasions, emailing the ward manager about all the ill-treatment I was receiving. She was formulating a backbone to the argument to get me transferred to The Priory.

By the middle of August 2010, having been in hospital for nearly two months, I had gained just over 4kg and weighed 36.8kg. I was still on complete bed rest, being fed through the NG tube with a twenty-four-hour feed, and not allowed to shower. I felt disgustingly dirty and dangerously depressed. There were occasions when they were short-staffed with not enough health care assistants to provide all the one-to-ones needed. Then it was fine for me to go to the lounge and sit with other patients while one member of staff watched several of us. And this really angered me. If I was allowed to come out of my room when it was convenient for them, then surely I must be ok to come out of my room generally? There were also times when they couldn't find the wheelchair so I would walk to the toilet. How can it be fine to walk one moment of the day and not another? It was all about doing what they wanted when they wanted... and they wanted to make my life as difficult as possible.

But my parents were doing quite a good job of making their lives difficult, too. Since arriving back at Avalon, I had a new consultant as the world-renowned one I had been told I was going to have had retired. My parents sent regular emails to and had regular meetings with my new consultant, the ward manager, and the social worker to complain about my treatment. The three of them, like the Witches of Eastwick, would work together to refute the complaints, but they weren't pulling the wool over my parents' eyes. They were fighting them tooth and nail. There were so many faults in their system, so much ineptness in their treatment, my mum would not let a single thing lie. While I had given up hope and was suicidal and helpless, my mum was strong, continually fighting for my transfer to The Priory... the only thing that could save me. My mum could she see was losing me and if I stayed at Avalon she knew it would probably be the end of me. Their methodology was very backward, not giving any consideration to the individual – which was what had helped me at The Priory.

I had my tribunal at the end of August 2010, to appeal against the Section, which had been extended to a Section 3. I had been having regular meetings with my advocate and solicitors who were very helpful. They could not believe the treatment I had been subjected to, even commenting that it would be a story to go to *The Sun* with! The staff at Avalon hated them and hated that I had contact with people fighting for my rights, because they didn't want me to have any rights. They warned my parents against the advocate, saying he was a suspicious figure who didn't have my best interests at heart.

Quite simply, they didn't like the fact he posed a threat to my remaining in Avalon.

At the tribunal, the main point of my consultant's argument was that I was too ill to be un-sectioned. In order to support this, she explained to the panel that I was so ill I had fainted in the shower. Now you may be thinking 'I thought she wasn't allowed to shower?' And yes, that is true. I had not had a shower in the two months I had been there, so when exactly was this shower I was meant to have fainted in? I had never had a shower and I had never fainted. With this approach, the tribunal was an uphill battle. But we did get one point across during the tribunal, and a crucial one at that. We highlighted how much more conducive it was for my treatment to be nearer home where I could have regular visits and support from my parents and where the aftercare could take place near home rather than in a strange area three hours away. The panel accepted this and recommended in their report that it may be better for me to be nearer home. The Priory was only five minutes from my house so this recommendation supported our request for a transfer back there.

However, the staff at Avalon and my care team from home were still refusing to transfer me. There was nothing I could do, and my parents had tried nearly everything they could. They were still going to keep fighting, they weren't giving up. But me? I was counting down the pills until I had enough for an overdose.

Chapter 27
Complications

I was due for an endoscopy at the beginning of September 2010 at St George's general hospital. I decided this would be my opportunity. I was going to run away. I had my debit card with me so I had the money to get away. I didn't care where I went, and I wouldn't make the same mistake as last time. This time I wasn't going to come back. My one-to-one escorted me to the hospital for the endoscopy and afterwards we were waiting in the corridor for the taxi to arrive to take us back to Avalon. My heart was thumping hard in my chest. I was waiting for the ideal moment to make my escape. As the taxi arrived and we made our way out of building, I knew this was it: I had to go.

I started running away from the taxi and my nurse, hearing her shouting behind me. But I hadn't anticipated the effect severe anorexia and two months of complete bed rest would have. I was hoping it would be a Forest Gump moment, that I would start sprinting and soaring down the road. But the reality was my legs couldn't function. My muscles had completely wasted away and I couldn't run properly. I was shouting at myself in my head 'run, just run, keep running', but my legs couldn't do it. Within 100 metres, my one-to-one had caught up with me. She grabbed my arm and pulled me to a stop. I fell to the floor, sobbing and exhausted.

I couldn't believe I hadn't been able to run properly and that I had been caught. My one chance was gone. Now my thoughts turned to 'what the hell are they going to do to me? How are they going to punish me?' When we returned to Avalon and I was taken back to my bedroom, I collapsed on my bed in floods of tears. I fumbled for my phone to ring my mum. She was at work, but she picked up. I was incomprehensible and she was worried about what had caused my upset. Eventually I managed to tell her, and she wasn't happy.

"What were you thinking?!" she said. "That's it now, you've blown it. They are never going to transfer you."

I was utterly devastated. I really had ruined everything. My mum advised me to ring my community nurse straight away to explain to her what happened before the staff at Avalon gave her their version and twisted the tale.

The community nurse's phone rang through to answer-phone.

"I'm really sorry," I cried hysterically. "I didn't know what else to do. I tried to run away. I can't bear it here. I'm sorry. I just had to get away. But they caught me. I'm sorry."

She sent me a text not long after, saying not to worry and as long as I was ok that was all that mattered. But I wasn't ok. I wasn't ok being there, in that hospital, in what was frankly, Hell on Earth.

However, rather than sealing my fate of endless torture in Avalon, running away seemed to prompt my community nurse to realise that Avalon was not helping me and was not the best place for me to receive treatment. With my parents continuing to fight from every corner, my community nurse agreed in principle to a transfer to The Priory. Throughout the months of fighting with Avalon, my dad had been in regular contact with The Priory and Dr Williams, explaining our situation. Dr Williams had always said he was happy to have me back at The Priory, as long as I was medically stable and that the care teams agreed. Finally, with my nurse now asking for the transfer as well, the staff at Avalon agreed with Dr Williams that I be transferred to The Priory with the condition that I was medically stable.

However, becoming medically stable was another challenge in itself. It seemed as if Avalon were still trying to put up obstacles and make it as difficult as they could. Dr Williams had explained he wanted my feed to be bolus (feeds at meal and snack times) rather than a continuous twenty-four-hour feed. But the staff at Avalon were reluctant to do this, making excuses to delay the change and therefore my transfer. Adding to complications, on 13th September 2010, my daily blood test revealed that my haemoglobin count was dangerously low and that I must be bleeding internally.

I was taken straight to A and E and hooked up to various drips. My haemoglobin levels had fallen below four which is critically low, the norm being around twelve. I felt dizzy and light-headed, and one of the nurses explained to me that most people are dead with haemoglobin levels as low as mine. I was transferred to a ward where I was urgently given a blood transfusion. It was now late at night, I didn't feel well, the blood transfusion hurt, and I wanted to sleep. We had finally got an agreement to transfer to The Priory when I was medically stable, but now I was terrified this was going to put an end to it.

My dad came to visit me the following day (my mum had to go to work). He sat with me as I had the second blood transfusion as one hadn't been enough. None of the doctors at St George's seemed to know what was causing the internal bleeding. They wanted me to have another endoscopy but was uncertain when. Until I had it, my feed had to be stopped, as the stomach needs to be empty for the procedure.

The days rolled by as I sat on my bed in a ward. I'd had three blood transfusions and was waiting for my turn for the endoscopy. I went three days without a single calorie entering my body before I was called for the endoscopy. This felt like an achievement… seventy-two hours without anything but water in my body. My consultant had been to visit me, explaining her main concern was getting the tube connected again to start the feed. My main concern was to find out why I had nearly died from an internal bleed.

The results of the endoscopy revealed that my stomach was inflamed and the only possibility the doctors could think of that may have caused such a dramatic loss of blood was that my stomach lining had been wearing away. But the reality was, nobody actually knew what had happened. On 17th September

2010 (my twenty-second birthday), with my blood levels stable, I was sent back to Avalon after five days in the general hospital. But this latest trip to St George's had only postponed my transfer to The Priory. Clearly, if I was internally bleeding and requiring blood transfusions, I wasn't medically stable. But I knew now it was only a matter of weeks until I would be stable enough for the transfer, provided nothing else untoward happened.

Back in Avalon, I was now allowed to have a seated shower twice a week. After two and a half months without, thee feeling of hot water rushing over my body, and massaging shampoo into my grease-ridden hair, smelling the fruity fragrance was amazing.

I had a visit from the consultant who told me that they had spoken to Dr Williams and he had told them he would make me get to a similar BMI to what they wanted – around the 20 mark. He asked, with knowing that, would I stay in Avalon? They must have thought I was as thick as them if I was going to fall for that. For one, my experience with Dr Williams showed me that he was not the type of person to make statements like that without speaking to the patient first, and two, even if he had, there was no way on Earth anything would make me want to stay at Avalon, target BMI included. I knew the treatment at The Priory was what I needed to help me recover, regardless of BMI. I would have killed myself if I had to stay in Avalon, that is certain. The Priory was my only hope in saving my life and I was going there no matter what.

The days slowly ticked by until finally 30th September 2010 arrived: my date for the transfer. I packed my clothes into my suitcase, putting my stash of antidepressants into one of my socks. I wanted it there as a back-up in case things got really bad. Not one member of staff came to say goodbye and, as my taxi arrived, I quietly left the building with my one-to-one. As I sat in the back of the taxi and it pulled away down the road, I looked out of the window towards Avalon. I could not believe I was finally getting away, I was finally going to be free from that hell. Three months of torture, three months of fighting, three months of sheer misery and hopelessness… it was finally over. We had won the fight against Avalon, but now I had to face the fight against anorexia.

Chapter 28
A Welcomed Return

I made my way with my one-to-one to The Priory's reception, pulling my suitcase behind me. As we stood in reception, Janet, one of the health care assistants who I had got on very well with on my first admission, walked in to greet me.

"Rebecca," she said sympathetically, as if to say she knew everything I had been through. She put her arm round my shoulders and I started to cry. Tears of relief trickled down my face. I felt like I should have been black and blue from the abuse I had gone through at the hands of both anorexia and St George's. She led me down the corridor to the eating disorder unit, leaving my one-to-one at reception struggling with the paperwork.

It all looked exactly the same as it had done when I left it six months before. I was even given the same bedroom, Room 4, which had been reserved for me by Jackie, another brilliant health care assistant, when they knew I was going to be transferred. My suitcase was searched... and my antidepressants found. My heart sank. I needed them just in case. The staff member searching my belongings didn't ask too many questions at the time I was due to see Dr Williams, the ward manager and the medical doctor within the hour and everything would be discussed then.

Dr Williams asked me why St George's had been so bad, but words could not do it justice. It was hard to believe that what actually happened there did really happen. That human beings could be treated in such a way. He questioned my stash of antidepressants. I explained I had never taken antidepressants, even though they had been prescribed in both St Ann's and my first admission at The Priory. I had always spat them out and disposed of them, worried they would interfere with my brain and change how I thought, and that my thoughts would no longer be my thoughts and that I would lose anorexia. I explained that, in Avalon, rather than disposing of them, I'd been storing them up for an overdose. I'd needed to make sure I had enough for it to be fatal and then I was going to take them. Because that is what they had driven me to. I wanted to die.

I wasn't feeling much better now. While I was grateful to be in The Priory, anorexia and Avalon had taken so much out of me and destroyed so much of me that my mood was still dangerously low. But Dr Williams explained, even though I was under section, he was not going to force me to take antidepressants. Yes, he wanted me to have them and thought I needed them, but he wanted me to be in agreement with it, and not force it upon me against my will.

The initial plan was to continue with tube-feeding and continue with the one-to-one.

Later that evening I had a visit from my parents. I threw my arms round them, thanking them for everything they had done to get me to The Priory. I think they were as relieved as me, and just as exhausted. While I had been living in the hell of Avalon, they'd had to watch me go through it, witness me on the brink of suicide and fight for me when I could not fight for myself. It had been hell for them, too. They were glad I was now in the place that was going to help me.

I was weighed first thing the next morning at 40.1kg making my BMI 12.9. I had thought long and hard about it and decided that I wanted my target BMI to be 15. As much as I wished to not go above 14, I recognised that this had given me very little leeway last time so that as soon as I had started losing a bit of weight, it soon rapidly fell dangerously low. I didn't want that to happen again. I desperately wanted this to be my last admission and, for that to happen, it had to work. I didn't want anorexia to

169

take over again, but I also wasn't ready to give it up completely. I wanted to be able to manage it. My thinking had completely changed from how it had been in St Ann's when I wanted to give my whole life to anorexia. Now, I actually wanted a life.

In my mind, BMI 15 was the maximum I could tolerate. I knew I couldn't cope with any more and I genuinely thought I could give life a go at that BMI. But obviously, because I was still sectioned, the decision was out of my hands. Ultimately, it fell to Dr Williams and he would also take into account the views of my community nurse who had to manage me in the community. It was not a decision he was going to take lightly… or quickly. He acknowledged and listened to my view but, as it currently stood, he had not made up his mind as to what he thought would be the best target for me. It was agreed that I would get to a BMI of 15 and, once there, I would maintain it until he and my community nurse had made a decision about the target suited for my best interests.

It was very difficult for me not knowing and I agonised about it all day, every day. I felt like my life depended on this decision. I was certain that if I was made to go above BMI 15 then that was it: anorexia would win. I knew The Priory, with all its excellent support and therapy, could help me build a life if I were able to stay at BMI 15 which I was determined to tolerate. A higher BMI would flick the switch in my head that would allow anorexia to completely take over once more. I was scared of living that life again where I was completely powerless to my mind. I was scared of the exhaustion and mental torture. I also felt like my body was a lot weaker now. The damage I had done to it over the past few years was really starting to take its toll. I was scared that, if the switch was flicked and anorexia ruled, I wouldn't make it. I had that gut feeling that if anorexia was to take over again, then it would be my last time. My last time of being alive. I probably wouldn't make it through another anorexia-driven weight loss mission. But I also knew that going above a BMI of 15 would trigger just that. I had to wait until a decision was made to find out what my fate would be.

The staff were always very kind to me, always trying to help and didn't push me day to day beyond what I could cope with. I wasn't ready to contemplate starting to consume food and drink (except water) orally, so they continued with the NG tube. Food had become a terrifying prospect and even contemplating trying to eat again was too much. For now, I was simply trying to survive, and feeding myself required more strength than I had, so I was very grateful to the staff for not pushing me until I was ready.

I also explained to Dr Williams that I could not sit down all day, that this was too much of a struggle and created immense anxiety for me. Rather than tell me that those were the rules and that standing was not allowed and that it was just something all anorexics say, he acknowledged me as an individual and we, with my primary nurse, devised a 'sitting/standing' regime. This designated several fifteen-minute time slots during the day when I was allowed to stand. And it worked. For the first time, my exercise obsession was becoming controlled. I wasn't given a blanket ban; we negotiated and devised this regime which allowed me enough standing to ease my anxiety but was by no means excessive. I stuck to the regime religiously. I didn't even try to pace. For me, this was a major achievement.

I soon started to attend the group therapy sessions which, I have to say, I hated. My mind was so preoccupied with what my target weight was going to be that I did not engage in them. I couldn't. My mind did not have the capacity. I had spent the past three months trying to survive Avalon, and the years before that living ruled by anorexia. I was physically and mentally exhausted and all the little energy I could muster was spent worrying about what my target weight, and therefore fate, would be. There was certainly nothing left for engagement in group therapy. I would sit in the group and listen, seeing other people benefitting greatly from taking part, but I did not actively participate. However, I did engage in individual therapy once a week.

My spare time outside of groups and therapy was spent alone in my room with my one-to-one. The idea of socially interacting terrified me. For years now it had just been me and anorexia. Anorexia had chipped away at me and left me completely broken. When your head is telling you what a horrid, disgusting, unlikeable and vile person you are every second of every day, you wholeheartedly believe it. The thoughts become ingrained as fact. Anorexia had abused me and left me with nothing. I was scared of absolutely everything. And that included talking to people.

After a month of being in The Priory, I reached my temporary target of 44.5kg (although they were still using the wrong, shorter height for the BMI calculation that they had used on my first admission) and was put onto a maintenance diet which was to continue until Dr Williams made his final decision about my target. As the weight gain had finished temporarily, I felt ready to try and make progress in order not to be so dependent on the tube, so I started to orally consume some of my *Ensure* drink. It was very difficult; it had been four months since anything had passed my lips except water and I had become dependent on the tube to feed me and keep me alive. I was now completely detached from food and drink. I didn't miss it; it repulsed me, and I never wanted to have to eat or drink again. But I knew this wasn't feasible if I wanted to be discharged and have a life, and the first step was to start drinking the *Ensure*. The guilt of knowing I was responsible for putting calories into my body was overpowering. The nurses would sit with me in my room and I would bring the cup up to my mouth when they prompted me to take a sip. That was the only way I could do it at first. The staff would eat their meals as I drank my *Ensure*. Looking at them eating, I would think, 'there is not one part of me that wants to eat that.' But I knew at some point I would have to eat.

As I got used to drinking the *Ensure*, I was brought into the dining room with the other patients for one of the meals. I would sit there with my drink while they ate their meals. However, in early November 2010 things took a turn for the worse and each day, each hour, felt like a battle to survive.

Chapter 29
Rock Bottom

One Sunday evening, after my mum had kissed me goodbye from her visit, I was sitting at the dining table with my *Ensure* and all the other patients and staff with their meals. I was thinking how much I missed my mum and dad, how I wanted them near me, to hug me, to make me feel better, and I started to cry. Soon, the tears became uncontrollable and I was struggling to breathe. I was taken out of the dining room having lost all control of my body.

I was quickly taken in the wheelchair back to my bedroom and moved to my chair. My mind had gone: it was blank, and my body was out of control. I was having fits and repeatedly banging my head against the back of the chair. I couldn't breathe. It was like an out-of-body experience. The staff called the doctor, but no one knew how to help me. They gave me an oxygen mask and soon my body became all floppy and I couldn't keep myself upright.

Paramedics were called and I managed to force out the words, "I need my mum."

By now, it was gone 8.30pm and I had been in this state for over two hours. My mum was rung at home and came immediately.

The paramedics removed the oxygen mask and tried to help me control my breathing. With their help and my mum by my side, I started to calm down and regain my thoughts. I felt absolutely shattered. I had no idea what had happened to me, my mind and body, those past few hours. Extreme crying, fitting and distress had taken it out of me. All I wanted now was to go to sleep. But it wasn't over. For the next two months, I was to experience episodes similar to this several times a day, every day.

Dr Williams explained to me that I was having panic attacks. I felt in a state of severe stress and anxiety every moment of the day, and this was culminating in panic attacks. Sometimes they would last about twenty minutes, other times they would go on for hours. All the staff were extremely worried about me. They had never seen such prolonged and distressing panic attacks before. There was also the danger that I could injure myself during them as, when one started, I would collapse instantaneously to the floor. My body would fit, my head would bang, and I would make the most horrendous noises. When I was having an attack, my body was completely out of my control.

Every day was a struggle to get through, living in fear that I could go into one of those attacks at any minute. And I did. They were triggered by anything. Sometimes when I was walking to or from ward round (the twice-weekly meeting with Dr Williams and other members of staff) I would have an attack and hit the floor, fitting and gasping for breath. Feed times, or when my parents left me, or even when I was only thinking about them… all could set off hours of an attack. Even the fire alarm going off was enough to set me off.

I felt constantly on edge, constantly exhausted. With my consent, they started to give me diazepam (a sedative) to try and help calm me down. I was on a strong dose on a daily basis. Sometimes I could be in the middle of an attack, feeling like I was going to die, and I would beg them to help me, to stop this happening to my body, to give me something that could help. But not a lot did. They were horrendous experiences and anyone who has ever had a panic attack will know what I mean. And to have them day in, day out, occupying most of the day was just awful.

With the persistence of the attacks, it wasn't possible to make progress with other areas of my treatment. I could not introduce more oral *Ensure* into my diet and I certainly couldn't contemplate solid food. I couldn't have any timeout and I didn't want any time out. I had been within hospital walls for practically six months and the outside world now terrified me. For the time being, the priority was to try and get the panic attacks under control, but I went through the whole of November and December in a panic attack cycle.

Dr Williams agreed for me to have a few hours at home on Christmas Day. But when my mum arrived to take me home, I started to feel panicky and couldn't breathe. The kind nurse on duty and my mum managed to calm me down and, when ready, I left in the car with my mum. However, when we parked up on our drive, I looked at my home and I felt terrified. I associated my house with how it had been when I left it – full of anorexia, worry, tears, and exhaustion.

I stood at the front door and burst into tears. I couldn't go in. I desperately wanted to be able to go in, to look at the decorations, to sit by the tree with my family; everything most people do without a second thought. But for me it was a task too great: too difficult and too scary. I stood in the doorway, crying. I felt overwhelmed with panic, sadness, and fear. I could feel my heart in my chest, the flutter of nerves in my stomach. I could feel an attack brewing. So my mum had to take me back to hospital. I must have been gone no more than half an hour and it felt a relief to return to the safety of the hospital and my bedroom. Although I was relieved, I was also overcome with sadness. It was Christmas Day and I couldn't even step into my own house. What had happened to me? What had anorexia done to me? It had destroyed me and made me a nervous wreck.

My parents and sister came back to visit me early Christmas evening and we all sat in my room and opened our presents. But it wasn't an occasion of celebration. While they tried to be positive and jolly, none of us could escape the reality of the situation: how ill I had been, how ill I still was, and how far I had to go. I have never felt so sad. Christmas is meant to be a time of happiness, of having fun and spending time with your family. But anorexia ruined this. I was lonely, scared, and overwhelmed with sadness.

That was when I started to hate anorexia. It had caused all

this pain and made me a broken person. On Christmas evening 2010, when I sat alone in my room, the hospital incredibly quiet as most people had gone home for the festive period, I started thinking about my family at home eating Christmas dinner together, playing games and watching TV. I so desperately wanted to be there and join in, to be a part of it and enjoy the special occasion. I wished I could sit on the sofa and have a chocolate from the *Quality Street* tin that always popped up around Christmas. Instead, I was in hospital alone, riddled with anxiety and fear. I felt I had hit rock bottom, that things couldn't get much worse than they had been the past six months. Something had to give. Life shouldn't be this difficult.

On the next ward, I told Dr Williams what had happened at Christmas. In recent weeks, he had suggested that, if my panic attacks continued being so severe, he would think about prescribing an antidepressant, even if I didn't agree to it, as he thought they would help. The trauma of all the panic attacks and the culmination of sadness and distress at Christmas had pushed me to the point where I knew I needed something, so I agreed to start taking antidepressants.

I had it in liquid form via the tube as, even though I agreed to it, I didn't feel able to take responsibility to give it to myself. Taking antidepressants felt like a betrayal of anorexia. I had fought against taking them since my escape from St Ann's and, while I could now see the misery anorexia had driven me to, I still did not want to be completely without it. But now I was tired. Anorexia had exhausted me and made life unliveable. I had to give the antidepressants a go. I had nothing to lose. I couldn't live in the state I currently was and maybe the antidepressants could help?

In the new year, the frequency and severity of my panic attacks started to reduce. And with not being in a frenzied state of panic all day every day, I started to think a little bit clearer. I realised I wanted more from life than anorexia, which was locking me in a vicious cycle of hospital admissions. I wanted to have friends and go out. I wanted a life. I still wasn't ready to give up anorexia, but I wanted to manage it and to have a life alongside it. I knew the only way for this to be a possibility was if my target was allowed to be a BMI 15. Any higher and the drive to lose weight would take over. If I wanted to give life a go, I needed to be at a size I could manage, BMI 15 being the golden number. But Dr Williams and my nurse were still undecided. They listened and accepted my view but feared they may be doing me a disservice in attempting full recovery if they didn't enforce a higher weight.

I knew if I was to have any sort of a life I needed to be able to eat. But food still terrified me. It had now been seven months since I had eaten food and I could not avoid it anymore. It was hanging over my head like a black cloud. I knew at some point I would have to start eating again and the longer I put it off the greater the fear was becoming. I told Dr Williams I wanted to start to re-introduce solid food into my diet in baby steps. He had always said he would only do it when I was ready and I felt now was the time.

As I put the first spoonful of custard into my mouth it was a sensation like no other. I couldn't remember how to eat. The custard sat on my tongue, kick-starting my tastebuds as I tried to remember what to do. It was smooth and soft, but swallowing felt difficult, almost as if I had to gulp it down. I felt wracked with guilt for putting food into my body, but the staff and my mum reassured me it was a necessary step if I wanted a life out of hospital.

I persevered with the custard at lunch, keeping the *Ensures* and NG feed in place the rest of the time. Once the custard at lunch became an established routine, I suggested replacing my *Ensure* at dinner time with soup and bread. So that was the next step, introducing *Heinz* tomato soup for dinner with a slice of wholemeal bread. I was daunted and guilt-ridden at the prospect of more food in my diet – and me having suggested it – but I knew it was necessary.

It had now been eight months since I'd eaten proper food (except custard) and it seemed my tastebuds had become a lot more sensitive. All I could taste as I slowly ate the tomato soup was salt. I have never known anything like it. The saltiness was so incredibly strong. I tore my bread up and put it in the soup so I still didn't have to chew anything, I could just swallow. The more I ate the soup, the more I got used to eating it (and also the taste).

However, I was still struggling to have any time out of hospital. The thought of being in the outside world seemed very threatening. I had never had an abundance of confidence or self-esteem, but now it had become extreme. I was a nervous wreck, scared of everything, emotionally and physically needy. When my panic attacks had started, back in November, I became very dependent on my mum. I wanted her by my side 24/7. Obviously, this was not possible as she had to go to work and I had to follow the routine of hospital. Originally, my parents had been visiting me on weekends and talking to me over the phone during the week. But, with the onset of the panic attacks, every evening at 7pm when visiting started, my mum would walk from her work to The Priory and sit with me on my bed for an hour and a half. I couldn't get through the day without her, desperate to have physical contact with her. She told Dr Williams I had become incredibly needy of her and he assured her this was normal behaviour and would ease in time.

When I started having timeout, my parents would take me for a drive. I would sit in the back of the car and watch the world pass me by through the window. It was a world apart from my timeouts at St Ann's when I would march the streets hour after hour, not giving a second thought to my parents and only using them to get my exercise. Now I did not want to step foot out of the car, wanting to stay hiding in the back seat. We would park up at a local reservoir or park, watching people walk their dogs. I felt like I inhabited another world. I could not see myself ever stepping foot outside again. I was terrified. Everyone was getting on with their lives, walking around the park care free. And there was I, looking at them, thinking that joining them was an

179

impossibility. I could never get out of the car; it had been a difficult enough task getting me to go out in the car at all. To step outside was like looking over the edge of a cliff and being asked to jump. I couldn't do it, though I knew in time I would have to. But that was a brilliant thing about Dr Williams and the staff at The Priory. They never rushed me and never forced me to do anything before I was ready.

As time progressed, I really wanted to be able to go home. When I was ready, I had a few hours at home on weekend afternoons. This time was spent on the sofa cuddled up to my mum, with my dad in the armchair, all of us watching rubbish afternoon TV, mainly *Jamie's 30 Minute Meals*. Neither of my parents had any interest in this – my dad hates most TV, especially cookery shows, and my mum is not Jamie Oliver's biggest fan to put it mildly. But they would sit there with me, keeping me company and keeping me feeling safe. For those couple of hours at home with my parents, there was nothing else I would rather have been doing. I didn't go anywhere else in the house as that was too scary. I would walk from the front door straight to the lounge and sit on the sofa, keeping my coat on. It continued like that for several weeks until I felt ready to attempt my afternoon snack of an *Ensure* at home.

I was continuing to make progress, slowly but surely. I introduced *Weetabix* at breakfast and had to relearn how to chew. It felt alien, having food in my mouth going up and down. It made my mouth feel dirty; the whole act of eating felt dirty. But I had to persevere, and I did. I started eating breakfast with the rest of the group in the restaurant but always sitting at the end of the table and making sure a member of staff was next to me. Again, this was completely opposite to when I was in St Ann's and wanted to hide food at every opportunity and was at constant war with the staff. Now I didn't want to fall back into the habit of hiding food and I was worried what I might do if left to myself to take responsibility. Sitting next to the member of staff helped take this responsibility away from me, encouraging me and giving me reason to eat. I needed their support and I wanted them to make sure I didn't hide anything – no longer the naughty, rebellious patient I had been in St Ann's.

The staff at The Priory and my parents would praise me when I made progress, and this encouraged me to continue making steps forward. I had missed out on so much of life, I was desperate to give it a go again. I wanted to have friends, have fun and do everything twenty-year-olds should be doing. So I had to keep progressing, to develop some sort of 'normal' eating habits. I continued to introduce more solid food, including a half-portion dinner in the evening. This was absolutely terrifying – my first proper, solid meal. I hadn't used a knife and fork for nine months and the idea of a normal meal was overwhelmingly daunting. I would eat in my bedroom with a member of staff, requiring their constant support and reassurance. I didn't choose off the menu like all the other patients. My meal was always the same: half a portion of white fish, half a jacket potato and vegetables. It was a huge struggle, but I was always determined to eat it. The tube was still used at certain times and I felt partly dependent on it. Taking responsibility for all of my eating and drinking seemed too much – too much guilt. But in time I would have to: it was essential to be discharged.

But the big question still loomed. What was my target BMI going to be? Would I be allowed to maintain at fifteen like I so desperately wanted, or would it be decided that I needed to go higher, my ultimate fear? I was desperate to prove I could manage at this weight. I did still struggle greatly but I had to keep pushing myself. I wanted to have a life and I knew the only way I could attempt this was with a BMI 15. Anything greater and I would simply revert wholeheartedly back to anorexia, determined to lose weight and destroying any psychological gains I had made… and any chance of rebuilding my life.

Chapter 31
The Big Decision

I had a CPA (the big meeting with everyone involved in your care) near the end of March 2011 and this was going to be the one where Dr Williams made his decision about my target weight. We were all called into the small room and my progress and future directions were discussed. My stomach was churning with extreme angst as to what his decision was going to be. My life depended on it.

"I, your community nurse, and the staff here have thought about this long and hard," he said. "We have gone to and fro, arguing the reasons for and against. Me and your nurse have discussed it at length and have both been on either side of the argument. It really has been a difficult decision what to do for your best interest. But I have come to a decision." I held my breath. "We are going to push your target higher."

I could not believe what I was hearing. Well, I could believe it, but I didn't want to. I had expected he would make that decision, but I had been hoping he wouldn't. My worst nightmare was being realised.

"Please no, don't do this," I begged in desperation. "It won't work. You've got to let me stay at a BMI 15, please."

"I'm sorry, Rebecca," he said. "I think it is for the best."

"You can't do this!" I shouted. I ran out of the room crying. I went straight to my bedroom and slammed the door shut, ripping out my NG tube as I crashed against the door in hysterics. 'I'm not going to eat a single thing now,' I thought. 'There is no way I am going to continue complying to make my weight higher.' I was absolutely distraught.

After a while, I was persuaded to open my door, being told it would be forced down otherwise. The staff were surprised to see I had ripped the tube out and when presented with my soup at lunchtime in my bedroom, I sat and stared at it, tears still trickling down my face.

"You need to eat it," the nurse tried to encourage me. "If you carry on complying then he is more likely to agree to a BMI of perhaps 16."

But I just couldn't do it. I could not eat another thing. I could not allow this to happen to me. I was going to fight tooth and nail as they pushed me up higher. I was going to again become the patient from hell and rebel in every way. The switch had been flicked and anorexia was on full power. They had forced me to it. Gaining more weight was going to make me fight for anorexia and I was convinced it would be the end of me.

I texted my parents, telling them I hated them and I never wanted to see them again. 'How could they have let this happen to me?' I thought. 'They should have fought my corner.' I was so angry with everyone. Afternoon snack time came around and again I refused to drink my *Ensure*. And now, with the tube removed, there was nothing they could do. I couldn't stop crying. I was totally exhausted in every way, shape and form.

I was called back in to see Dr Williams in the afternoon. He asked me why I had pulled the tube out and told me they were going to reinsert it. He also explained that, with my history of running away, if I were to do so now, I would have to be transferred to a different eating disorder hospital that was a secure, locked unit which The Priory wasn't. He must have read my mind as I had actually been planning on running away. I had it all worked out in my head and I had my debit card ready to take me far away. I was only waiting for the ideal opportunity. I had to get away.

But with Dr Williams telling me I would be transferred I had to think twice. After everything my parents and I had been through, after all the fighting we had done to get me moved to

The Priory, the last thing I wanted was to be taken somewhere else. I knew the best place was The Priory. It felt they were against me at the moment and had made a decision I was violently opposed to, but somewhere else could be a lot worse. I decided against running away, but I continued to not comply.

That evening I lay on my bed, still crying. I had been put back on a one-to-one through fear of what I might do. Despite my texts full of hatred to my parents, bang on cue at 7pm my mum walked into my bedroom. As soon as I saw her, I started sobbing uncontrollably again. She stroked my head as I lay there, a complete mess.

"I can't do it, Ma," I cried. "I just can't do it. I can't gain any more weight."

"You've got to try," she said, "and if you really can't do it then he will see that and he might change his mind."

I truly felt like my world had collapsed and there was no point in living anymore. 'If only I still had my stash of pills,' I thought, 'I would take them without hesitation.'

It is hard to convey how excruciatingly difficult, terrifying, and unbearable the thought of gaining weight is to someone suffering from anorexia. It is unimaginable how it makes you feel, how even 100 grams (which is 0.2 pounds) feels huge and disgusting and makes you want to rip your stomach out. The fear of weight gain, the fear of being fat is indescribable. I was coping with a BMI 15. I didn't like it, but I could just about deal with it. I knew 100% there was no way I could cope gaining more weight.

I cried myself to sleep that evening and awoke in the morning unable to control more tears from flowing. I became hysterical when being taken down to breakfast. The thought of having to gain more weight was sending me into breakdown. My key nurse took me back to my room and tried to calm me down. She was always very kind and supportive and I got on really well with her (she was a similar age to me). We could have a laugh and a joke about normal things, although she would be strict with me when she needed to be. But this time I had been pushed over the edge and was beyond her help as I was falling rapidly into self-destruction.

Dr Williams arranged to see me that afternoon. He said they hadn't anticipated such a severe reaction and my heightened distress was a cause for concern. He said he was going to arrange for a second opinion from another doctor to see what they regarded the best decision to be with reference to my target BMI.

"I am going to arrange for an independent consultant from another eating disorder hospital to do the assessment. It will be very fair, and she will give her professional view. I am trying to get this arranged as soon as possible, but it will likely be in about three weeks," Dr Williams said.

"What am I going to do in the meantime?" I asked. "I don't want to start gaining weight until I have seen her." I was scared I would be made to gain weight in the meantime so that by the time she came to see me it would be pointless doing the assessment because I would already have reached a higher weight.

"You will continue on your current care plan as it is," he explained. "Your meal plan won't increase and you will continue maintaining BMI 15 until she has done her assessment."

The next three weeks were consumed with anxiety and stress – feeling as if my life was hanging in the balance – awaiting my trial to see if I would be put on death row. That is literally how I felt. The days rolled by incredibly slowly, each day seeming like Groundhog Day, until D-Day finally arrived.

I saw the independent consultant on 13th April 2011 for the second opinion. We spent a long time discussing my past, my previous hospital admissions, my intentions and hopes for this admission, and my plans for the future. I told her how I wanted to socialise and go out with friends again and hoped to get what I thought was my dream job of working in a café. I explained, completely honestly, that if I were to leave with a BMI 15, I would work very hard to try and maintain it, whereas any higher and I would be completely committed to losing weight. I knew a BMI 14 hadn't worked, but BMI 15 gave me that little bit of extra leeway and I wanted the chance to prove I could make it work. Life without anorexia was inconceivable and I simply could not cope without it, but I didn't want it to take over. I wanted to manage it and I knew the only way for me to do this was to stay at a BMI of 15.

A week after seeing the independent consultant I was called into ward round to see Dr Williams. He had received the assessment from the consultant, outlining her second opinion. Within her four-page summary she wrote:

'The modest improvement in brain function associated with a 1-point increase in BMI must be balanced against a high risk of losing the gains in psychological and physical health achieved during the admission and losing Rebecca's engagement now and in the future. I conclude that it is likely to be in Rebecca's best interest to support her having an opportunity to prove that she can maintain herself safely at BMI 15 in the community while she begins to rebuild a life for herself outside of her illness.'

I couldn't understand what I was hearing; I couldn't be certain of what the decision was. I questioned Dr Williams frantically, looking for clarification.

"I have come to the decision that I will keep your target at BMI 15," he tried to reassure me.

"Are you sure?" I asked, reluctant to allow myself to be relieved and happy in case it wasn't definitive.

"Yes. That is my final decision and it won't change."

My views had been listened to and acknowledged and I was so grateful for this. They were giving me the chance to try life again. I couldn't have done this if I had been made to gain weight. I would have sunk into terminal anorexic decline which, not only for the first time did I not want, but which I could not see myself ever recovering from. I think it would have killed me. I know that, to many, a BMI of 15 may seem very low but the decision was not taken lightly and was based on my individual needs and history. And it turned out to be a decision that helped save my life.

But it wasn't the end point: it was only the start.

Chapter 32
Discharge

Now it was full steam ahead to try and continue making progress so that I could reach a state ready for discharge. There was still a long way to go, for instance I still had the NG tube in. But now my target weight was decided, I could start tackling my other fears.

Outside the group sessions, I never allowed myself to do anything, I just sat (or stood if it was my designated time) and worried. Worrying, to me, was reassuring. By not distracting myself and not allowing myself to do anything it meant I could make sure that I hadn't lost anorexia completely. I worried that if I allowed myself to be distracted and to think or do something else, I would completely lose my grip on anorexia. This was something Dr Williams and my therapist wanted to tackle, so they slowly introduced different tasks for me to do during the day.

I started to watch a bit of TV and do some puzzles – I became a whiz at cryptic crosswords and Sudoku! I felt incredibly guilty when I didn't just sit and think. 'How dare I allow myself to do this,' I would think, 'I shouldn't enjoy this. I shouldn't enjoy anything. It means I am losing anorexia.' But I fought those thoughts and I realised that I could actually do something else for a little bit and enjoy it, and not lose anorexia which I still felt I needed. If I wanted to regain some sort of normality in my life I had to be able to do 'normal' things, rather than spend all day every day staring into space 'thinking' about anorexia. That was not the life I wanted. I wanted to be out there doing things, enjoying things. So as difficult as it was, I knew they were right and I worked with them. They were helping me to slowly build up a life again.

My mum was still visiting me every evening but instead of sitting and talking we started watching Peter Kay DVDs together. Only half an hour at a time as that I was all I could manage, but in that half an hour I did find myself laughing and enjoying it. Little challenges like this that Dr Williams and my therapist were setting me were making a big difference and getting me closer to being ready to go back into the real world.

I also started attending 'social phobia' group, which was intended for general patients and outpatients but one which the eating disorder staff thought would be beneficial to me. And it was. I got in contact with Jess, Allana, and Sarah from school and they started to come to visit me. I still felt very socially awkward – I didn't know how to talk to people and I didn't know how to behave. I had missed out on so much of normal life for years that I basically had to relearn everything. It was going to be a slow process, but I had to start somewhere and I couldn't keep running away from it.

I so desperately wanted friends and I would imagine myself after being discharged, going round their houses, going out together, having fun – that was going to make it all worthwhile. I was given more timeout and started eating lunch at home and doing more things out of the house with my parents. I was still very quiet, scared and reclusive but I was making progress. Everything still scared me, but nothing scared me more than going back to my life dominated by anorexia. It was not a life but an existence. I desperately wanted to start living and catching up on everything I had missed out on.

At the start of May 2011, I had the NG tube removed, nearly a year since it had been put in place. It felt very strange being without it; not only had I got used to it but it had also become a slight comfort. The tube in place was a constant reminder that I had to comply – if I didn't, the calories would go down the tube. It helped take the responsibility away from me. It wasn't me choosing to feed myself, I was doing it because I had to, otherwise, I would be tube fed. But now the tube wasn't in place I had to take more responsibility and with that came large amounts guilt. Eating when I didn't have the threat of the tube felt like a betrayal of anorexia. 'How could I possibly eat?' I would think. 'I don't have to, and I could get away with not doing so now I haven't got the tube.' But if I wanted to be discharged and have a life then I had to do it... I had to eat. I would tell myself that I was doing the right thing for a life outside of hospital.

At the start of May, after weeks of deliberation, I decided I wanted to be able to eat my mum's cooking again which I hadn't done for so many years. A petrifying thought, yet one I was longing to do. A decision was made between myself, Dr Williams, and the staff that on three days a week, instead of having my usual half a portion of white fish, jacket potato and veg, I was to pick a meal off the menu. Whereas most people look at restaurant menus and think about what they fancy and how nice some of the meals sound, I (along with many anorexia sufferers) looked in fear, analysing the ingredients of every meal and its calorific value, feeling I couldn't possibly eat anything. An intuitive and natural task for many is torture for a sufferer. But I wanted to be able to do it... so I did.

The first day of picking from the menu I was torn between choosing the 'safe' option – what I had calculated would be the lowest calorie and, therefore, least fearful meal – and a meal that my mum regularly made at home and which I used to enjoy: braising steak. I discussed it at length with my key nurse who encouraged me to go for the braising steak as it was my mum's cooking I wanted to be able to eat and this was a good step towards that. I decided to throw myself in at the deep end and go for it. With the rich tomato sauce and tender beef, the flavours were delicious. But this was a cardinal sin – to like the taste of food. And again, that familiar debilitating guilt encompassed my entire body. It was impossible to ignore. But I could not let it set me back and I *did* want to broaden my eating repertoire. After years of restriction, I was keen to try a range of foods. I wanted to be able to eat freely and join in with meals. So I had to put in the hard work now to get to that point. During the three meals a week I was picking off the menu I started trying a variety of 'fear' foods that I used to eat but hadn't for a long time, including roast chicken and roast potatoes, pasta, and scampi.

My mum had dinner with me a few times in the restaurant so I could get used to eating with her again and for her to get an idea of portion sizes. I had to be able to trust my mum that when she cooked for me she would serve up the correct sized half a portion. And she didn't want me hoodwinking her that I was meant to have smaller portions. I didn't want to be deceitful anymore. I wanted this to work and the more involved she was, the easier it would be for me.

I had my first overnight leave at the start of June 2011, eleven months since I had last slept in my own bed. My first dinner at home was my old favourite which I hadn't had since my eighteenth birthday: chicken chasseur. It tasted as good as I remembered. It was a nerve-wracking experience, not only eating different food but also allowing my mum to cook and portion it for me when for years I had taken sole responsibility for my food. Again, I was wracked with guilt, but I also felt a strange sense of achievement, like I had done something big. For me, this was a major step.

It pleased my mum as well. Not only that I was eating, but that I was eating her cooking. After years of fraught meal times, me scraping and picking at food, trying to get away with the bare minimum, I was now actually eating a meal she had prepared. That is not to say meal times were not still tense, they were, and she could see the anxiety in my face as I sat down to eat. But she was finally able to feed me. For years she had been helpless and unable to get me to eat anything. But now I was eating, and eating her cooking!

Dr Williams had suggested using a Community Treatment Order (CTO) when I was discharged. While initially unsure about this, I soon came to acknowledge that it would probably be beneficial to me. Previously, following discharges, I had wanted to lose weight, but now I was desperate to try and maintain my weight, keep myself out of hospital and get back into life. Left to myself I wouldn't be able to do this. I would need the CTO to stop me falling straight back into the clutches of severe anorexia. A CTO is basically like being sectioned when you are in hospital – you have to be sectioned to be put on one, but you are allowed to live out in the community. You have certain rules that you have to follow and if you break these you can be immediately sent back to hospital. The rules that have to be followed will be different for each person. For me, my rules outlined a weight that I could not go below – 43.5kg. If I did I could be immediately sent back to hospital. Without formalised limits to my weight, I knew that once I started losing I could get very low again. But the CTO would stop this. Unlike previous discharges, I knew that with any significant weight loss I would be admitted straight back to hospital and I desperately didn't want this.

I was discharged on CTO from The Priory on 1st July 2011, a year since being admitted to St George's, with a weight of 44.7kg. Dr Williams told me that given how ill I had been it was a miracle I had survived. Most other people would be dead. Now I was being given my chance at life. I was to go back to The Priory for day care three times a week for four weeks. This was hugely beneficial in helping me adapt and cope with the outside world after a year in hospital. I attended groups, I had trips out with staff and other more independent eating disorder patients. I also met with Dr Williams and my therapist and I was weighed and ate lunch and snack there.

However, my lengthy stay in hospital had shattered my confidence, esteem, social skills, and life skills and four weeks of follow-up at The Priory was not enough to make me ready to face the world alone without their support. As my local health trust could not provide any more funding, my parents paid for me to have several more weeks of day care while I adapted to normal living. Day care gave me something to do. Nothing was more dangerous to me than having endless days with no structure, no routine, and no activities; my mind would go into overdrive, anorexia would become stronger and the opportunities for exercise would build. This had happened before and we all recognised it would likely happen again, leading to weight loss feeling like my only purpose.

The Priory had become my safety blanket. I liked the staff

and some of them had become like friends in a world where I didn't have any. In The Priory I was surrounded by people all day every day. I never had my bedroom door shut as I liked hearing and seeing people all the time. But now I was back in my home, my parents were my only source of company and I often found myself completely alone. My mum still had to go out to work and my dad had to look after my grandparents several times a week. I was grateful to be at home with my parents, but having just the three of us did seem a lot quieter than what I was used to. I didn't know how to behave in the 'real world' and I continued to miss the one thing I had missed all my life: friends.

My first admission to hospital had been when I was nineteen and I was now nearly twenty-three. I had lost four years of life and, while everyone else my age was now adult and living adult lives and being independent, in my mind I was still a teenager. Getting a job and moving out was inconceivable to me as I was wholly dependent on my parents, as much so as if I was a small child. I felt like a freak of nature unable to fit in anywhere. It didn't help that I had no social skills and I had lost all confidence in my ability to interact with people. As much as I wanted friends, I didn't feel I was capable of having any as I struggled to hold a conversation. I had kept in touch with Allana and Sarah after they visited me a few times in The Priory, but I only saw them occasionally as they both had full-time jobs so were busy. Plus, Sarah now lived in Portsmouth so it wasn't easy to see her much.

That first summer I had out of hospital was like dipping my toes in the paddling pool. My parents were helping me establish some sort of daily routine. Meals and snacks were at set times and I would always eat with one or both of them present. I couldn't be left on my own to eat, I wasn't capable of it. I couldn't handle the responsibility and guilt of eating alone, and if my parents weren't there I knew I wouldn't pass any food into my mouth. I needed them present to keep me maintaining my weight, keep me out of hospital and ultimately, to keep me alive. The CTO was also a driving force behind my eating because I knew if I lost weight I would be immediately recalled to hospital. I was determined not to let this happen. It wasn't me choosing to eat, I was eating because I had to. My life had to stop being like a revolving door, going in and out of hospital.

Thankfully, with it being the summer, my mum had more time off work so she was around to keep me company. She made me feel safe from myself as I was scared of what I would do if left alone. It is strange to think someone can be scared of themselves, but I was. In fact, I was scared of anorexia, but at the time I just felt scared of myself. I didn't want to start exercising all the time, restricting food, being slave-driven by my mind. The CTO helped stop this, as did the support from my parents. It took a lot of effort from all parties to keep my eating regime, keep my exercise regime and keep me building a life. This time was different from the others because this time I really wanted it. I didn't want to be secretive and hide things and get away with things. I had to be honest and open to stop this happening. I had made the decision that I wanted to live life so I was determined to keep fighting for it. However, facing the real world and trying to build a life proved to be one of the hardest battles.

Chapter 33
New Struggles

I was trying to live in the real world while also managing anorexia. I had never tried to manage anorexia before, I had always given in to it. Battling my anorexic mind made life feel incredibly hard. When I was completely dedicated to being anorexic, life was simple. There was only one thing to think about: weight loss. Focusing on anorexia had helped me avoid thinking about and experiencing real life and the stresses that accompany this. But now I couldn't run away from it anymore. Life was passing me by and I had missed out on so much. I wanted to be involved in life again, while also trying to control my anorexia.

Managing mental illness is tiring and challenging, both for the sufferer and the people around. Living life actually terrified me. As much as I wanted to be a part of it, I was too scared to give it a go. Following my discharge from The Priory, I spent a lot of my time sitting in the armchair in my living room with my eyes shut. It was a habit I had got into in The Priory as a way to escape the world and my thoughts. It was my relief from life. I could sit there and not have to face the scariness and disappointment of normal life. Although I wasn't being manically driven to dangerously low weights, anorexia was still stopping me living.

One thing was clear in my mind: I wanted to complete my degree at Loughborough. My dream job was to work in a tearoom but it seemed impossible to get anywhere with this without any experience. And I wanted to finish my degree. I had started it and I did not want to leave it incomplete. I feared what my career prospects would be without a degree.

I decided to return to study at Loughborough on a part-time basis. This meant that one year of full-time academic study would take me two years to complete. As much as I would rather have done it quicker, I knew I wasn't capable of studying full-time while still managing anorexia. I was not able to live away from home so, by studying part-time, I was able to continue living with my parents while commuting to Loughborough for lectures.

I returned to Loughborough for my first lecture in October 2011, three months after being discharged. My lecture was at 9am on a Tuesday, so my mum and I had got up at 4.45am for me to have breakfast and set off for the two-and-a-half hour car journey to Loughborough. I was incredibly nervous returning to university and it felt very strange being back there. I had no idea where any of the buildings were and I felt like an ant lost in a huge forest.

At that first lecture, I could hear all the students talking about their summer holidays and where they were going that evening. They had their established groups of friends and all sat together. I sat on my own at the end of an aisle. I felt eyes burning on my back. I knew people would be looking at me; they wouldn't recognise me from their first year and would be wondering who I was. I didn't attempt to talk to anyone and no one spoke to me. It was a relief not to have to socially interact, but it also provided me with more evidence that I was a social reject and incapable of being liked or befriended.

It was sad being back there and seeing my old halls of residence, the athletics track and the fields we used to run round. It was a stark reminder of what had happened and what I had thrown away. My dream of becoming a professional athlete was gone and I had missed out on a full, proper university experience with friends. Anorexia had robbed me of this. Yes, I was glad to be at the point now where I was able to return to study and start to complete my degree, but it was very sad to be doing it in the circumstances I was; without friends, without engaging, without the full experience.

For my first term I only had to be there one day a week. My mum took me in the car as she had gone down to a four-day working week. We soon got used to the 4.45am start and the home study helped give my life some necessary and wanted structure and purpose. Once a fortnight I had an extra lesson which required me to travel up and down on the train, an experience I hated. Those days were very long, tiring and stressful, but there was no other option.

I threw myself into my studies, trying to get back into that mode of thinking after so long with nothing but weight, food and exercise to think about. After the first term, once I had got back into the swing of things, I would spend all day, every day studying. I would stand at a bedroom window with my books and laptop for sometimes over eight hours a day. I had to stand, it was the only way of keeping my anxiety under control. By standing, I could focus on my studies, rather than worrying about how long I was sitting down for.

I found the whole thing incredibly difficult. I hated studying and I was convinced I was going to fail; that the next exam or the next piece of coursework was going to be the one. The failure. During my first year back I really wanted to quit. I absolutely hated every part of it – the studying, the stress, the work, the commute, the loneliness. Being in hospital had provided an escape from life and, at a time when managing life and anorexia seemed too much, I'd been desperate to escape the living reality. Trying to complete a long-distance degree alongside trying to manage severe anorexia was a huge task. Trying to be anorexic is a full-time job in itself, let alone trying to complete a degree at the same time.

I always felt so incredibly tired, partly because I was taking Respiridone (an antipsychotic) three times a day which made me very sleep. So when I was trying to study at home, I would often have to lie down on my bed for an hour with my eyes shut, drifting off to sleep, drifting off to a place where I could escape reality. Because, although hospital would be a way to escape the real world, with the threat that the CTO could recall me with only a slight weight loss, I was determined to not let that happen.

Deep down I knew it wasn't the solution and I knew it wouldn't make me happy. And deep down I also was determined that I wanted to complete my degree and there was still, despite all the pain and sadness, a tiny flame of hope flickering that one day, if I kept fighting, things would get better. So I ploughed on, persevering with the course, year after year after year. And actually, the more I got into it, the less I hated it. Yes, I still didn't like it, but I got into the routine of it and I got used to it. Importantly, studying provided me with a purpose and a distraction from thinking about anorexia all of the time.

It also helped that at the start of my second year back, just over a year since being discharged, my mum retired from work. For the previous term I had lectures on a Thursday and Friday and the only way it was possible to do this was for my mum to drive me up to Loughborough on a Wednesday afternoon and drop me off at a small hotel where I stayed alone for two nights, before catching the train home on a Friday night. I absolutely, wholeheartedly hated it. It was so much easier once my mum started staying with me and I actually began to enjoy our little trips away. It was like a relief from the monotony of home. Plus, it meant I didn't have to eat alone like I had to in the previous term when I was staying on my own. I had really struggled with this, it being the first time I had to eat without my parents there. I would pack all my food with me but having gone from not being able to eat a morsel of food without my mum or dad sitting right with me, to now having to cope with eating alone for two days; it was so challenging and mentally draining. I did restrict very slightly, I couldn't stop myself. I couldn't cope with the guilt of eating everything when my mind was telling me I didn't have to. But it was only very small and not to the point that it had any effect on my weight. So, I was still, just about, managing the anorexia so that it didn't take over and make me seriously ill again.

But while the trips away had become less miserable once I started my second year back at university, my daily life was still a great struggle. I had been out of hospital for just over a year and had developed a strict routine for what I did at every point in the day, and I never allowed myself to deviate from that. My life had become a regimented routine and it was a tiresome chore, but I wasn't giving in to anorexia and the temptation to lose weight. As much as I loathed routine, I was too scared to break it for fear something bad would happen. My life was predictable, I knew exactly what I was doing and when, and this reduced the chance of anything bad happening (that bad thing being weight gain). Since being discharged from The Priory, I had a wardrobe full of new clothes. Lovely different coloured jeans, pretty jumpers, dainty skirts. But I couldn't wear any of it. I was scared that wearing something new would make something bad happen, that it would make me gain weight.

I was balancing on a fine edge and I was miserable and lonely. While I wasn't relapsing, I still felt controlled by anorexia's rules, with the addition of the studying to do. With my life narrowed to studying, walking and eating, meal times had become the highlight of my day; a time when I could stop studying. But I hated myself for looking forward to food when previously I had been terrified of it. I would beat myself up with scathing remarks: how could I possibly be anorexic and look forward to my meal times? I feared I was losing anorexia which I ultimately felt I needed in order to cope with life. But even though I enjoyed eating my meals, I still struggled greatly when my parents left me at the table alone, as they had now started to do. Every mouthful was a battle to eat – my mind telling me I should do the 'anorexic thing' and restrict, and having to fight this with reasoned arguments such as 'if I lose weight my meal plan will increase' and 'I can't lose weight because the CTO will send me straight back to hospital'.

My return to university, while providing me with focus, acted as a great source of stress. I felt like a freak with no one ever talking to me. I wasn't part of any conversations or groups. I wasn't even sat next to anyone in any of my lessons. In the time I was back at university I hadn't made a single friend. I didn't fit in and people looked at me strangely. With my studies and anorexia taking over the whole of my life, I also only ever saw Allana and Sarah a couple of times a year. That deep-seated loneliness I had felt ever since I started secondary school was still there, and still hurting. I worked hard not to let my weight fall as I wanted to stay out of hospital. But it was clear I wasn't really living much of life, just an existence dominated by anorexia. This existence was taking its toll on me and I often felt it was all too much to cope with.

12ᵗʰ September 2013,

I feel like I am wasting my life away. When I was in hospital, I was motivated to get better by all the things I wanted to do with life, but now that I'm out I don't do any of them. So I console myself with being anorexic and then the more anorexic I become, the less I am able and the less I want to do other stuff so it's like a vicious circle. I never see friends. When I'm not studying, I struggle to fit anything else in around walks, runs and meals — which again shows how anorexia is leading my life.

I'm dreading starting back for the new term at uni. I hate it so much. I hate having to do all of the work and study practically all of the time. And I hate being up there and worrying about gaining more weight and I hate having to be with all those people that hate me. I know the work is going to be really difficult and I'm not going to be able to do it and I'm just going to get really depressed again and wish I was back in hospital.

For the first few years after The Priory, I had been maintaining my weight at a BMI of 15. But by 2014, I was maintaining at the lower end outlined in my CTO at which I would need to be readmitted. I was really struggling with the stresses of university and my anorexia. Life after hospital hadn't turned out how I had hoped. It wasn't even close. My dreams of going out with friends, having fun, being happy; none of it happened. I was left with a dark, empty hole. For years anorexia had been my way to avoid living life. Life had terrified me, and I didn't want to have to face it. But in 2011 when I was in The Priory, I wanted to give it a go. I was full of hopes and dreams of what life could be if I was just brave enough to try. But there I was, three years into trying to live life and it had been nothing but struggle and disappointment.

I had become fixated on trying to keep my weight on exactly the same number. I was terrified of losing weight and finding myself falling back to anorexia, but also of gaining weight and what this might entail. When my nurse weighed me on her weekly visit, if it had changed by as little as 100 grams, we would make a change to my meal plan, be it ten or twenty calories added or removed. Whereas in The Priory, they strongly discouraged calorie counting, now it had crept back in and everything I ate, apart from my main evening meal, was counted to the exact calorie. My rigidity and inflexibility in order to keep my weight exactly the same only heightened my anxiety and fears of gaining weight.

My depression and anxieties were made worse by the fact that I had decided to start running again with my mum in 2012. While it had initially started out as a short run a couple of times a week for enjoyment, it soon became all-encompassing and I would spend every day worrying about it. I had to follow a strict routine in the morning before going out – everything at the exact time and in the exact order, even to the point where I stood in the exact same spot in the kitchen while having a ten-minute rest between finishing my breakfast and getting ready to go out.

If I didn't run the distance I was meant to in the set time (it was good if I ran further, but not if I ran less) then I would get really upset. I would spend the evening before a run obsessing and worrying about it, and I became obsessed with the weather because that would affect whether I could go out running and, if I did, it could affect how I ran. I was wearing my mum down as I would take my stress out on her. Really, it shouldn't have mattered whether I finished one metre less than I normally did, or if I wasn't able to complete three runs a week. But to me, this had become more important than anything and my life revolved around it and it only added to my worries. But I struggled on, fighting this battle to manage anorexia and live some sort of life.

Chapter 34
Two Parts to My Brain

In January 2015, still hovering at the bottom end of my weight band, I sat my last exam. My results came through in February: I got a First! I was overjoyed. But although I had slogged away at the degree for year after year, I still did not want a job in the sport science industry. My dream job was still to work in a café. I had spent a lot of time baking during the summer holidays and trying out different recipes from my collection of recipe books. I knew the first step was to try and get some experience in the catering industry. I applied for hundreds of jobs, handed out my CV and went to interview after interview. But I was never successful. From chains like McDonalds and KFC to independent tearooms and cafes; I tried them all and they all turned me down. I didn't have any experience so none of them would give me a job.

With the constant knock back from jobs, along with not having any studying to focus on and there now being a lack of routine to my life, it gave anorexia an opportunity to grow stronger and my obsession with food, weight, and exercise had become increasingly dominant. My anorexic mind was torturing me every waking minute. I would weigh myself every day and panic over any slight fluctuations, and I was fixated on what I was eating and what exercise I was doing. But thanks to the CTO and my parents, I was able to keep myself going without falling back completely into its clutches. All my food was still being strictly portioned and calorie-controlled except for one thing. Vegetables. I really enjoyed vegetables, so allowed myself to eat them freely and throughout my time back at Loughborough, the amount of vegetables I was eating with my dinner gradually increased. But this acted as one of my biggest sources of stress.

When it came to eating vegetables, I felt I lost all control and I hated myself for this. Without my studying there to distract me, I would often spend the whole day worrying about how many vegetables I was going to eat with my dinner. It was torturous and it drove me, and my mum, crazy. Every day I would stress to her about how worried I was and every evening after dinner, when I felt I had eaten too many vegetables and my mind was going stir-crazy with worry and guilt, I would go on at her about it, trying to relieve some of my stress and look for reassurance. My mind was a living hell and it was bringing my mum down too as she never got a break from it. She tried to be supportive, but I was beyond consoling. I was like a broken record on repeat, the same words, the same worries, the same horrendous feelings day after day after day.

Each day I would go to bed feeling so full up and so disgusted with myself. I wanted to rip my stomach out most evenings, so I would make a promise to myself that the next day, I would eat fewer vegetables. But when it came to it, I was never able to restrict my vegetable intake. I hated that I had lost that self-discipline and self-control. I would think back to how I was in St Ann's when I would refuse to eat a full portion because I could not cope with the feelings of extreme fullness and there I was now eating large portions. It disgusted me. 'How could I possibly have lost all my will power?' My mind would shout at me. 'I used to be so good at resisting food and now I just can't stop eating vegetables!' My mind was making me feel guilty for eating vegetables. When I thought about that, my hatred for anorexia grew. It felt so unfair that I was made to feel horrendous for eating vegetables. No one should feel guilty for eating anything. I hated anorexia. But at the same time, I still felt I needed anorexia.

In the past, anorexia had completely taken over my mind and body and I would behave exactly in accordance with what my mind was telling me. There was no other option, there were no other thoughts except those of anorexia. But I started to notice a difference in my head. Whereas before all my thoughts had been 'my thoughts' and there wasn't a separate anorexic element, now I was starting to recognise that actually, there was a difference between my real thoughts and my anorexic thoughts. My mind wasn't just one anymore; now it was divided into two and there was a constant battle between them. Anorexia had previously consumed my whole mind and I was not used to being able to identify when one of my thoughts was anorexic. I think when you are deep in the clutches of anorexia and it is all-encompassing (as had been the case for myself for many years) you don't hear it as a separate entity, I certainly didn't. But now my mind had become a site of conflicting thoughts and while I wanted to engage with life, I was still utterly terrified, and anorexia was still keeping a strong hold on me.

I felt like I was living on a roller coaster. There were times when I would feel positivity and hope, that things could change and life could get better. 'Recovery' and 'getting better' had never previously been ideas in my mind and it was very unfamiliar for me to have these small parts of my mind contradicting anorexia. But when I felt these glimmers of hope, I was almost instantly dragged down with overwhelming feelings of guilt for even contemplating a life without anorexia, a life where I might get better. I was tired of my anorexic thoughts and I hated them for how they had ruined and continued to ruin so much of my life. I didn't want to worry about my weight and my size and exercise every moment of the day, having to do things exactly how and when anorexia wanted, having to worry about how many peas I was going to end up eating.

By March 2015, I was a kilo heavier than I had been in December and was over the top of my weight band. I was convinced it was the vegetables that had made me gain weight and I hated them. I was in complete despair and the conflict in my mind was heightened; one half of my mind telling me to restrict, the other half knowing restricting was wrong and would not get me the life I wanted. My whole mind and body existed in a state of confliction. Sometimes I would think I wanted to get better and have a life, and other times I wished to be 'properly anorexic' again, where I was thin and dedicated everything to losing weight.

February 20th 2015,

Being anorexic is all I've got. For every bit of me that wants to get better and have a life, there is a strong pull backwards. If I listen to the good things, I feel guilty for contemplating a life without anorexia, but if I do the wrong things (the anorexic things), it's not going to help me live the life I want (except being thin and being thin is sometimes all I want). But there's got to be more to life than being thin?

I truly believe that for me to be able to reach the position where I am able to think I will put on weight, I need to be happy (at least partly happy anyway). And I think I would be happier if I had a job. But no one gives me an opportunity. So I think what's the point in trying anymore? Nothing's going to change. I might as well stay as I am... if I can't have anything else in life, at least I can be thin. It's all I've got to console myself with. But then there's the tiny bit of me that's clinging onto some hope that maybe life can get better than this. It would be the easy option to give up trying and just stay as I am. But that is all I want to do right now.

Losing weight gives me a purpose and makes me feel worthy. But I do nothing to try and lose weight anymore. And I hate myself for it. Maybe it's the part of me that wants a life that is preventing the weight loss? I wish I could stop feeling one thing one second and another thing the next. It's a constant battle and all I feel is guilt.

I just spent the whole of my lunch thinking I should be hiding my bread in my pocket and hating myself for not doing so. There has got to be more to life than this. Constant misery. Not able to eat a meal without someone watching over me all the time. I don't want that from life. But my weight means so much to me. Is there a better life out there worth fighting for? Worth giving anorexia up for? This is not what I want from life. But in the same breath I don't want to gain any weight.

I had a trial in a pub kitchen on 7th March 2015 as a pot washer. It was not a good experience, I was not familiar with professional kitchens, the staff were not particularly helpful and I hated every minute of the six-hour trial. I had such high hopes for getting a job, that it would change everything, that it would be the start of my life. I thought it would make me happy and from then on things would improve. But I came home from the trial in floods of tears, physically and mentally drained and wanting to completely give up on life.

Saturday 7ᵗʰ March 2015,

If I'm going to be faced with that as my life then I'd rather be dead. If there's one way to guarantee me not getting better and to stay anorexic and lose weight, then it is to have a job like that as my life. I'm destined to be miserable. My life is going to be absolutely shit. I'm never going to achieve anything I want to. What's the point in anything? I might as well just focus on being anorexic. At least I can do that. A day like today is just making me suicidal. I went in with really high hopes. Why does life have to be so difficult? I hate it. I just want to curl up in a ball and never step outside again. I don't know what to do with my life. Everything seems pointless. I might as well try and get as thin as possible and go back into hospital. At least I won't have to live life then. Everything is a battle. I'm tired. I'm tired of living.

Being in hospital is an escape from life. In hospital there are no expectations, you don't have any decisions or worries (except weight gain) and everyone cares about you. Just that feeling of being thin. I crave it.

The work trial had shot me and my hopes to pieces. I was convinced that I was not going to be able to escape my anorexic prison cell and that my life was destined to be awful. The trial had been so physically and mentally demanding that, for the next few days, I was too tired to do anything. I felt completely wiped out. I was depressed, numb and helpless, with no vision for a future. 'Should I take the job?' I started to wonder. 'I hated it, but jobs aren't there to be enjoyed and everybody has to do things they don't like. I should be a bit tougher. Work is hard and I'll have to get used to it.'

I had become very good at making myself do things I didn't like (living by anorexia's rules being a fine example) so maybe this job had to be another of those situations. In some twisted way, punishing myself made me feel good. It is as if I only get a sense of self-worth if I push my body to the extreme. That is what anorexia used to give me; a feeling of worth. Knowing I had pushed my body to the absolute limit felt good. But I couldn't do that anymore, I couldn't starve myself beyond what most people could even begin to comprehend, and I couldn't exercise to the point of collapse. So, I had to get my self-worth from something else.

When I had been studying for my degree, I did get a feeling of self-worth from that. Making myself study for over eight hours a day, slogging away doing something I didn't enjoy. That had made me feel worthy. Like I had a purpose and was pushing my body. Albeit not to the extremes that anorexia pushed me, but I was pushing, more so mentally than physically. But it was a push and it felt good. But then, without feelings of self-esteem coming from anorexia or studying, I was left feeling completely worthless. I couldn't feel good about myself because my body wasn't being pushed and this just compounded my depression and negativity.

So, I thought that maybe taking that awful job would give me the hard work and punishment I needed to feel good? I didn't want to do the job in any way, shape or form, but I did start to think that I should force myself, like I had forced myself to do all the other things.

I had a conversation with my sister over the phone about how the trial had gone and what I was currently thinking.

"I hated it, Nico," I explained, "it was awful. But I think I should take it because lots of people don't like their jobs and you just have to make yourself."

"Life is short. Very short. Do you really want to waste it doing a job you hate?" my sister replied.

This made me think. Actually, no. I didn't want to waste my life doing that job, and importantly, I didn't want to continue wasting my life with anorexia.

Tuesday 10ᵗʰ March 2015,

I have to remind myself of the reality of anorexia. When I am actually living it at its worst, it is not fun at all. It's torture. It's exhausting and you never feel satisfied, never feel you've done enough. And importantly, it's not fair on Ma and Pa. The love, time and care they have given me… I shouldn't put them through all that again. It's up to me if I waste MY life but I can't keep wasting theirs. And I don't want to waste my life anymore either. But I guess the only way for it to improve is to keep fighting, to not let me slip back to anorexia. I must keep fighting.

Not long after the awful trial in the pub kitchen, I had a three-hour work trial in The Lordship Tearoom (a branch of tearoom in the 'Tiptree Jam' company) in a nearby village. I was so nervous, and I had absolutely no expectations that it was going to be any good, not after the last trial I had done. But I absolutely loved it. From the moment I walked in and was asked to chop mushrooms, I knew this was the place I wanted to be.

A few days later, the manager rang me and offered me the job on a six-week trial basis. I couldn't believe it. I was so happy! I had finally got the job I had wanted for so long. Someone was finally giving me that opportunity I had been so desperate for. I had thought getting a job would be the start of my life. But now I was about to enter into this six-week trial period of complete unknown, I started to panic. I had pinned all my hopes and expectations on how life would get better once I had a job, but now I was starting to worry this may not come true. What would happen to me then? I had so strongly believed that having a job would make me happy, but then I started to have doubts. I use negative thinking as a form of protection. It is a maladaptive coping strategy: if I think negatively and don't have hope or expectation, then I avoid disappointment. If I always expect the worst to happen, then I will be prepared and avoid upset from shattered dreams. It is not a productive way to think but, at the time, I was trying to stop getting my hopes up to avoid any disappointment.

When I got the job, I became convinced that I was not going to be good enough and, come the end of my six-week trial, they would let me go. Alongside my worries about my ability and that the job wouldn't be the life-changer I had hoped for, I was also scared of it being exactly that. Scared that it would help me lose a bit of anorexia. That thought was terrifying, having felt dependent on and unable to live without its strong presence for so long. I knew anorexia wasn't making me happy and that I shouldn't want to hold on to it, but I still couldn't let it go. And having the job meant I would have to let go just a little bit. This was a terrifying prospect.

Monday 23rd March 2015 was my first day in the kitchen. It was the start of a new chapter. I was finally going to start making anorexia smaller and take a step towards life.

Chapter 35
My First Job

I started my job as a kitchen assistant, chopping vegetables, making scones, making lunch orders on the 'cold-side' (sandwiches, salads, ploughman's etc) and doing the dishwasher. I loved it. I loved going to work and having something to do, I loved being involved with food and I loved having company. The days were long and physically demanding. I would start at 8.30am and not finish until 5.30pm, with only a twenty-minute lunch break (and you were lucky to get that!). The kitchen had to be cleaned thoroughly at the end of every shift with the floors swept and mopped. It was hard work, but there wasn't an element to it that I didn't like. The only negative to the job was that there was a lot of pressure and I would worry beforehand about the days being really busy and me being unable to cope with the demand. However, by the end of my six-week trial, I had found my feet, was up to speed in the kitchen and was offered the job.

Because of the demands of the job, I didn't eat while I was there. I would have a banana and a glass of milk in the morning at 7.30am before I set off, and the next time I would eat would be my dinner at 7pm. I knew not eating lunch was not a good habit to have gotten into but I had to find a method that worked for me and enabled me to go out to work and do the job I wanted, and so bring more into my life and slightly reduce anorexia. I did not feel comfortable eating at work and with often not having a break planning lunch was impossible. So, instead, I added the calories that I would have consumed at lunchtime onto my evening snack so that I wasn't restricting.

After starting my job, I found I was eating more vegetables than ever with my dinner. I felt even more out of control with them than I had done previously. My mum and my nurse both explained to me that because I was now very active at work and wasn't eating lunch, I was starting my dinner in a state of starvation and vegetables, being the only food I allowed myself to eat without precisely quantifying them, were the only food I could increase in order to satisfy my hunger and energy demands.

The best thing about starting work was that, for the whole day I was there, I would not give anorexia, or any element of it the slightest thought. This was a whole new world to me. I never imagined it would be possible to have eight or nine hours a day when anorexia and all my worries about weight, exercise and food, which had previously occupied my every waking moment, would not even feature for a brief minute. It was amazing. But as soon as I got in my car to head home, my worries would start and anorexia would come at me full pelt. Worrying how many vegetables I was going to eat and how much weight I was possibly gaining. And I always had to go out for my daily power walk after having worked a nine-hour shift on my feet. But the time I was at work and not thinking about anorexia was incredible and opened me up to a whole new world.

Although I enjoyed being able to go to work and not give anorexia any thought, when I had a day off I would then worry excessively that I had not been thinking about anorexia. I had gone from doing nothing all day every day (except power walking for fifty minutes) to working full-time, five days a week. Despite the excessive worry on my days off, it didn't change the fact that it felt so nice to have the time at work when I wasn't worrying and thinking about anorexia.

Alongside the positive of the job allowing me time without anorexia was the social interaction. Apart from seeing Allana, Sarah, and Jenny a couple of times a year, I never saw anyone. I had lost touch with all my friends through the years spent in hospital and dedicated to anorexia. Even when I returned to

Loughborough I had never spoken to anybody. So I was incredibly lonely and fairly socially inept. I found it difficult at first going to work and trying to interact with the other staff, all of whom were absolutely lovely. I was very quiet to start with but as the weeks passed by and I became a regular fixture in the kitchen I started to talk more, my confidence in my ability to hold a conversation growing. Sometimes, with particular members of staff that I got on really well with, we could spend virtually the whole day in the kitchen chatting away while we worked.

At the start of July 2015 when I had been working at the tearoom for three months, a girl who worked in the kitchen with me, and one of the weekend waitresses, Megan, both had birthday parties on the same night. And I was invited to both! This was the first time in so long that I had actually been invited to something. But me being typical me, scared of social events and anything that changed my normal routine, I was reluctant to go. I thought I would be better off going home from work, putting my pyjamas on, having my dinner and evening snack and watching TV. That was what I knew, that was my routine and that was safe. But that wasn't going to get me what I desperately wanted: friends. I had longed for years to have friends, to go out, go to parties, and here I was, being given that opportunity and I was too scared to go.

But deep down I knew that if I did want to have friends, if I did want to build myself some sort of life, I had to make the effort and I had to put myself out there and make myself do things. So, with strong encouragement from my mum, I went to the two parties, spending about an hour at each. I arrived home about 9.30pm and that was the latest I had been out since I was a fresher at university. I felt jubilant. I wasn't at the parties for long and I didn't talk much while I was there, but I went. And that was a major step forward in my life. A big bit of progress. I was still a long way from where I wanted to be, but I had started to unlock the door and open the entrance to life where previously I had been locked away in my anorexic prison cell.

A month after the two parties, I went out for my first meal in a restaurant for over seven years; the first time since becoming severely anorexic. It was incredibly daunting. A big group of us from work went for the manager's leaving do. We went to Prezzo and I had looked up the menu and calories online to find something that I was able to have. I know a lot of people, including many anorexia sufferers, are actively against calories being shown on menus, suggesting it encourages eating disorders and makes it more difficult for sufferers to be able to eat out. But for me personally, I felt the opposite. I knew how many calories I needed and with restaurants displaying the nutritional information of their meals, it allowed me to select a meal that I could fit into my calorie allowance. I know you are probably thinking that this isn't a very healthy approach, counting calories and picking meals based on this, but with my anorexia in the stage that it was, it was the only way for me to be able to eat a meal out.

I had decided, after much deliberation, to go with the 'Pollo E Spinaci'. A chicken salad with spinach, avocado, and croutons. I sat near the end of the table next to one of my favourite waitresses, Mel. As the meal came out and was placed in front of me, a wave of panic flushed over.

'How on Earth can I make myself eat this?' I thought.

But as I looked around and saw everyone else tucking into their meals – pastas, pizzas, salads – and not giving it a second thought, I told myself 'I want to be a part of this and I want to join in. Just get on and eat it.'

So that is what I did. I picked up my knife and fork and started to eat like everyone else was doing. I was even able to talk while doing so. My head was in overdrive, thinking constantly about what I should I leave on my plate in order to get rid of some calories. My anorexic brain was screaming at me to leave a bit of chicken, leave a bit of bread, avoid the avocado. But stronger than that was my desire to join in, to be out socialising with friends and enjoying myself. That was the most important. That was what I wanted more than anything. I fought the anorexic cries in my head and finished my meal. And truth be told, I did actually feel quite proud of myself. I had achieved something I had wanted for so long.

It was that evening as we sat round the table chatting, that I told them about my anorexia and my past. They had already guessed but this was the first time I had spoken about it. They were so supportive and encouraging, appreciating what a major achievement eating out had been. Mel went on to say how happy tonight must be making my mum, for her to know that her daughter who has been through so much over the years, is out with friends, eating a meal and enjoying herself. This comment made me feel happier than ever. And I so hoped it was true. Now I was finally fighting anorexia and I wanted my mum to be proud of me.

Chapter 36
Weight Gain and Parties

Summer and autumn of 2015, I really found my feet at work and settled in. I loved cooking and had established myself as a fellow 'cook' in the tearoom. I was able to do all aspects of the cooking, ordering, and daily running of the kitchen. It also felt really nice that I had started to become friends with some of the other cooks. But despite all this progress I was making, every evening at home I was still plagued with worries about my weight. My weight was maintaining near the middle of my band and I did not want to gain any more.

Monday 6th July 2015,
I'm worrying about how much veg I will eat. And my nurse wants me to gain a bit of weight to go back nearer the top of my band but now I'm lower I want to stay here and I really don't want to go up. How can I, in one breath, want to have a life not controlled by food, weight, and exercise, yet in the next breath be so determined not to gain any weight and to keep my weight as low as I can? I really annoy myself. How can I want complete polar opposites? But I know I don't want to be worrying all the time and that is all a life with anorexia will end up being. But my fear of gaining weight outweighs and overtakes everything. Nothing is simple. Surely I can't live the rest of my life like this?

By November 2015, eight months after starting work, I was over the top of my band and had gone into the dreaded next kilo up. I had hit 46kg. The day this happened I was utterly devastated. I cried uncontrollably while I ate my breakfast before my nurse arrived. My parents were unable to console me. When my nurse weighed me it confirmed my worst fears. I was hysterical. I could not believe I had gained that weight, that I was more than half a kilo above the top of my band and that I had allowed it to happen. I felt I had shown such disgusting lack of self-restraint when eating vegetables. I wanted to curl into a ball and sleep, to avoid this hell of a life and avoid this torture. But I had to go to work.

As soon as I walked into the kitchen, Mel could see I was upset, and I burst into tears again.

"I've gained half a kilo," I cried when she asked me what was wrong.

"I don't understand kilos," she replied. "What's that in pounds?"

"It's about one pound," I managed to say.

"A pound?" she questioned. "Rebecca, a pound is nothing. To most people it's insignificant."

"To me it's loads, Mel. I haven't been this heavy in years." I started crying more as the realisation that this was the heaviest I had been since 2009, six years ago, hit me.

Mel looked at me with complete sadness. "What a horrible, horrible illness. To make you feel like this, to see you in such distress after gaining a pound. It's awful." She gave me a hug and tried to reassure me, "I can honestly say you don't look any different. You certainly don't look any bigger."

I forced a small smile amidst the tears. I tried to compose myself to start work, putting my apron on and tying it round what felt like the biggest stomach in the world. "Sorry for causing a fuss."

"Don't be silly," Mel replied, "you certainly weren't making a fuss. We're all worried about you and we care for you. And to us, you gaining a bit of weight can only be viewed as a good thing."

I got on with my day at work, barely speaking a word to anyone, too upset to hold a normal conversation. It must have been difficult for the people working with me. Anorexia is a difficult illness to understand, particularly for people that know

215

nothing about it and have no experience of dealing with it. Even I don't understand it and I have lived with it for years. It must have been hard for them to know what best to say when I was in that state, how best to approach the day with someone who is so terribly upset but can't be consoled by logical reasoning.

Weight gain is one of the worst fears for someone with anorexia. Previously, I had only ever dealt with it in hospital when it was forced upon me and when I would agonise all day about it. In hospital I was able to talk to staff and seek their help and reassurance. Now I had to deal with it in the real world and get on with real-life things like going to work. Anorexia has a tendency to freeze you in time. You focus all your efforts and thoughts on it, making your weight your number one priority, and while you are doing this normal life is passing you by. But now I was living in the real world, I couldn't focus everything on weight and anorexia. I couldn't dwell on it for hour after hour, crying in my bedroom over any weight gain. No, this was not an option. I had to get on with life. The world doesn't stop (as it used to in my little anorexic world) with a bit of weight gain. Jobs still have to be done. We couldn't shut the tearoom because I'd gained half a kilo. Everything carries on and so I had to, as difficult as it was. I made it to the end of the day, collapsing on my bed in a crying mess when I got home.

We had our staff Christmas party booked for the 4th December 2015 and in the week beforehand, four weeks after originally going over the top of my band and into the 46kgs, I was still above my band limit. I decided I couldn't face going to the party, not with being so heavy and having to eat a meal in front of everyone. I told Mel I wasn't going to go.

"Is that because of your weight?" Mel asked.

"Yes, I just can't face it. I don't want to go out or do anything. Not being this big."

"Rebecca," Mel sighed, "you're young and you have missed out on so much. Now you have an opportunity to go out, spend an evening with friends who also want to spend time with you. Isn't that what you want?"

"But I can't face eating," I said. "Not in front of everyone. Not when I'm this big and need to lose weight."

"Could you come to the party after everyone has eaten?" One of the cooks suggested trying to be helpful.

"That's not going to help the issue," Mel replied. "You don't want to be stuck in the house every evening for the rest of your life watching *Casualty*, with no friends and nothing to live for. This is the first time you have had an opportunity like this, to come to a Christmas party and be with friends. You have come so far. A year ago you never imagined you would be where you are now. You don't want to waste any more of your life. I know I'm being harsh but sometimes you need tough love."

I knew she was right, and I thanked her for encouraging me to come. Deep down I did want to go; it was anorexia telling me I shouldn't and that I had to wallow in misery to satisfy it. What Mel said was true. I didn't want to be alone, never going out for the rest of my life. I had to make the effort and take opportunities when they arose. So, I went to the Christmas party. And it was bloody brilliant. My mum bought me a new dress from *New Look* – a shimmery ivory-coloured dress with pink flowers. I planned with my mum beforehand what I was going to eat and drink to make it roughly the right amount of calories.

However, I also devised my own plan of what I could restrict while at the party to try and have less calories, lose weight, and get back into my band. So there I was – while everyone else was planning to have a good time, a dance and a drink – planning how I could reduce calories and lose weight. However, when the food came out, although I had been nervous about going beforehand and was worried what the food would be like and how I would deal with it, I made a decision. I would not carry out my secretive plan of leaving food and I would eat everything I had agreed with my mum. I wanted to join in and eat normally like everyone else. I wanted to enjoy myself and I didn't want to sit there thinking about how I can leave this and avoid that. Once I had made that decision, I got on and ate, talking and laughing, embracing the moment of my first ever Christmas party. I even had half a glass of white wine (which my mum and I had planned) and everyone gave me a 'cheers' as I drank it.

After the meal was music and dancing which I took part in and loved every minute. It felt incredible to be out doing that sort of thing after so many long, hard years locked up with anorexia. The party finished at midnight and I even went on to a nightclub in town with Mel and a couple of others until the early hours of the morning. I got into bed at 3am on Cloud Nine. I couldn't have wished for a better evening. And an evening like that was worth being a bit bigger for.

Tuesday 8th December 2015,

I'm still over my band. When it first happened, it felt horrendous and I cried, and I got to work and burst into tears again. And now, four weeks later, I still haven't got back into my band. In the past I would have really restricted what I was eating to make sure I lost weight, but I haven't this time, which makes me feel guilty. But the longer I have been out of my band, the less it has bothered me. Obviously I hate being this heavy, but I am starting to wonder whether I could tolerate staying here? But then it's dreadful for me to be thinking like that. I should be trying to be anorexic. But being anorexic is not going to get me anywhere.

My nurse suggested that I try and tolerate being this weight and I feel so guilty for even considering it. I don't want people to think I am less anorexic. I cling on to it because it's all I've got that makes me different. But I know if I had gone out of my band like this a year ago, there's no way I would have been as ok about it as I am now. It's not that I don't want to lose weight, because I do and I definitely don't think I could tolerate more than this, but life hasn't been too bad being out of my band. I have still managed to enjoy things. I really enjoyed the Christmas party even being out of my band. But then my head tells me I shouldn't have enjoyed it. But I think because I've got a lot more in my life now, weight has become less important. I still worry very much about gaining weight but 80% of my day is spent NOT thinking about it which is a huge difference from before when I was thinking about it 99% of the time.

Not only was I thinking about weight, food, and anorexia less, but I was enjoying not thinking about it and no longer feeling guilty for it. No longer did I spend my days off worrying about not having given anorexia any thought while at work. I was enjoying things and I wanted to enjoy more. But then I would tell myself I should lose weight to get back into my band. The contradictions were all still there. But the worrying was less, and the guilt was less. And this could only be a good thing.

Another good thing, which was also helping me reduce my worries and anxieties, was that I had stopped weighing myself every day as I had been doing before I started working. Within a few months of starting work, I was weighing myself only once a week, on the day my nurse visited. Reducing the frequency I was weighing myself greatly helped alleviate my obsession and anxiety. Because I wasn't weighing myself regularly, most of the time I would simply get on with my day, without getting obsessed and worried if I had gained 0.1 or whatever of a kilo. It seemed pointless weighing myself all of the time. It would only depress me because how I felt was dictated by what the scales said, and this was no way to live. I still majorly stressed about it the evening before and the day of the weigh-ins but, on the other days I could plod on just about alright.

With weight gain still being a big fear in my life that I didn't feel ready to tackle, I started to consider change in other areas. I began seeing a psychologist in the middle of February 2016 to whom my nurse had referred me on the NHS.

Previously I always thought, 'I'm scared to change, I don't want to change, so I'm going to stay anorexic.' But now I was thinking, 'I'm scared to change and I don't want to change… but I don't want to think like that. I don't want that to be my thought process.'

I had always previously gone along with my thought process of 'I'm too scared so I'm going to stay anorexic'. But now, although still too scared, I wanted the psychologist to help me think, 'I *do want* to change'. And that was a huge step forward. Yes, I was too scared to change, but this wasn't good enough for me anymore. I wanted to want to change. This was a completely new feeling.

Chapter 37
Making Progress

Despite all the positives and progress I had been making, after a year of being at work I started to dislike my job and was feeling distant from the kitchen workers I had formed friendships with. Also, when I started my job, I lost touch with Allana and Sarah and didn't see or speak to them anymore. That painful feeling of loneliness was as strong as ever. But rather than accept that I was destined to be lonely and without friends, in February 2016 I plucked up the courage to ask two of the weekend waitresses from work who I really liked if they wanted to go out for dinner and to the cinema. To my amazement they said yes. I didn't know them particularly well, only having contact with them at work on weekends when it was very busy with not much opportunity for chatting. But they had always been nice to me, friendly and welcoming, and I had been to Megan's birthday party the previous year. I really liked them and wanted to build a friendship with them. I never imagined they would agree to actually go out with me – the freak, social reject, loser me. But they did and I had a brilliant time.

We went to Prezzo for dinner and, as before, I planned what I was going to eat beforehand – spaghetti with king prawns and a side salad. A new meal in a completely new situation. It was very daunting but I wanted to do it. I ate every last strand of spaghetti, chatting away while doing so; enjoying myself *and* enjoying the meal. It did sometimes pop into my head that I should leave some of the food, but I was able to override that thought. I told myself if I wanted these girls to like me, to want to do more things with me, I could not let anorexia feature. I had a brilliant evening but negativity still had its way of getting into my mind. Yes, I liked them and I had a really nice time, but I couldn't see us ever becoming proper friends. Not like how I imagined having proper friends was like: doing things together all the time, going round each other's houses, doing everything and anything together.

My mum tried to tell me that my version of 'best friend', where we spend all our time together, is not what happens in adult life. Adults are busy and they don't go round each other's houses and hang out together all the time. It is difficult making plans and you don't necessarily get to see each other that often. But you can still be good friends. My idea of a 'best friend' was still that of a teenager. But it is not like that in reality as an adult. When I was a teenager, I had been taken away from my life and my friends by anorexia and then thrown back into reality years later in my mid-twenties. I missed the transition from adolescence to adulthood; I still had the mind of a teenager. I expected things to be as they had been when I was last in reality. Time had moved on and I hadn't. But I had to accept this and try to approach life with an adult mindset, even though I felt like a young teenager.

My weight had been above my band and in the 46kgs for a few months and I had resigned myself to the fact that I was going to have to be this higher weight. I hated myself for doing so, but I had much more going on in my life now. I had a job which I wanted to progress in, I had started making friendships with Megan and Saffron who I wanted to do more things with; maybe, just maybe, weight was becoming less important? But if I even so much as entertained that idea, the anorexic voice in my mind would beat me down and bully me into remembering that weight is *the* most important thing and I must not let myself lose my grip on it.

But anorexia was becoming gradually smaller and quieter. I was now able to eat my food without having a battle in my head as to whether to eat it or not or whether I should be hiding food.

Now I got on and ate everything without thinking about it. The anorexic thoughts about trying to hide food, which had previously been all-encompassing when left to eat on my own, weren't there anymore. However, anorexia made me feel guilty for this and my mind would shout at me things like 'I shouldn't sit and eat everything without thinking that I should hide it,' and, 'I should not eat mindlessly.' Every time I made a step forward, I was riddled with guilt for doing so, terrified that I was losing anorexia. It still had the ability to convince me I could not cope without it.

At the time, any sign of enjoyment was portrayed by anorexia as a betrayal. I am pleased to say this is not the case anymore. Anorexia is still there, but it is so much quieter and in the background. I can now go out and enjoy myself and do normal things without worry or guilt. I don't let anorexia stop me anymore. Recovery is a long, hard journey but it is so worth it. I am freer now than I have ever been and, yes, there is still a way to go, but I am a million miles from where I was and life has got so much better now anorexia is smaller.

But back in 2016, it was the first time I found myself enjoying things since being a young teenager. This feeling of enjoyment felt incredibly strange, but it felt good. And I wanted to feel it more. I felt it very strongly when my parents and I went on holiday to Marbella with my sister and her partner at the end of March 2016. Every summer since I was discharged in 2011, we had go on holiday to Spain as my sister lived there with her partner, Gonzalo, who I love like a brother.

But they weren't like most people's holidays. I would sit on my sun lounger in the late afternoon and 'people watch'. Germans, Spaniards, Brits. Families with children, couples young and old, groups of friends – there was a complete mix of people. But they all had one thing in common. They were all enjoying themselves. Whether they were playing in the pool, reading a book on a sunbed or taking a stroll on the beach, they all had smiles on their faces, were having fun, and simply looked happy.

But that never happened for me. Yes, technically I was 'on holiday'. I had gone to another country, I was staying in a hotel with a pool and near the beach. But it didn't matter where you took me or what environment you put me in, there is one fact I couldn't escape from. You don't get a holiday from anorexia. Anorexia succeeded every year in destroying a lot of the enjoyment that should come with being on holiday. Anorexia hung over me like a black cloud. I would constantly worry about the food and I was obsessed about getting my walking and swimming done. And I hated anorexia for this.

Not only did it always ruin my holidays, but it affected the rest of my family who had to deal with my stresses and bad moods. For example, the holiday of 2013, we had an early flight out to Spain, setting off from our house at 3.30am. Anorexia made me do something most people wouldn't think of in their wildest dreams. Because of the anxiety anorexia causes, it made me go out, at 3am, to do part of my daily walk as the worry of having to do it all once I arrived was too great. So there I was, walking round the streets at 3am. That isn't how life should be. My exhausted body was doing what my warped mind told it to.

Similarly, on holiday at breakfast, there was always an array of lovely-looking food to choose from. An abundance of different varieties of breads, rolls, and cakes; dozens of different types of cereals, traditional Spanish churros and pancakes. It all looked and smelt wonderful. Every morning for breakfast do you know what I had? A miserable bowl of cornflakes with milk. That was all my head would allow me, the only thing I could cope with. As much as I longed to be able to try the different foods, the fear and anxiety it would cause was too much. Even the thought of it made me panic. Looking at the different foods and imagining myself eating them seemed equivalent to looking at Mount Everest and imagining reaching the top. An impossible task.

But that holiday in Marbella in March 2016 was different and provided evidence of the progress I had made. I was still worried about food and exercise, but nowhere near to the same extent as the previous holidays. I made a decision beforehand with my mum that I wasn't going to do any swimming while I was there. Previously, I'd had to swim religiously on my summer holiday so this decision eased a lot of stress. Without that hanging over me, it made it much easier to relax, join in, and enjoy myself.

Being in March, it wasn't a beach holiday and we went out

and about visiting different places and looking round. I really enjoyed that – going out together as a family and being able to spend more time with them. Normally on our summer holiday, I spent most of the time by myself either exercising or lying on the beach worrying about not exercising. But going sightseeing, keeping busy, spending time with my family, I didn't have the same intense worries. I didn't want to have to worry about it. For the first time, I wanted to not care and simply enjoy myself. I went out for walks with my mum instead of getting up at crack of dawn to go out on my own. I ate what I was meant to and I was able to actually enjoy the holiday. Every summer holiday since then has been so much better. I no longer obsess about exercise, I feel much more at ease with the food and the whole holiday itself. I have definitely made a lot of progress!

I had always thought I could have exactly the life I wanted and stay at BMI 15. I thought it was not inhibitive and I could do everything I wanted to do being that size. But doubts about that theory had started to creep in. My life continued to feel so restricted and so dictated to by anorexic rules that I was beginning to wonder if life could possibly be better if I was a bit bigger and a bit freer from anorexia.

I had been out of hospital for five years and while I had made a lot of progress in that time, I was still far from living the life I had imagined and hoped for following discharge. That wasn't all down to anorexia, but up to that point I hadn't even given anorexia any part of the blame. I had always insisted that anorexia was not limiting my life, that my life was shit anyway and anorexia helped me cope with it. But now I was starting to wonder whether anorexia was in part responsible and was in fact making my life more difficult and inhibiting me achieving my dreams. This way of thinking was another progression in my mind and it was like wobbling a loose tooth. If I kept wobbling away at it, it would get weaker and weaker. So, I told myself to keep wobbling away at this anorexic loose tooth because it felt like I was getting stronger and the tooth was getting weaker.

Chapter 39
Blogging

There was a lot of progress being made with my thinking. I was realising that if I allowed my life to plod on and didn't try to make changes, then my life would stay exactly the same. Anorexia would continue to dominate and cause me stress and anxiety, lack of freedom, spontaneity and friends. And ultimately I would stay miserable. Because, although I had slightly more things in my life now, I still felt incredibly sad, lonely, and depressed.

I recognised that I was all-or-nothing, black-or-white, with my thinking. I believed that unless I was really happy and everything in my life was perfect, then everything was dreadful and I was utterly miserable. I needed to start recognising that, although my life wasn't perfect at the moment, it was a lot better than a year ago before I had started making any changes. Not only was I able to do more now than I had done previously, such as going out for dinner or out to show, but I was now able to actually enjoy doing it.

My weight increased into the 47kgs and, although I hated being 47 kilos, I coped a lot better than I had done when my weight was creeping up in the 46 kilos. I had got a taste of how life could get better and I wanted more of it. I knew that if other areas in my life were to grow then anorexia needed to shrink. I was determined that I would not go back to my old anorexic habits and lose weight. I was going to stick with my heavier weight and continue with life. This had previously been unimaginable and unthinkable, but I was now going to do it. It wasn't easy and seeing higher numbers on the scales was very difficult to cope with. I wanted to try and tolerate being this slightly higher weight, but I did find that my mental state was struggling to catch up.

At the start of June 2016, I began writing a blog to give myself a focus and work towards achieving the things I wanted. I also hoped it would help others. Other eating disorder blogs all seemed so positive and pro-recovery, which was fine, but not something I could identify with. As much as part of me wanted to recover, I still wanted to hold on to anorexia, which made the idea of recovery even more difficult. I think this is an important point to highlight about recovery. Many anorexia sufferers have portrayed an image that when you are attempting recovery you do it with 100% commitment and that it is what you wholeheartedly want. But, for me, recovery hasn't been like that. I felt I must not be normal or doing recovery 'right' because I didn't feel positive about it, and half the time wasn't sure that I actually wanted it. So I wanted to write my blog to share my experiences in the hope that there would be others who might identify with how I was feeling, who would be able to read my blog and know that they are not alone and realise that it is ok to feel like that. Also, I hoped that reading about the small progressions I was making would inspire them to think that they could too.

Here is an extract from first the blog post on 13th June 2016:

Anorexia. In the game that is life, it's like playing Monopoly. Living with anorexia is being locked up in jail. You don't pass 'Go', you can't take a 'Chance', you can't live life and experience things other people do. But does it have to be a life sentence?

...So, after three long hospital admissions, I'm now twenty-seven, on a Community Treatment Order, have been out of hospital for nearly five years, maintaining my weight, in a full-time job working 40 hours a week, a graduate and, for the first time, starting to want to break free from this prison sentence of anorexia. I want my 'Get out of jail free' card. Before, I was happily locked up in my cell of anorexia. I lived, slept, and breathed anorexia. But now I want more. Anorexia is exhausting and I'm tired of it.

I am now starting to roll the dice, hoping to get closer to the double to set me free. Yes, these moments may be short-lived and the fear of losing what has been my only friend for many years often makes me too scared to roll the dice and risk breaking free from my anorexic prison. But they are there and becoming more frequent.

Having looked at other anorexia recovery blogs, the way anorexia and recovery is talked about makes it feel to me as if I will never get there. How can I ever recover from it when 90% of the time I feel I desperately need it to cope? I don't think like these other recovering bloggers, who seem so overwhelmingly positive. To have the occasional time when I imagine recovery is a huge step forward from where I was. Every attempt, no matter how small, to roll the dice and step towards breaking free is building the stepping stones to the prison door that will one day unlock.

This blog doesn't flower up recovery… you don't have to feel you want to get better 100% of the time and everything isn't always fully determined to beating it. And that's why I'm writing this blog. I want it to help. To help other people try and understand eating disorders, to help me and to help others who also want to roll the dice to break free but often find their other hand turning the key to stay safely locked up.

So, amidst my struggles, I was still persevering and trying to make progress. My care team suggested that I join a club in the hope that it would help me to make friends and socialise. Having discussed it at length with my mum and with the approval of my nurse, it was agreed that I would go to my old athletics club and see if there was a running group I could join. I was running twice a week at home anyway, and the idea of being able to do this with other people seemed so much more appealing. But it carried a huge risk.

The running track was where it had all gone wrong in the first place, where anorexia was first allowed to creep in, to pounce on my feelings of negativity and lack of self-worth, making my burning desire to be an athlete dependent on losing weight. It would be the first time I had trained since becoming diagnosed with anorexia and, while I wanted to be able to do it, I was worried about how it was going to make me feel. I feared that it may act as a trigger again and bring back all those feelings, making my anorexia and obsession with exercise worse. I hoped not, but training before had brought with it so much sadness and disappointment, feeling like my dreams were never going to be achieved and that I was never going to be good enough. I wasn't sure I would be able to train again and not put extreme pressure on myself and experience continual disappointment.

Despite having those fears, another part of me thought that actually going back to athletics might help. Whereas before I had always thought that if I lost weight I would run faster, now I knew this was not the case and that if I were to gain weight this could make me run faster. So, I hoped going back to athletics might give me that push and encouragement to gain a bit of weight.

After my first session back at athletics in June 2016, I wrote in my blog:

I dedicated all my time to focusing on being the best I could be, trying to get personal bests to help me achieve my ultimate goal of becoming a professional athlete. That was the dream. But instead I became a professional anorexic. That is the nightmare.

… I never imagined after four years of a revolving door taking me in and out of hospital that I would ever step foot on a track again. That part of my life had gone. But now, five years since my last admission, I am stepping back on the track. And I am pleased to say it didn't pick up from where it left off. Last week I completed my first training session and it felt incredible. It wasn't a slog like before. Yes, I ran slowly and didn't complete the whole session, but that wasn't shattering my dreams, it was taking me away from my nightmare. The dream of being an athlete has gone, and I know I risk the negative emotions and drive to be the best coming back but, on the other hand, if I can stay mentally (and physically) strong enough, it has huge potential to help me.

On reading my blog, one of my friends from university, Selin, got back in touch with me. I plucked up the courage and asked her if she wanted to meet up. And she did. We went out for dinner in London and I was so nervous beforehand, worried that I wouldn't be able to hold a conversation. But it couldn't have gone better – and I tackled my fear food, of cheese! That evening truly reignited my friendship with Selin, who I have gone on to meet up with at least every couple of months. She has been a friend who I cherish and who has helped me keep fighting for recovery. And while eating out was initially quite hard, now I do it with complete ease and really enjoy it!

For nearly a decade I had been shy and reclusive, living in my own little anorexic bubble. Some people who are in a similar situation to this may feel that doing things such as going out with friends is something you will never be able to do. I used to feel like that, but I desperately wanted to have friends and to go out and socialise, and the things you want most in life you have to work hard to try and achieve. This will probably involve taking risks and going out of your comfort zone but, if you never take a risk, nothing will ever change and you will stay locked in your prison cell. The anorexic prison cell may feel safe but ultimately it is not going to make you happy. I have tried really hard to progress my recovery these past couple of years and it has been so worth it.

It was that first date back with Selin that really inspired and motivated me to keep fighting to achieve my dreams. Up to this point, I had pictured what I wished to happen in my life but had never done anything about it other than moan that my dreams would never come true. I lived in hope that one day it might simply happen. But meeting with Selin, I realised I had to go out and get my dreams. They aren't going to come to me. Anorexia doesn't like to let you dream. It puts a high price on dreams – so high that you give up on them and concentrate on anorexia instead. And that is what it wants you to do. But I knew I wanted my real dreams to come true and I sure as hell was going to keep fighting for them.

However, by the end of 2016, I was really beginning to struggle. I had grown to hate my job. Living with anorexia and feeling like I couldn't let go was incredibly tiring, and I had lost touch with Megan and Saffron so was feeling incredibly lonely again. Life didn't feel worth fighting for if I didn't have friends and it wasn't going to get any better. I might as well stay anorexic because the alternative wasn't any better.

At the start of February 2017 I was faced with a new battle. I had gained a few kilos for no apparent reason. I hadn't changed anything in my diet or altered my exercise regime, yet the scales showed I was heavier. My stomach had become increasingly distended (which is incredibly common during anorexia recovery) and I hated that my clothes were all now too tight and that to wear my work trousers I had to undo the button and try and squeeze into them. I also hated that my nurse and a lady at work told me my face didn't look as gaunt and that I looked a lot better. I hated it. I absolutely hated it. At the end of March my weight reached new heights. I hit 50kgs for the first time.

Monday 3rd April 2017,

I entered a whole new 'decade' of numbers. I am no longer in the 40s... oh no... now I have hit the 50s. And it feels utterly shit. Coping with the weight gain was bad enough before but at least I could reassure myself that I was still in the 40s, I hadn't quite gone over that all-important number. But, low and behold, my worst fears came true. I couldn't help but break down, crying to my mum and my nurse in disgust, in despair, in desperation, in fear.

It is crazy how a number can have such significance. Why, just for example, does 50.1kg feel so much worse than 49.9kg? Just because you have gone from a four to a five? That gain of 0.2kg feels so, SO much worse than say, 48.5kg to 48.7kg.

Previously I had been contemplating recovery but now I can't face it. I haven't got the energy to give it any thought and with feeling so down, it's not the time to start thinking about leaving the one thing that gets me through difficult times. I know this is wrong – anorexia doesn't really help get me through anything, it is destructive. But I do use it as a coping mechanism and at the moment I am struggling to cope.

When life is difficult and I feel down, as I have been this week, I cling on to anorexia. And that gives it its chance to creep back in, to take over. I look back on losing weight and being very skinny with rose-tinted glasses. I start thinking about how nice it would be to start losing weight again, to be skinny, to feel like I was achieving something. But the reality is, it wasn't a nice feeling. For one, you are never skinny enough... there is always more weight to lose. And with being so skinny comes repercussions... hospital, isolation, and all the horrible consequences as a result. Ultimately, you lose more of your life. And I can't afford to lose any more of mine.

To revert completely to anorexia would have been the easy option; the escape route out of my awful reality. But I knew I had to try and keep myself going and I had to keep fighting the anorexic voice, as difficult as it was. I was determined not to give in to anorexia and end up living my life as a professional anorexic. I decided that I wanted to do a Masters in sport science. I had started doing some work experience in sport and I really liked being busier, getting out and doing things, interacting with different people and feeling independent. I had to keep believing deep down that life could get better if I just kept trying.

Chapter 42
A Big Decision

I decided I would start the Masters in September 2017. But I was worried about how I would focus on my studies and continue to progress my recovery so that I could have more freedom and flexibility. I didn't want anorexia to go, but I wanted it to become quieter and smaller. I wanted it to sit in the corner of the room, rather than taking up the whole space. However, I didn't feel at all ready to try and gain more weight. So I decided that, for the year I would be completing my Masters, I would concentrate on other aspects of recovery that weren't as encompassing and daunting as weight gain. I believed this would allow me to keep making progress on the road to recovery alongside completing my studies. I also decided that when my Masters finished in October 2018, I would commit to gaining weight. This was a huge decision for me. By then, I would be thirty years old and I was determined I could not waste any more years of my life. I still was not prepared to lose anorexia completely, but I could not allow it to lose me any more of my life.

I decided on a weight I would try and get to after my studies were completed. It was a weight I felt I could cope with and was a million times better than where I had been for the past decade. It was a weight not too much lower than when I started at Loughborough ten years ago, and I was determined that I *had* to do it. Once I got there, as time went on, I might feel able to go a bit higher. I wasn't ruling that out but, to start with, I knew my limits and what I could cope with and, given that it was 10kg above what I was discharged at, I felt it was a positive decision.

With the decision regarding weight gain made and scheduled for October 2018, I now needed to try and take control of aspects of my life which weren't weight-related. I wanted to tackle my rigidity with food and calories, to eat more spontaneously and because I fancied something, not because it was a number. But my number one priority was my exercise obsession. A few months after being discharged from The Priory in 2011, I had started power walking for fifty minutes a day. Since then, I had done that walk every single day; it was a compulsion. I *had* to do the strict, regimented fifty minutes of power-walking every day come hell or high water. I wanted to reach the point where I would be at liberty to exercise if I felt like it, not because anorexia told me I had to, and for it to be ok not to walk for a set amount every day.

My power-walks were a real chore and I reached the point where I thought I couldn't carry on with them, getting up early every day before work to go out and do the bulk of the walk. I didn't want to have to power-walk for fifty minutes every day for the rest of my life. But my walking held more significance for me than being merely walking. It gave me a sense of self-worth, that I was pushing my body to do something when most people wouldn't bother. It proved that I could beat laziness and that there was still a part of me that had anorexia. Part of me feared that with reducing my walking I would lose that sense of self-worth.

My mum suggested that, to address this issue, I pay to see my old therapist from The Priory who I got on really well with, as my current NHS therapist hadn't been able to help. My first appointment with her was at the start of July 2017 and we began to address my issues with exercise. We developed a plan – or more of a 'test' – to start to address my exercise obsession. This test was to reduce my walking by five minutes on one day a week until the next time I saw her in a couple of weeks. She understood the struggles and anxiety that would come with this but, rather than tell me to think in a certain way to overcome this and resist any compensatory behaviours, she proposed that it was a 'test' – to see how it made me feel and how it made me want to respond. Once we knew this we would have something to work on. With regards to the compensatory behaviours, she explained that it didn't matter if I did them. I was testing how the reduced walking made me behave and think, whether it made me want to introduce compensatory behaviours and whether or not I could control these or if I responded to them. If I did respond, that was ok because we were only testing, and we could develop an appropriate plan according to what happened.

Reducing my walking was incredibly difficult. I felt nervous and panicky and it was always popping into my head, 'Oh my God, you've done five minutes less,' and I felt a strong urge to go out and do that last five minutes. It took great strength to resist going out and finishing off the walk, but I did it. However, in the evening when I was preparing my evening snack, I found myself unable to maintain my calories. I didn't reduce them by much, but it gave me that bit of reassurance. I knew it was wrong, but I hoped that the next time I saw my therapist we could come up with a strategy to beat it. We did come up with a strategy, reminding myself of why I was doing it, that I didn't want to be walking like that for the rest of my life and that I wanted more flexibility in my life. Over the summer of 2017, I managed to start reducing my walking without any compensatory behaviours.

Another huge positive at the start of that summer was that I re-established contact with my old school friend Allana and we went out for dinner.

18th June 2017,

I cannot tell you how nice it was. We are both quite different from the last time we met – I have come a long way these past few years and I realise that actually, back then, it was probably very difficult for her to know what to say and how to act around me. But anorexia is sitting slightly smaller in my life now than it was then and I think that makes it much easier for me to socialise relatively 'normally'.

I felt very regretful for the years I didn't keep in touch with her but I have to accept that I cannot get that time back but I can control the future. And I hope that now we have met back up, it will be the start of a new, old friendship that can grow even stronger.

Both Selin and Allana have been incredible friends to me and I couldn't believe I had let the pair of them drift out of my life because of anorexia. Never again will I lose a friendship because of anorexia convincing me that I only need my friendship with anorexia. Anorexia is not a friend but a devil. There is no substitute for real friends.

Chapter 43
A Year on My Masters

In the summer of 2017, I did my final shift at the tearoom. It was sad saying goodbye to all the staff and I did feel fearful of having no structure or purpose until the start of my Masters. The closer the start of my Masters came, the more anxious I was becoming, and anorexia was an increasingly appealing option. With the stress of it all and a big life change about to happen, I felt like I couldn't deal with it. I had chosen to do my Masters at St Mary's; however, a few weeks before I was due to start, my doubts about my capabilities to complete the course, particularly in completing a dissertation, were growing ever stronger and I was close to pulling out. I was scared of this imminent change in my life. If I couldn't manage, it would be confirmation that my life was destined to be awful.

But giving in to anorexia was not an option and I had to face my fears. Registration and induction day was on Saturday 9th September 2017, with lessons due to start on the following Monday. I slept at Selin's on the Friday night and this was a huge achievement for me. For so long I had wanted to be able to stay round a friend's house and to now do so felt incredible. It was a great start to a new chapter in my life.

Saturday 9th September 2017,
Being able to sleep round a friend's house has been something I have wanted to for the best part of a decade.

To spend an evening with a friend, chatting and relaxing in front of the TV, to stay over for the night – it has always been a wish yet felt a million miles away. Firstly, I didn't think I would have the friend(s) to do it with (but the return of this friend in my life last year has been wonderful) and secondly, I never thought I would be able to manage my anorexia to the point which would enable me to sleep round a friend's house. This time two years ago, probably even one year ago, I wouldn't have been able to do it. The anxiety over food, exercise etc would have been too much – how I'd fit my eating plan around staying at someone's house, how I'd fit my exercise routine in – I just wouldn't have been able to cope.

But on Friday night I did it. Without much stress and with a lot of happiness. To most, sleeping round someone's house is nothing out of the ordinary. To me, it is huge. And to fulfil a decade-long wish – something I have desperately wanted to do for so long but have been locked up by anorexia – it feels liberating, it feels incredible. A step towards unlocking my anorexic prison cell.

My first week at St Mary's went surprisingly well; better than I had been expecting! It was a full week of 9am to 4pm every day, learning research and statistical methods. I stayed over each night in a nearby hotel with my mum. While I was still daunted by the work (and convinced I wouldn't be able to do the coursework), it was really nice talking to the people on the course. There were only about ten of us, which was completely different from what I had experienced at Loughborough, and I genuinely liked all of them.

While the social side of the course was good, the stress of the workload soon started taking its toll. I instantly got back into the studying routine and, on the five days a week when I didn't have to go into the university, I was back at the window all day, every day doing my coursework assignments or revising. It was very stressful as there was never a time when we didn't have at least one piece of coursework to be getting on with.

My eating routine changed and, although most of the time I continued to eat breakfast, dinner and an evening snack as I had done while at work, sometimes I would go all day not eating until dinner and I would make up the calories in my evening snack. I knew this wasn't a good habit to get in to but once it had started, it was difficult to stop. Not eating until the evening gave me a feeling of strength and made me feel good amidst all the stress of university. It provided me with a 'buzz' that I hadn't experienced in so long I had forgotten how good it felt. I was terrified I might be slipping back into anorexia: it seemed like a tempting escape from the stresses of university.

Altough the workload was stressful, I was actually enjoying the whole experience of university and I knew I could not let anorexia take over. My first couple of months on my Masters were a million miles away from my experience at Loughborough when I had gone back to complete my degree. I had spent my time at Loughborough completely isolated, whereas now I was part of a group, involved in conversations, laughing, joking, and making friends. My experience at St Mary's really highlighted to me how much I had changed over the past few years and how far I had come. I had become so much less reclusive. I've had to work really hard at it, to make myself more sociable and to talk to other people, but life is so much better for doing so. That's not to say I don't still struggle with social situations, because sometimes I do find them daunting, but I don't hide from them anymore.

During the first couple of months of my Masters, I went to the pub with Selin and out shopping and for dinner with Allana. This was completely different from how I had behaved at Loughborough when I would spend all my time studying, never seeing anyone or doing anything. I could recognise that all-or-nothing trait in me again; everything is either amazing or awful, I have to study all the time or I'm going to fail. These were thoughts my therapist and I were challenging. I was trying to accept that there is middle ground; it's not simply one thing or the other.

One of the hardest things I was having to deal with while completing my Masters was my continual, unexplained weight gain. Since leaving my job at the tearoom in the summer, my weight had continued to slowly creep up. Not by much each time, but it was a continual, steady increase and I was really struggling to deal with it. The weight gain wasn't part of my plan. I was meant to be gaining weight when I finished my Masters.

It's bad enough gaining weight when it is planned but when it is happening for no reason it is incredibly hard to deal with. At a time when I needed to be focused on my coursework, I was preoccupied with my weight and feeling overwhelmed. Fighting the anorexic temptation was a huge battle.

In the first few months of 2018 I was showing I could keep building that life I wanted and that I had the strength to fight anorexia. I didn't realise this at the time but, looking back, the things I was achieving and doing were signs of strength and fighting. I was doing things socially which in previous years I could only have imagined possible and all at the same time as doing my university work and fighting anorexia.

Monday 22nd March 2018,

I went out to a nightclub for Allana's birthday, the first time I'd been to a nightclub in years! Was I scared and daunted? Very much so. Not just with the prospect of going to a nightclub, but also with being with her other friends – people I don't really know. But did I enjoy it? Very much so. To be out, having fun, doing normal things – I've missed out on all that. It really hit me that evening how I lost virtually of all my 20s. The time when you are meant to be going out and having fun – being young and free – I wasn't. I was locked up by anorexia (and locked up by hospitals for several years). And that is a decade of my life I will never get back. And yes, it made me feel sad, very sad… but it made me more determined to not let the next ten years go by in the same way. Because that can so easily happen. The years tick by and before you know it, you are ten years older and still living by the rules of anorexia.

As terrifying as fighting anorexia and leaving it behind is, the thought of being forty and still imprisoned by this devil – that's even scarier. So I resolved to stick to my plan formed nearly a year ago now, that when I finish my Masters I am going to have to tackle recovery head on. No more ifs and buts or waiting for the right moment – I've just got to do it.

As well as the nightclub, I also went out for dinner with three of my friends from my course at uni. That too was really nice, the first time we have done anything socially outside of uni. And I also met up with Allana and my friend from school, Sarah, who I had lost touch with over the past few years. It was so nice to see her again, I just wish I hadn't let anorexia strip me of such a good friend. But we are back in touch now and I'm determined to keep it that way. I am now in a position where I truly feel, and will happily say, that when it comes to friends and friendships – anorexia can bugger off! Ten years ago, anorexia was my best friend. I wanted nothing else in life, nothing else mattered as long as I had my best friend, anorexia. Everyone else could bugger off and leave me and anorexia alone. That is how I felt for years. And the outcome of that? Over a decade of misery, isolation, reclusiveness, and torture. Hovering on the brink of death. It took me a long time to realise that it wasn't everyone else that was the enemy, but anorexia itself. Given the chance, anorexia will destroy everything. I am not going to give it that chance again.

In September 2018, in the space of three days, I said goodbye to my 20s and my Masters came to an end. Two major life events and they hit me one straight after the other. They were both hard to deal with, as they would be for anybody. But I finished my Masters in a much better place physically and mentally. I had grown in strength during my Masters year and my life had started transforming. My confidence was growing and anorexia had become smaller. I didn't want to run back to anorexia, I wanted to continue growing and grab life with both hands.

Although I had originally planned to gain weight once I finished my Masters, by the time my Masters had come to an end, I had already reached my target weight. The unplanned and unexplainable weight gain had been hard to cope with. But I was coping. As much as I hated being bigger, I liked the life that had come with it. I had Selin and Allana, I was going out and about, my walking was reducing, I was enjoying my running, life was getting better. And I wasn't prepared to sacrifice it all for the sake of losing weight. I finally felt like life was improving and I was determined this would continue.

Chapter 44
Friends and Life

As my life continued to grow in 2019, anorexia continued to get shrink. I wanted to use all of my lived experiences to raise awareness of eating disorders, campaign for change and improved services, and help others. I decided to start my own YouTube channel, *Bex's Anorexia Recovery*, so that I could vlog about my experiences and recovery. I hoped that in sharing my thoughts and life it would help others and help me to keep challenging myself.

I signed up to be a campaigner for the eating disorder charity *Beat*. I attended a *Beat* campaign training day early in 2019 and later in the year attended Parliament to talk to MPs and contribute to discussions on eating disorder services. My passion for helping others with eating disorders and desire to improve services was growing into something I wanted to commit to. I started working part-time in admin at my local general hospital which gave me the flexibility to do paid work alongside my campaigning and awareness-raising work. I settled into the job quickly and really enjoyed it. I didn't tell anyone at work about my eating disorder when I started. I just wanted to be me. I wanted to be Bex. Not Bex who has anorexia. Anorexia has always tried to convince me that the only reason people give me any time is because of anorexia; because it makes them concerned so they feel they have to. By not telling my new colleagues about anorexia, they could get to know me and not be influenced by the fact I have an eating disorder.

To my surprise, my colleagues seemed to like me and I made a few good friends straight away. I loved going to work. We always had a laugh and a joke and I felt like I could be the real me. Bex. There was no anorexia. My confidence in myself and my ability to make friends grew and I started to feel like I was really putting anorexia in the corner of the room. It was still there, and I still felt I needed it there, but it was very much moving to the corner.

Another new element to life that was helping me move anorexia to the corner was my new friend, Bex. We had met on a few occasions through our work with *Beat* and hit it off straight away. I absolutely loved spending time with her (and still do). I was able to be me and talk to her about anything. I had never felt so close to someone so quickly and I knew she had become a friend for life. Her support has been unconditional and she gave me so much motivation to keep pushing my recovery. Having friends and being able to go out and do things was making sticking with recovery worth it.

It was also through my time with Bex that I finally felt able to try a new challenge. Until this point, I had been happy and comfortable to go out for meals only as long as I knew what the calories were. So this restricted where I could eat to those restaurants that displayed calories. But, going out for dinner with Bex, I started to challenge this, eating in restaurants without displayed calories. It was very hard at first, but the more I did it, the easier it got. Now when I eat in a restaurant, I don't look at the calories. I eat a meal, not a number. Not counting calories has brought with it so much freedom and happiness.

It felt so nice to be at the stage in my recovery where I could go out and do so much more with my friends. I had also got back in touch with Megan who I was meeting up with regularly and, as someone who had helped show me what life had to offer when I was starting to unlock my anorexic prison cell, it was lovely that we could now do more things together. I had also started meeting up for coffee or food with Rebecca, a friend from my running group and she too had become a very close friend. Rarely a week went by when I wasn't out socialising with someone and I loved it. As my world continued to grow, anorexia got smaller.

That's not to say I didn't still struggle, because I did (and sometimes still do). Anorexia was, and is, still there. But now I had friends in the room who were helping me to push anorexia into the corner. I hated my size, my weight still caused me stress, and I was still a bit rigid around food. But it wasn't all-encompassing anymore. And as much as I didn't like my size, I was prepared to tolerate it for the life it was giving me. I still had a very long way to go in terms of building a bigger and better life, but it was a million miles better than it had been a few years previously.

I knew that if I wanted to continue living a more flexible, free, and fulfilling life, I had to keep challenging myself. The eating routine that I had gotten into at university involved not eating during the day and consuming all my food at night, and, although this wasn't restricting in terms of calories, I recognised it was very much an anorexic habit and therefore feeding anorexia. So I committed to shifting my intake around so that I would eat breakfast, lunch, dinner and an evening snack, and I also stopped having a half-portion dinner and ate a normal sized dinner with a normal amount of protein and vegetables. It was hard to start with, but I soon got used to it. The temptation was always there to save my food for later. But I knew this wasn't healthy and wasn't helpful to recovery. So I had to keep fighting that temptation. I now eat and enjoy breakfast, lunch, dinner, and snacks without a second thought. I don't try and save all my food to have a big evening snack and I am no longer obsessed with vegetables because I allow myself other food and to eat during the day. And I could never possibly go back to half-portion dinners!

But some things have been more difficult to change. One of those being my feelings around my birthday. Every year when September approaches, I find myself feeling more depressed and anxious. September is my birthday month and as you know, birthdays have been a struggle for me since I was a child because I hated growing up. Also, when in the depths of anorexia, a birthday was just a reminder of the time I had, and still was, wasting, and how I didn't have any friends to do anything with. However, it was my friends who, for my birthday in September 2019, reminded me of my reasons to keep fighting for recovery.

At the start of September, I went on holiday to Benidorm with two friends from work. One of them, Sharron, was having such a positive impact on my life and really helping me discover my true self. I had known Sharron for less than four months but it felt as if I had known her for years as we got on so well. It was my first holiday without my parents in twelve years. I was incredibly daunted by the prospect and how I would cope but I had such a good time. I did find the food challenging at times and there were a few occasions when I would panic, but these were brief moments. Being on holiday with friends was more important than making sure I ate the 'right' amount while I was there. The holiday was a milestone and showed me how far I have come. Also on the holiday I told them about my past and they, and my other colleagues who I told when I returned, have given me so much support.

A few weeks after I returned from Benidorm, my close friends, including Selin, Allana, and Bex, arranged a surprise birthday for my thirty-first. We spent the day in London, went out for dinner (un-calorie-counted) and out to a bar. I had such an incredible time and the whole event would not have been possible if I hadn't challenged myself to get to the point in recovery that I was. I wouldn't have been able to cope with the food, not exercising, the spontaneity. Yes, anorexia was still there, but I had freedom I had never had before and it felt amazing. Anorexia has convinced me for so long that I am completely unlikeable and that I don't have any friends other than anorexia. But this birthday really showed me how much my friends care and made me determined to never sacrifice a true friend for anorexia again.

I had made a lot of progress by this point in terms of reducing my walking obsession. It had been challenging but we attacked it gradually and my fifty-minute power-walk had been reduced to fifteen minutes, and I could have the occasional day when I didn't go for a walk. I felt like I was getting very near to the point where it would it be my free choice whether I decided to walk or not, as opposed to being driven by anorexia.

Chapter 45
2020: The Year of Covid, Athletics, and Presentations

2020 proved to be a mixed bag for me. It started off really positively, picking up from where 2019 had left off. In February, Bex and I went on holiday to Barcelona together. I can honestly say that this holiday and being with Bex is one of the happiest moments I can remember and a major step forward in my recovery. For the three days we were there, I ate completely un-calorie-counted and I ate food I would never have let myself eat before. Unlike the holidays when I was first discharged and could only allow myself cornflakes for breakfast, this holiday with Bex was totally different. Our favourite way to spend the afternoon was to find a café that served crystal bread and eat it while chatting, people-watching, and enjoying each other's company. I didn't feel stress or anxiety around the food or what exercise I was or was not doing. For so very long I had wanted to be able to go on holiday like this with a friend. I never imagined I would be able to do it but here I was having the best time. Anorexia would shout at me occasionally and make me worry that I'd eaten too much and would be gaining lots of weight. But far more important to me than that was being on holiday with Bex and having a good time. Which we did!

When I compared what I was able to do now with what I had been like a few years previously, it was like I was looking at a different person. Well, I had become a different person. I was no longer governed by anorexia's rules. I now had freedom. And with freedom came less anxiety and more happiness.

It was also at the beginning of 2020 that I started delivering talks and presentations on eating disorders. Raising awareness and understanding of eating disorders is something I feel passionately about so I decided I had to put my passion and my experiences to good use and start educating and inspiring. I started off delivering talks on my experiences, including important facts about symptoms and knowledge of eating disorders, to university nursing, medical and psychology students. I really enjoyed doing it and the feedback I received was so positive. I have gone on to deliver talks and presentations both in the UK and internationally to schools, charities, businesses, sports clubs, and I've presented at conferences. This is my focus now – sharing my story and raising awareness and understanding to provide hope and inspiration, and give sufferers the best chance of recovery.

However, when Covid hit, things took a turn for the worse. It was as if the eating disorder switch in my head had been flicked on and anorexia came at me full pelt.

April 3rd 2020,

The world seems very scary and uncertain at the moment with Coronavirus. Everyone is dealing with the stress and anxiety in their own way. For me? Welcome back anorexia. You had become so much quieter and I was making good progress with my recovery. But when faced with the extreme stress and anxiety over Corona and lockdown, you have leapt back into my life. The world is making me feel so scared and terrified and the eating disorder is telling me it can help me cope and will make me feel better.

In come the thoughts of wanting to lose weight, wanting to restrict, wanting to exercise. If I focus my mind on all of this, I haven't got to face all the terrifying things going on in reality. There is no denying that the eating disorder thoughts are hard to fight right now. Lockdown is a terrifying prospect. I am scared that I can't do the exercise I would normally and so I will gain lots of weight. In reality, my exercise is not really going to be much different to what it was before lockdown. But a new situation makes my head, makes the eating disorder, panic. And with overwhelming fears of weight gain and limited exercise, in comes the thoughts that I need to restrict my food in order to compensate. So you see, it is not just the want to lose weight to try and cope and control the situation, it is also the unbearable fears of weight gain arising from the new situation causing a drive in eating disorder behaviours.

It feels incredibly difficult to manage right now. My head is filled with all these eating disorder thoughts. Anxiety around Corona and lockdown and the effect on my weight is there every second of the day. And like I said, the eating disorder says it knows the answer. It tells me that if I exercise and restrict then my anxiety around weight gain will reduce.

At a time when you are struggling, it promises that it has the answer to make you feel better. It has convinced me of this many times in the past. It promised me happiness and that it would make everything better. And I believed it. But it led to nothing but heartache, misery, and complete devastation. Yet, despite that, it still creeps back so convincingly. Convincing? Yes. But truthful? No. Liars can be very convincing, but they are not truthful. So while anorexia is here trying to convince me, I am reminding myself of the facts. Anorexia does not solve anything. Anorexia does not stop anxiety and stress. Anorexia does not make me happy. Anorexia does not help me get the life I want to live.

As soon as the UK went into lockdown in March 2020, I found myself really struggling with my eating disorder. I found myself engaging in anorexic behaviours that I hadn't done for years. I felt an overwhelming fear of gaining and an incredible desire to lose weight. My exercise increased and whereas before lockdown I had managed to reduce my walking down to fifteen minutes per day, now I was doing an hour a day and I *had* to do it no matter what. I was scared of what was happening to me and to my brain. I could feel myself free-falling into relapse.

I still had to go into work as, with working for the NHS, I was considered a key worker. And I was so grateful for the routine and structure that it continued to give me. I think I would have struggled even more if I hadn't have had my job to go to. It also helped in the sense that I was able to see my friends at work. I was also having regular phone calls and always messaging with my close friends which helped to give me some motivation to keep fighting. I had to keep reminding myself that the situation with Covid was short-term but relapsing into the depths of anorexia would not be. It would lose more years out of my life. Once Covid eased, I wanted to be able to pick my life up from where it left off, not start from scratch and have to rebuild my life from anorexia all over again. My mum was also a huge source of support and, although my anorexia and desire to lose weight felt overwhelmingly strong, I did pretty much maintain my weight. With my anorexia having become so much stronger during lockdown, it highlighted to me that it was still very much there and how easy it could be to relapse. But I knew I had to keep fighting. I *wanted* to keep fighting.

As lockdown progressed, I did adapt and become more used to it and the strength of anorexia was weakening. I also had a new goal to keep me motivated. My running. After re-joining my old athletics club in 2016, I had started to take my training a bit more seriously in 2019. I really enjoyed it, the company, and as someone who had grown up as an athlete, it was nice to be able to train again. In 2019 I had made the decision to start strength-training. I had been wanting to do it for a while as I knew it would improve my running and general health. But I kept putting it off because I was terrified it would make me gain weight and get bigger. But anorexia had destroyed my body and although I had regained weight my muscles were still very weak. My head thought it was capable of things but, when it came to physically doing it, I was too weak. In 2019 I got so fed up with not being able to do basic movements, such as lunge down and step back up, that I decided now was the time. I started off doing only body weight exercises as that was all I could manage. But gradually I was able to start lifting weights. The feeling of gaining strength was so empowering. It felt like I was developing a stronger body to accompany my growing strength of mind. Little things such as being able to go up two steps at a time felt incredible. And during lockdown, my training and focus on running and getting stronger really helped to keep me going.

Training for my running, whether that be running, cycling, or weights, was completely unrelated to my eating disorder. Unlike my walking, I did not do any of my training to burn calories, lose weight, or satisfy anorexia. My training was all done with the focus on improving my athletic performance. And many of my anorexic urges to obsessively exercise during lockdown were overridden by the knowledge that it would hinder my training. More importantly, I had decided I wanted to race again. When I was a teenager I'd been convinced that losing weight would make me run faster, whereas now I had the knowledge and experience that this was not true. If I allowed myself to give in to anorexia and start losing weight that it would ruin all the gains I had made with my training, ruin my performance, and ruin any chance of racing. So when struggling during lockdown, this really helped to keep me going. My running was now more important than anorexia. And in the summer of 2020 I raced again for the first time in thirteen years. It felt utterly amazing. I never imagined that I would reach the point in my recovery where I would be able to step back onto a track and race. And not just race, but run a Personal Best! But there I was and loving every minute. And I was more determined than ever that I had to keep maintaining my recovery so that I could keep improving my running. I had gone from athlete, to anorexia, and now I was back as an athlete.

Chapter 46
2021: Medication, Racing, and a New Job

Because of the pandemic and lockdown, life in 2021 was not much different from how 2020 ended. I would go to work, I would train, and that was basically it. I was doing well with my recovery and keeping anorexia in the corner of the room. However, something that had changed was my medication. For the last two weeks of 2020, I was tapered off my antidepressant Mirtazapine, and started on Sertraline. Unfortunately, because I had been on Mirtazapine for ten years, tapering off this medication over two weeks was far too short (I was following advice from a psychiatrist). Therefore, I suffered quite severe withdrawal side-effects for many months. Basically, from January through to June, I had incredibly bad insomnia and had diarrhoea every day. This made life quite challenging.

I was often only getting four hours sleep a night and considered myself lucky if I got five. The daily diarrhoea was also very tiring and for both the insomnia and diarrhoea to continue for half a year, it was exhausting. Due to the medication change and diarrhoea, I did lose a bit of weight. There was nothing I could do about it. But seeing the numbers on the scale go down again, I remembered how good it felt. Anorexia was triggered.

But rather than let anorexia run riot, I fought it. That's not to say I didn't engage in certain eating disorder behaviours at times, but I was fighting the overwhelming urge to continue with the weight loss, to see how much lower I could keep getting. Because

I knew where that path ultimately led: to more suffering, more sadness, more isolation, and less living. Even though tying to lose weight was tempting, I didn't actually want to go back to anorexia. Also, of key importance to me, was that it would lead to a deterioration in my running performance. I was not prepared to sacrifice my running ambitions for anorexia.

Thankfully, in the summer the diarrhoea and insomnia settled down. Although still not completely back to normal, I was sleeping better and dashing to the toilet far, far less. With the side-effects reducing, my weight also stabilised. As much as the anorexia in me wanted to keep trying to get the numbers lower, I knew that the stabilisation of my weight was a good thing.

The withdrawal effects of my medication might have stopped, but the effects of the pandemic were still ongoing. Because we had spent so long in lockdown, I had got used to not going out and seeing people. I had become reclusive. I could remember how I was in The Priory when I was too scared to leave the hospital grounds and I was now experiencing similar thoughts and feelings, although not to the same extent. Over the summer of 2021, I have been able to challenge these thoughts and force myself to go out and meet friends occasionally. But it has been difficult, and it is still also restricted by Covid. Covid has affected everybody in so many ways. But I am a firm believer in holding onto the light at the end of tunnel.

However, it was during 2021 that I received some of the worst, most devastating news of my life. My friend, Nikki Grahame, had sadly passed away from anorexia. Nikki had been my idol ever since she went into *Big Brother*. She gave me so much hope and inspiration. At times when I was really struggling, I would think about her and what she had achieved, to help keep me going. She helped me in ways she will never know. Over the years, since my first admission in 2008, I would go and watch her in shows and pantomimes as much as possible. She would always meet up with me after the shows (I'm sure you can appreciate how significant meeting your hero is) and she was always so lovely. On one occasion, after her Easter pantomime in 2017, talking with her about recovery, she said, *Recovery is worth it. There is a whole world out there and you can have it if you want.* This has stuck with me ever since.

It was during lockdown in 2020 that Nikki went from not only being my inspiration, but to being my friend. We would speak regularly on the phone and would often discuss our plans for when lockdown was over. On 9th April 2021, I heard the tragic news that Nikki had passed away. The cruelty of anorexia is overwhelming. I made a promise to myself and to Nikki that I had to keep going with recovery. I had to keep fighting. I am not just doing it for me now, I am doing it for Nik to. I am doing recovery for both of us. Nikki lost her life to anorexia, but she helped to save, and continues to help save, mine. I wouldn't be where I am today without her.

Nikki helped to save my life, and I want to help others. In June 2021, alongside my admin job and public speaking, I also started a new job as a Peer Support Worker for an NHS trust in London. I was using my lived experience of mental illness and being in recovery to help others also suffering. I was giving other people hope. My passion for helping others was becoming my career.

I was progressing so much with my recovery in the summer of 2021. I had so much more freedom and it felt incredible. To think that several years ago I used to monitor my diet to the exact calorie, and my walking to the exact second. Now I hardly calorie-counted or portioned my food at all, and I no longer had to walk for a certain time every day. And I felt relaxed about it

Although Covid had stopped so much, it was not able to stop the athletics racing season in the summer. The athletics leagues and championships were back, and racing in these formed the basis of my summer. As an athlete, you spend all of the winter doing the hard graft in training, in order to race and be at your best in the summer. For me, it had been a long, hard winter. Coupled with the insomnia and diarrhoea, I had a constant stream of injuries. I managed it all so I could still train while also looking after my mental and physical health, but I was left feeling very unprepared for the 2021 athletics season.

However, to my surprise, my first race of the season was a Personal Best! I had improved my time from 2020 by one second. It may not seem like much but, as an 800m runner, every second counts! During the 2021 season, I took part in my first Essex Championships since 2007. I was so proud that I had got myself to the point where I was able to race in these championships again. Ten, five, or even two years ago, I would never have imagined that I would physically or mentally be well enough to compete in any race, let alone the Essex Championships. But I was. And not only did I compete, but I won a gold medal in the 800m! Over the season, along with some not so good performances, I improved my best even further. My season culminated in September, two days into my thirty-third year of life, with a Personal Best of 2m 23.4. I was running quicker than I ever had before.

Someone I met on a training course described my journey as *A Cinderella Story*. Athletics and my dream to be an athlete was a key driver in leading me down the anorexic path to destruction. For many years after, anorexia was all that mattered to me. I lived and breathed it. Athletics was all but a very distant memory. However, with starting recovery, my inherent love of athletics started to return. And now I keep myself well for athletics. So athletics led me to anorexia, but now it keeps me fighting anorexia. I am running free from anorexia.

Chapter 47
Here and Now

I have been out of hospital now for eleven years. For the first five of those years, in order for me to manage my anorexia and not succumb to its urges, I had to live a very isolated, reclusive, regimented life. I did go back to complete my degree but, as I have said before, I didn't talk to anyone, I never did anything, I never went out. I had my strict routine of studying, walking, and eating set meals at set times with my mum present. That was my life on repeat year after year. It was better than being in hospital, but it wasn't a life; it was an existence. I wasn't ready to challenge anorexia. I had to manage anorexia before I was ready to challenge it.

But it was during those first five years, when I was managing anorexia, that I realised I wanted more from life. Because of the CTO, the cycle of me going in and out of hospital stopped. Initially, the CTO acted as a deterrent to me losing weight as I knew I would end up in hospital if I did. The longer I stayed out of hospital, the more I realised there was so much more to life than anorexia and I actually wanted to build my own life. Without the CTO, I couldn't have done that. The CTO has saved my life and I feel it could save so many more sufferers with eating disorders. I am building a campaign to increase its usage for eating disorder patients as I feel this could save lives. I have been meeting Members of Parliament and psychiatrists to discuss this and working on building my campaign.

It has only really been in the past few years that things have started to truly get better, and I have made a lot of progress. Going to work in the tearoom was a game-changer and was the beginning of me socially interacting, making friends, and re-establishing old friendships. It was also key to me starting to have head space away from anorexia. From there it was a domino effect. Doing my Masters, working at the hospital, going out more with friends, my running – it all helped to grow my life. And as my life has grown, anorexia has become smaller.

I get on better now with my family than I have ever done and it is because of them that I am where I am today. I love going to Spain to visit my sister and her partner, Gonzalo, and we do so as regularly as we can. Before, I hated going away, which is why I only ever went once a year. But the past few years, because of the increased freedom I have through making anorexia a much smaller part of my life, these are now trips that I grab at every opportunity.

Having friends has always been key to my recovery and I am now so content with the friends that I have. Socially, I'm in a different universe to where I was several years ago and sometimes, when I look back, I can't quite believe how far I have come. That's not to say I don't still find social situations daunting sometimes, because I do, and I still sometimes worry that I don't have anything to talk about. I know it is anorexia that has crushed my self-esteem, confidence, and belief in my ability to socialise. But I am no longer letting anorexia stop me. I cherish my close and never would I want to sacrifice them again for anorexia.

My running is hugely important to me and is a key driver keeping me well. Alongside my job, public speaking, campaigning, I also consider myself an athlete. I am training hard and getting stronger (and making sure that I am fuelled properly) and looking forward to more races in future. As I write this, the 2022 season has just begun and I have improved my PB again to 2m16 for the 800m, and 4m45 for the 1500m. I hope that when I reach thirty-five and become a Veteran, I will run for England in Masters competitions. For so long my identity was solely based on anorexia, but now I have more, and I love that being an athlete is not only a key feature of my identity again, but is bigger than anorexia. And my focus on being an athlete helps me continue to fight anorexia.

I take so much motivation and inspiration from other athletes. They inspire me to keep fighting anorexia, rather than how I was in the past when all I wanted was to be anorexic. Recently, I have used my two favourite and most inspiring athletes, Lina and Laviai Nieslen, to devise myself food challenges. Once a week I challenge myself to eat a meal that they have eaten and posted a photo of on Instagram. Whether that be a pasta dish, a cooked breakfast, an afternoon snack, any meal that they eat, I challenge myself to replicate once a week. This is a huge challenge for me and something I wouldn't have been able to even contemplate a couple of years ago. But challenging anorexia is the only way for your life to grow.

Regarding my weight, it pretty much stayed stable until 2021, after reaching my target weight during my Masters in 2018. As explained earlier, the medication change in 2021 did cause me to lose a small amount of weight. That weight has been regained and my weight is once again stable. There have been times when my weight has increased for a while and I do panic. I think that if I can just lose a few kilos, everything will be better. But then I have to remember that I must not give a few kilos the power to completely rule my life. I do still struggle with all-or-nothing thinking and using negative thinking as a form of protection in an attempt to avoid disappointment. But these are thought processes I am trying to work on, and I am getting so much stronger in not letting my weight and anorexia have control. I am able to make plans for the future: towards the end of 2020 I underwent fertility treatment to freeze my eggs should I wish to have a child in the future. I can now honestly say that I actually enjoy life and am looking forward to what the future has to bring.

I focus on the good things I now have in my life, all the things I am able to do, and all the things I still want to achieve. I'm not going to say it isn't hard, because it is. But I am not letting my weight, or anorexia, dominate my life anymore. The life I have managed to build is not worth sacrificing for anorexia.

And it certainly isn't worth sacrificing for the sake of a few kilos. It has taken me a long while to accept that weight fluctuates, but now I do, and I can cope with my weight being as it is. I wouldn't say that I am happy with my weight, but I tolerate it. Tolerating the increase in weight over the past six years has brought with it increased freedom and a better life. I still wholeheartedly believe that I was discharged at the right BMI. At the time, I just couldn't cope with any more. Had I been forced higher, I know I would have relapsed. But by being discharged at what I was able to cope with, I could start to build my life outside of anorexia. And weight gain naturally accompanied this. I was gaining weight, and gaining a bigger and better life.

I am not fully recovered and I don't know that I ever will be completely. I think the hurt, pain, and years of torturous struggle with anorexia have left their mark, and that ball of pain and loneliness I have felt since being a young child may always be there. I am left with the physical repercussions of anorexia, including osteoporosis. I still take antidepressants – I know they help me and I will continue to take them for as long as I need them.

I have lived with anorexia for longer than I lived without it and, as I said, I don't think it will ever leave me completely. But anorexia doesn't control me like it used to and I have come such a long way. I don't see recovery as an end point where you cross a line over which you are defined as 'recovered'. For me, recovery is ongoing. I am still making progress and, with each day and each time I fight anorexia, a bit more freedom comes with it. I am so much happier now than I have been in a very long time. Anorexia no longer haunts me every day. Most of the time, I get by day-to-day without it really featuring. It is still there and I can still feel restricted by it, and sometimes it pops out loudly, but most of the time it is lying low in the background.

For example, the other day when I was having my lunch, I fancied a popadom with it. So I had a popadom. I didn't think anything of it: I fancied it so I ate it. It made me think back to when I was unable to consume *anything* that wasn't portioned, weighed, calorie-counted and part of my meal plan. I never would have believed you if you had told me I would be able to eat as freely as I do now. That's not to say I eat totally freely, but it is a million miles from how it used to be. The freedom I have gained through challenging anorexia over the years has been so worth it. It isn't easy to challenge anorexia and its rules, and I do still have a wobble sometimes, but I have learnt over the years what helps me to keep fighting anorexia and get through the wobbles.

Some of the things I have found helpful when challenging anorexia are:

1. Anxiety doesn't increase forever.
This is one of the key things that helped me to challenge eating disorder (ED) behaviours. Challenging ED rules can cause anxiety. For example, when I started to reduce the amount of walking I was doing, I felt I could not deal with the anxiety this caused, so I needed to do the walking in order to stop the anxiety. But my therapist taught me that anxiety doesn't increase forever. It does eventually settle down naturally on its own. But every time I engage in an eating disorder behaviour to relieve the anxiety, it reinforces to my brain that I have to do that behaviour to stop the anxiety. But you don't. So a lot of the time, it is a case of having to sit with the anxiety – grit your teeth and get through it. Because then you start to learn that you don't need the eating disorder behaviour.

2. Writing
Writing down my thoughts and feelings has really helped me over the years. It gets my thoughts out of my head and onto paper. Once I've written it all down, it helps me to rationalise my thoughts. For example, when I used to get stressed about eating vegetables, I would write my thoughts down and it would help me to think more logically and factually, rather than just with my feelings.

3. Talking
Talking has been a huge help for me. Anorexia thrives in secrecy. It took me many years to start to talk to people about how I was feeling, but once I did, it really helped. Whether it was

259

my family, friends, therapist; telling people about how I was feeling meant anorexia couldn't grow in the strength of silence. Also, when you talk to people, the reassurance they can provide can be incredibly valuable.

I also talk to myself. If I have an eating disorder thought, I try to talk myself out of it, or I don't let myself engage with it. I will say to myself, "No Bex, that's an eating disorder thought and I'm not engaging in this conversation." Sometimes I have to say this to myself repeatedly until the eating disorder thought weakens, and then I move on. Simply talking to myself and saying "No, I'm not engaging with this" has been hugely helpful.

4. Goals

Setting goals and reminding yourself of these when you are struggling can be helpful. Being able to eat in a restaurant and go out with friends were huge things I wanted to achieve. So if I found myself struggling, I would remind myself of these goals and that anorexia was not going to help me achieve them. Improving my running is now a big focus of mine. Reminding myself of this goal, and what I need in order to achieve it, helps me to fight anorexia.

5. Future years

When I am struggling with an eating disorder thought, I ask myself whether I want to spend the rest of my life worrying about this. For example, sometimes I might think I've eaten too much cereal and that I should eat less. I will then ask myself if I want to spend the rest of my life worrying about eating cereal and if, when I'm in my 70s, I am going to look back on my life and think *I'm so glad I ate less cereal*. The answer is always no. This helps me to go against anorexia. If I don't want it to be an issue in five years' time, I'm not going to give it five minutes of thought now.

I talk to myself, I focus on my goals, I remind myself that anxiety doesn't increase forever, and I continue on my run from anorexia.

Life can be terrifying. It is easy to not face your fears and stick with the safety of what you know. But sometimes you have to take a leap of faith. Scary? Yes. But who knows what you can achieve? The only risks you'll regret in life are the risks you didn't take. For many, many years I couldn't do what I am doing now, and the progression has been gradual. Trying to manage a mental illness alongside living in the real world is difficult. Life can be hard but anorexia is not the answer. I am continually making small steps which slowly, without me even realising, creep me up the recovery ladder towards a bigger and better life. My life has completely changed for the better. I still want to make further progress but a long time I couldn't even imagine that I would be able to do what I am doing now.

Each day, I'm fighting and I'm getting there. That is not to say that I don't still sometimes struggle to fight anorexia or feel tempted to lose weight, because I do. Recovery isn't a smooth journey. It is full of ups and downs, and some days are harder than others. But the longer I keep fighting anorexia, the less frequent are its outburst and the quieter it becomes. I am no longer prepared to give up more of my life to anorexia. I am terrified at the thought of life passing me by and me being forty or forty-five and totally locked up by anorexia. That is not what I want from life and this now overrides any desire to lose weight and be thinner. Anorexia can sometimes seem like the answer to my problems and an escape from reality, but I have to remind myself of the harsh realities of what living in the depths of anorexia is like. It leads me nowhere but to exhaustion, misery and pain, and this is not a life I want. I remind myself that going back to anorexia is not going to help me achieve the things that I truly want and, ultimately, it does not make me happy. It will try to convince you otherwise but you have to tell yourself that this is not the reality. As the saying goes – *if it makes you happy, why are you so sad?* Anorexia brings nothing but sadness. I hope I have come too far now for anorexia to tempt me back. I am determined to keep progressing and not relapse back to wasting my life in dedication to anorexia. I wouldn't have believed it if you had told me anorexia could be fought and that I could live a better life by fighting it and making it smaller, but I am living proof that is true.

I am starting a new chapter and I am going to keep building on the progress I have made. In 2020 I won *Mental Health Blogger of the Year* at The Mental Health Blog Awards and I appeared on BBC Panorama sharing my experiences of eating disorders in sport. This is something I am currently working on a campaign for to ensure that all coaches across all sports have knowledge of eating disorders. My work in public speaking and delivering talks on eating disorders and my experiences is giving me a sense of fulfilment and I hope that by sharing my story, I can help others. I hope that, through being an active mental health campaigner and advocate, I can help improve treatment for eating disorders and reduce the stigmas and stereotypes. This is my passion now. I want to share my story which I hope can help others in a similar situation and stop vulnerable people falling down the same hole, as well as improving general understanding of eating disorders.

Courage doesn't mean you don't get afraid. Courage means you don't let fear stop you. With courage, you can achieve anything you set your mind to. If you are struggling with an eating disorder, or know someone who is, I hope this book has helped to show you that recovery is possible. Regardless of your age, or how long you have been unwell, it is possible to have a life that isn't dominated by anorexia.

Eight years ago my letter to anorexia would have read:

Dear Anorexia,

You have broken me. I am destroyed. I have nothing left, I am just an empty shell. This is how you have left me – without hope or a happy ending. You took my life and you killed me.

Rebecca.

But with years and years of fighting, good treatment in The Priory, the CTO, amazing friends who have stuck with me and, most importantly, the everlasting love and care from my family, my letter is different. Jenny and her daughter Laura have stuck by me, and my sister and her partner Gonzalo are always there at the end of the phone to offer me love and support. My parents, who are with me day in, day out, who sat by my bedside day after day when I was in hospital, who I marched round the streets walking like a maniac, who held me as I cried and loved me when I told them I hated them and never wanted to see them again, who drove me up and down to Loughborough week after week for me to complete my degree, who sat with me patiently while I agonised over my dinner, who have put up with all my stresses and worries and who simply love me unconditionally – it is because of them that I can fight. I would not be where I am today without my parents and they give me the strength to keep going.

My letter to anorexia now reads:

Dear Anorexia,

You tried to kill me with your lies and promises. You promised me that everything would be better if I lost weight, that nothing else mattered in my life other than you. I thought you were my god but you were driving me to hell. You are nothing but an evil devil that will destroy everyone and everything. You had me trapped for so long. You wanted me dead and I felt it inside. My soul was frozen cold because you had me in your complete control. You possessed me. You abused me mentally and physically. My mind and body ached with pain because of you. You took everything from me – my family, my friends, my dreams – and you left me with nothing. You beat me black and blue, you made me cry endlessly, you filled my life with darkness. You broke my world. But in breaking me, you made me strong. I developed the strength to fight you and I started to rebuild my broken wings. I am now emerging from the darkness, the warmth is returning and I have the strength to take on life and achieve my dreams. I am now ready to fly. I am running free.

Bex

To those reading this book, you can run free too. On your marks, get set, go…

Support & Information

If you or someone you know needs more information or support regarding eating disorders, here are some useful links:

BEAT: www.beateatingdisorders.org.uk

First Steps ED: www.firststepsed.co.uk

SEED: www.seed.charity

National Centre for Eating Disorders:
www.eating-disorders.org.uk

The Recover Clinic: www.therecoverclinic.co.uk

ORRI: www.orri-uk.com

Schoen Clinic: www.schoen-clinic.co.uk

To find Rebecca online:

Website: www.bexquinlan.com
Twitter: @LittlebexQ
Instagram: @bex.quinlan.319
YouTube: Bex's Anorexia Recovery

SRL Publishing don't just publish books, we also do our best in keeping this world sustainable. In the UK alone, over 77 million books are destroyed each year, unsold and unread, due to overproduction and bigger profit margins.

Our business model is inherently sustainable by only printing what we sell. While this means our cost price is much higher, it means we have minimum waste and zero returns. We made a public promise in 2020 to never overprint our books just for the sake of profit.

We give back to our planet by calculating the number of trees used for our products so we can then replace. We also calculate our carbon emissions and support projects which reduce CO_2. These same projects also support the United Nations Sustainable Development Goals.

The way we operate means we knowingly waive our profit margins for the sake of the environment. Every book sold via the SRL website plants at least one tree.

To find out more, please visit
www.srlpublishing.co.uk/responsibility

CPSIA information can be obtained
at www.ICGtesting.com
Printed in the USA
LVHW031104200722
723877LV00002B/2

9 781915 073082